THE FREE ENTERPRISERS:

*Kennedy, Johnson
and The Business Establishment*

THE FREE
ENTERPRISERS

Kennedy, Johnson
and The Business Establishment

HOBART ROWEN

G. P. PUTNAM'S SONS, New York

To Alice

Author's Preface

This book was begun early in 1963, and was perhaps two-thirds finished on that terrible Friday, November 22, when President Kennedy was assassinated in Dallas. Mr. Kennedy knew about this book and its theme. As a matter of fact, he had agreed to talk with me, retrospectively, about his relations with the business community, and on Wednesday, November 20, Pierre Salinger arranged an interview for the following week. The precise date was to be after the scheduled return from Dallas, and before the President was to go to Hyannisport to discuss the new budget totals with Kermit Gordon.

Mr. Kennedy was continuously intrigued by the persistent business criticism of his Administration. It was one of the important factors accounting for the discrepancy between his accomplishments and his more lofty goals. President Kennedy was acutely aware of the strain in relationships between him and most businessmen, and almost desperately wanted to improve them. He was especially sensitive to the prospect that attacking some of the more notable fixations of the American consciousness—like balanced budgets—would drive even more deeply the wedge between business and the Administration. Yet he hungered for the abandonment of the old clichés and the incantations.

It was this dilemma of Mr. Kennedy's—the struggle between what he wanted to do and felt he could do—that I wanted to bring into focus. I hoped to do it in a way that would encourage

7

a bolder attack by the President—wherever that mobilization of forces would lead in terms of relationships with business. And President Kennedy encouraged others to "zero in" on the principal economic myths; for example, after he had read an article of mine in *The New Republic* urging heavier federal spending, he passed word on through Ted Sorensen that he'd like to see more such articles in magazines of mass circulation.

Few of us will forget easily the shock of the assassination; I expect to remember it as long as I live. Needless to say, it changed the prospective impact of this book. The man I wanted most to read it is no longer with us. But the basic problems are still with us, and the myth that Kennedy was "anti-business" still abounds—especially in the framework of the more comfortable relationship President Johnson has managed to establish with the same cast of characters.

I am indebted to many persons in and out of Government who talked to me frankly and freely both in my capacity as a *Newsweek* correspondent, and in special interviews for this book. I have imposed on the time of Justice Arthur Goldberg, Walter W. Heller, Labor Secretary W. Willard Wirtz, Commerce Secretary Luther Hodges, Gardner Ackley, John P. Lewis, Kermit Gordon, James L. Tobin, James W. Knowles, Mortimer Caplin, William McC. Martin, Roger Blough, Joseph A. Pechman, Stanley Ruttenberg, Nathaniel Goldfinger, Stanley Surrey, Henry Fowler, Myer Feldman and many others. This does not mean that they have the slightest responsibility for what is said here, for in contrast to a practice I note to be common, no part of this book has been read in advance by the above-mentioned or any other sources or friends. Thus, any and all errors or misinterpretations of fact are entirely mine.

I am grateful to the management of *Newsweek* (which also must be held blameless for any of my conclusions) whose confidence in me gave me the range of reporting responsibility which made this book at all possible; and to Ben Bradlee, Chief of the *Newsweek* Washington Bureau, who gave me every encouragement. I feel especially indebted to Don MacCampbell, agent extraordinary, and to Bill Targ of Putnam's, who believed in this book from the start.

And finally, it is difficult to express the full measure of my ap-

preciation to my wife and three children, who not only understood the meaning of the locked door to my study at home, but
whose confidence and pride in "the book" while it was still a
long way from the presses sustained a first-time author all along.

HOBART ROWEN
May 7, 1964

Contents

PART ONE: *Crisis and Retreat*

I	*The Beginning*	*15*
II	*Coming to Grips With Recession*	*34*
III	*Tax Reform, First Stage:* *It's Still Deductible*	*46*
IV	*The Business Advisory Council:* *Divorce and Remarriage*	*61*
V	*Business Ethics*	*80*
VI	*The Big Steel Crisis:* *Kennedy vs. Blough*	*89*
VII	*Rapprochement, Second Phase*	*113*
VIII	*Black Monday on Wall Street—* *"The Kennedy Market"?*	*130*

PART TWO: *Groping for Full Employment*

IX	*The Economic Advisers' Pecking Order:*	*153*
X	*Kennedy, the Public Interest,* *Dillon and Heller*	*183*
XI	*William McChesney Martin and the "Fed"* *and the Labor Movement*	*208*
XII	*The Tax Reduction Act of 1964:* *Will It Work?*	*231*
XIII	*Unemployment in America—* *Ugly Side of the Affluent Society*	*253*
XIV	*From Kennedy to LBJ:* *The Unfinished Business*	*274*
	Notes	*298*
	Index	*311*

Part One | CRISIS AND RETREAT

I | *The Beginning*

For much of John Fitzgerald Kennedy's Presidency, right-wing critics complained that he harbored an inner conviction or feeling of hostility to the American business community. A good deal of this "anti-business" talk arose after the President cracked down on the steel industry's attempt to raise prices $6 a ton in April, 1962.

But the fact is that Mr. Kennedy in dealing with the complicated American economic machine catered so fully to the needs of business that he distressed some of his liberal friends. It is a curious thing, perhaps, that an administration with as much brains, good intentions, and style as Mr. Kennedy's found itself caught in this sort of cross fire.

He was urged to press forward—to "get the country moving again"—with the speed and urgency he set forth in the 1960 campaign. Mr. Kennedy did not always find this possible; where the liberals would plunge in, the politician in Mr. Kennedy exerted caution. Where they felt free to expend the "capital" of his popularity, he, thinking of re-election—the same spur that sent him on his final, ill-fated journey to Dallas—was determined to conserve it. And then, there were practical problems that no amount of heroics could surmount: no matter what John Kennedy wanted to do about taxes, for example, Senator Byrd and the oil lobby were and remain facts of life—unhappy ones, to be sure, but necessary to contend with.

Paradoxically, the complaints from the right and the left

often converged on the same set of actions. For example, business criticism of Kennedy's abrasive encounter with the steel industry was matched by labor's disappointment that he didn't press his advantage to set up some system of continuing price restraint. As a matter of fact, the President quickly backed away from his tempestuous struggle with Roger Blough, and found himself in 1963 the victim of slick price-hike maneuvers that negated, in large measure, his victory over the steel industry the year before.

Another element of the paradox is that the many specific actions taken by Mr. Kennedy which were clearly "pro" rather than "anti" business—ranging from an investment credit which was a genuine tax bonanza to orthodox methods of solving the payments-balance problem—were accepted by business with all the grace of a spoiled child. When, for example, the Administration decided to tie as much as 80 percent of foreign aid to purchases of goods here, this Democratic version of "Buy America" was received matter-of-factly by business—and with scarcely a raised eyebrow in liberal circles which would have blistered such a protectionist device had it been sponsored by a Republican Administration.

Meanwhile, the labor movement, lacking inspired leadership, had to submit to the insistence that it support the "public interest"—and when President Kennedy sent a thinly disguised compulsory arbitration proposal to Congress in the summer of 1963 to head off a nationwide rail strike, the useless fumings of labor boss George Meany were restricted to the seventh floor of his barony on Washington's 16th Street.

All in all, any calm analysis of the Kennedy Administration should convince one that John F. Kennedy was *not* anti-business. On the contrary, he went further than most Republican Presidents (with whom the business community would rather identify themselves) in making significant overtures to business. If there is a dispassionate criticism to be made, it is, rather, that after a brief period (in the flush of victory over Richard Nixon) in which he thought he would curtail special favors to business, Kennedy changed course abruptly. He decided, instead, that he must convince businessmen that he was even-handed—and that they should support him. And in this process, he leaned over backward for a long period to accommodate the criticisms and conservative views of businessmen and bankers.

Mr. Kennedy was new to the job and, as he liked to point out himself, had but a thin majority in Congress (reflecting his tight popular majority over Nixon). But a policy of appeasement, as Neville Chamberlain and others learned the hard way, neither contents the appeased nor satisfies the more basic needs of the larger body politic.

Throughout his Administration, Kennedy was able to exact a self-discipline from labor leaders that would have been quite impossible under a Republican. To be sure, the doors of the White House, shut during the Eisenhower Administration, were flung open to the union men. But where there would have been an angry snapback to a Republican demand for wage restraint or curtailment of strikes, labor accepted the imposition of guidelines on wage increases and official frowns on use of the strike weapon with only muted complaints. In fact, as 1963 came to a close, many economists worried that the rate of productivity increase in the private sector of the economy, was dangerously outstripping wage increases. This spelled trouble for economic growth—trouble which arose because in his zeal to close the balance of payments gap, Mr. Kennedy had given second priority to expansion of the sluggish underpinnings of the economy at home. But the business community returned the many Kennedy gestures with continued hostility and little support. It took the President quite a while to conclude that no matter what he did, it would be difficult to bridge the gap between a Democratic President and the business world.

Professor Seymour E. Harris, in *The Economics of the Political Parties*[1] observed that Democrats generally reject the view that the role of government "is to create the proper climate for businessmen by reducing government expenditure, balancing the budget, diminishing government responsibility for social welfare and economic regulation, and in general, transferring power from government and labor to the business community."

The traditional business point of view is essentially hostile to government—especially the Federal Government. According to a recent poll of key executives by the Research Institute of America, "business has a distinct distrust of the federal machinery." [2]

In its pure sense, the business point of view is almost anarchistic: the best government is the least government. Of course, concessions are made to the need for certain services such as a police force and a defense establishment. But in all other ways, the role of the government should be closely restricted, so that the marketplace can make the big economic decisions. Emphasis on monetary policy fits neatly into the pattern of leaving the big decisions to the private sector. When a Galbraith or Myrdal suggests a greater concentration on the public sector, the automatic response of businessmen is—"socialism." The Research Institute study, for example, when it polled businessmen on threats to the American way of life, found that they ranked "creeping socialism" second only to internal "moral or spiritual decline" among the dangers.

Thus, Kennedy's controversies with the business world have been essentially the same that any Democratic President was likely to encounter. As his brother Robert once said with refreshing candor: "The business community always has a greater mistrust of any Democratic President than of a Republican Administration. It is an ideological reflex—obsolete in my opinion —but that's one of the facts of life. I don't know that businessmen, the big ones, anyway, no matter what we do, will ever be in love with us." [3] President Johnson, on the other hand, may have discovered a significant new secret in relationships between his party and the business world: the American business tycoon seems to be as much interested in symbols as in reality. Thus, Johnson has effectively used the vehicle of White House dinners and tête-à-têtes with the President to make businessmen feel "comfortable," while continuing most of Kennedy's economic policies and even elaborating on them—for example, by initiating new federal spending to combat poverty.

In effecting the transition from the Kennedy Administration to his own, Johnson openly resorted to an emotional appeal for understanding. "I'm the only President you have," he said repeatedly and unashamedly. When necessary, as in the case of a threatened rail strike in April, 1964, he waved the American flag. Thus, the LBJ concoction of corn pone, sincerity, energy, and action—served up with all of the fervor of a Southwestern preacher—was hard to beat, and resisted by few. And no one is more susceptible to effective use of clichés than the American businessman or average labor leader. Johnson is a master of the technique—but Kennedy would have choked reading the best Johnson lines.

President Kennedy, sensitized during the 1960 campaign to the outspoken challenge by businessmen to his fiscal integrity, arrived on the Washington scene ready to meet their demands at least halfway. Kennedy's official welcome from the outgoing Administration was a warning, in Eisenhower's "lame-duck" budget message, against a "credit card" economy, a not very deft suggestion that Kennedy was an inflationist. "The budgetary outlook for the future," Eisenhower said in his budget message of January 16, 1961—four days before Kennedy took over, "reinforces the need for self-discipline. If . . . we deliberately run the Government by credit cards, improvidently spending today at the expense of tomorrow, we will break faith with the American people and their children. . . ."

It was to be a recurrent Eisenhower theme, and it irked the new President no end. But Kennedy soon gave evidence that his own real fiscal instincts were conservative, too. His biographer, James McGregor Burns, had written in *John Kennedy—A Political Profile* that he would fit in the center of the liberal Wilson-Roosevelt-Truman tradition. In social issues, in a feel for the problems that affect people, this was doubtless true.

But in fiscal and monetary matters, there was a conservative streak inherent in President Kennedy's makeup. As a practical and successful politician, he found his way to the top by a gradual espousal of the social and economic aims of progressive Democrats. But Kennedy was not a doctrinaire liberal, as he showed by reaching unhesitatingly for an urbane and sophisticated Republican, Douglas Dillon, to be his Secretary of the Treasury.

Dillon was no mere decoration in the Kennedy Cabinet, a good GOP name to dress up a Democratic lineup. He was, instead, the dominant influence on Kennedy's economic programs, although Dillon himself showed an amazing ability to adjust his views. His friends consider this agility a testimony to his flexibility, while his enemies think it a sign of weakness. Dillon, for example, was converted to the necessity of a modest-sized deficit to counter recession. It's true that he fought and scrapped with Walter W. Heller, chairman of the Council of

Economic Advisers, to keep it down. But it's hard to recall any other Treasury Secretary who embraced the principle of deficit financing of any kind for any purpose. Dillon's "flexibility" on this score embittered some of his old Wall Street associates.

To a private visitor a few short weeks before the assassination, Kennedy defended the wisdom of his choice of Dillon on the grounds that some gesture of the sort was necessary because of his narrow popular vote margin over Nixon.

"Do you suppose, Mr. President," his guest asked politely, "that if Mr. Nixon had been elected, he would have named Leon Keyserling Secretary of the Treasury as a gesture to the liberals?" Mr. Kennedy roared at the joke.

Dillon is considered something of a traitor by Nixon and Eisenhower for taking a high post with the Kennedy Administration—and they tried to dissuade him. As a matter of fact, three years after Dillon had blended into the Kennedy background so effectively that most Washingtonians—including the Dillons—had all but forgotten their GOP label, Eisenhower was complaining that it was a pity such top Republicans as Dillon, and Henry Cabot Lodge—who went to Vietnam for JFK in mid-1963—had deprived the party of their services.

Kennedy's appointment of Dillon was a grand and shrewd gesture, a resounding, symbolic tribute to sound money. Dillon had been a member of Eisenhower's subcabinet as Undersecretary of State, with credentials as a Wall Street banker to boot. As a heavy contributor to Nixon's campaign, he would have been a logical appointee as the Republican Secretary of the Treasury—if Kennedy had lost.

In the interregnum between election day and Kennedy's Inauguration, liberal Democrats, aware of the sensitive and powerful role of the Treasury Secretary, tried desperately to come up with the name of some one politically acceptable to Kennedy who would not, at the same time, outrage the Wall Street powers. They couldn't. Seymour Harris has recorded for history that he, Prof. John Kenneth Galbraith, Arthur Schlesinger, and Paul Samuelson sat around one day trying to find "a good name among Democrats" they might recommend to Kennedy.[5] Harris, later an adviser to Dillon, is convinced that the hard-working Secretary is a genius at absorbing new ideas:

"Dillon is not blind to modern theories of fiscal policy. . . . [He] promises to become the Alexander Hamilton of the twentieth century."

Neither Wall Street nor most regular Democrats accept such an effusive estimate of Dillon. But Kennedy shared Harris' enthusiasm. By instinct, heritage, and drive, Kennedy and Dillon were close together. Men of wealth, heirs to fortunes created by their fathers, Harvard graduates comfortable in the same Newport-Palm Beach-Georgetown social set, their relationship was a natural. Kennedy said when he originally announced Dillon's appointment: "Mr. Dillon would not have accepted this position if he had not been in agreement, in general agreement with me, and I would not have asked him to accept the position if I had not been in general agreement with him." The President knew what he was talking about: despite the difference in party labels, their thinking was on the same wavelength, and when it was necessary for Dillon to shift to stay in line with the President, he shifted. A member of the Democratic National Committee mused privately: "Dillon is the thinking man's Republican!"

If Wall Street thus didn't acquire an Andrew Mellon type Republican as Secretary of the Treasury, it didn't have to face a John Kenneth Galbraith type Democrat, either. And there were other signs that should have been of general comfort to the business world. Kennedy's appointments and the men he passed up, said something about the probable character of the new Administration. He didn't hesitate to appoint Allen Dulles, and then John McCone, both staunch Republicans, to run the Central Intelligence Agency. True, he appointed a full-fledged liberal in Walter Heller as chairman of the Council of Economic Advisers, and abolished the post of economic aide to the President. That established Heller as his chief economist-thinker. Moreover, he let Heller have his own choices for the No. 2 and No. 3 men on the Council.

But there were counterweights on economic policy, not only Dillon and Federal Reserve Chairman William McChesney Martin, but Undersecretary for Monetary Affairs Robert V. Roosa, a brilliant money technician who had been a vice-president of the New York Federal Reserve Bank. Roosa, in charge of debt management and international money matters, forged the Treasury, with Dillon, into a stronghold of traditional, but not archaic, economics.

For the key jobs of Secretary of State and Secretary of Defense, Kennedy chose essentially nonpolitical men in Dean Rusk, and Robert S. McNamara of the Ford company. Moreover, two Democrats that businessmen worried most about during the campaign, Harvard Prof. John K. Galbraith (author of *The Affluent Society*) and former Michigan Governor G. Mennen ("Soapy") Williams came up with only secondary appointments—in terms of their potential influence on economic policy. Galbraith, although called in on occasion by Kennedy for confidential consultation on economic matters, performed his principal service as Ambassador to India; and Williams was named an Assistant Secretary of State in charge of African affairs.

In terms of "dangerous radicals," there weren't any. Pointedly, Leon Keyserling, who had been chairman of the Council of Economic Advisers, was not invited onto the team at all, primarily because he was considered a "spender" by some Kennedy men. For "bêtes noirs," the Republicans were reduced to heckling Arthur Schlesinger, Jr., noted historian and author who was taken on the White House staff for miscellaneous speech assignments; and Heller, who as a prolific writer, lecturer, and Congressional witness had made the correct liberal, academic record on all economic issues.

But Schlesinger had virtually nothing to do with policy making in the White House. And Heller yielded principles gracefully to the pressures of the feasible, proving that even a professor can learn the political ropes. Schlesinger and Heller have been—regardless of Senator Barry Goldwater's nightmares —about as radical as sunflower seeds. But for the lack of anything better, which is a sign of how conservative Kennedy's appointments were, Schlesinger and Heller have had to stand in for whatever nineteenth-century abuse the right wing chose to dish out.

Appointments aside, Kennedy gave other notice soon after taking office that he was no tiger that the business world needed to cage to protect law, order, and the free enterprise system. For example, he rejected much of an economic expansion program that had been suggested initially by Professor Paul Samuelson of M.I.T.—who headed an economic task force established by Kennedy after the election. A cautious, rather than bold economic approach was taking shape as the Kennedy hallmark.

The President moved so carefully during those first few months that Walter Lippmann felt impelled to say that he had preserved "in all its essentials the Eisenhower economic philosophy and the Eisenhower international commitments . . . never explaining to the country that those can be changed. It's like the Eisenhower Administration thirty years younger." [6]

The trouble was that Kennedy, working with a bare Congressional majority and—for the moment—content to follow what he thought was public opinion, instead of molding it, rejected larger deficits in the national budget in order to stimulate economic growth. In a private conversation, Kennedy told one of his aides: "I don't want to be tagged as a big spender early in this Administration. If I do, I won't get my programs through later on." In early 1961, before the Berlin crisis forced his hand, Kennedy planned to hold the budget as close as he could to Eisenhower's last prescription for it. At that time, Kennedy was determined to get by with a deficit of some $3 billion or less, even though unemployment was about 6 percent of the labor force, and threatening to go higher.

The President paid close attention to his Republican critics and was extremely sensitive to shafts aimed his way by General Eisenhower. Ironically, just as General Eisenhower told a Republican rally in June, 1961, that Kennedy was spending too much money, Professor Arthur F. Burns, Eisenhower's first economic adviser, was acknowledging that the sharp contraction in federal outlays in 1959 was one of the three principal reasons for the recession that resulted in 1960. (The others, according to Burns: tight money, and the 1959 steel strike.) Eisenhower's campaign to pin the "fiscally irresponsible" tag on Kennedy stung the President. Although liberals like Heller, Senator Joseph Clark of Pennsylvania and Representative Henry Reuss of Wisconsin were urging heavier, rather than reduced spending, the "primitive misconceptions" of Eisenhower (Paul Samuelson's felicitous phrase) had a compelling impact on Kennedy.

In an interview for a *Newsweek* feature, Walter Lippmann sagely observed to me that "Kennedy's domestic policies don't reflect those of his economic advisers. They are sound, modern men, and the only reason he isn't going along with them is that he's got other matters to worry about. He can't take on a full fight with Eisenhower over budget policy, when he needs his support on other matters." [7]

The principal "other matters," of course, were Berlin and the cold war in the summer of 1961, and for these reasons, most labor leaders and liberals (as did Lippmann) softened their criticism. But business should have been cheering the President on: his uncompromising defense of the dollar, with fervent assurances that there would be no devaluation, dumped the London gold speculators. Gold, which had soared from the fixed U. S. buying price of $35 an ounce to $40, settled back.

That brilliant and perceptive economist, Per Jacobsson— whose untimely death in the summer of 1963 has left a gaping void—summed it up in a single sentence at a Washington cock- tail party: "When Kennedy came in," the managing director of the International Monetary Fund said, "the stock market went up, and the price of gold went down."

But there were some doubts and suspicions overhanging from the campaign, when Kennedy made tight money and high inter- est rates a major issue. The business community feared the onset of easy money. Nothing else so symbolized the impend- ing change, save, perhaps, the fact that after eight years of extraordinary influence in Washington, it would be on the out- side, looking in, if Kennedy became President.

Even discounting the Democratic platform adopted July 12, 1960, at Los Angeles for the usual measure of political over- statement, businessmen felt that the "Rights of Man" declara- tion might chart new paths for the economy.

"As the first step in speeding economic growth," said this platform, "a Democratic president will put an end to the present high interest, tight money policy." It went on to pledge a 5 percent annual growth rate, an attack on "administered prices," and a repeal of "anti-labor excesses" that had been written into labor laws.[8]

Even more than the formal words of the platform, Candidate Kennedy's own views were carefully combed over for hints of the future—and what businessmen read and heard, they didn't

like. At the Los Angeles convention, men close to Kennedy
spoke ominously about their dislike of William McChesney
Martin, chairman of the Federal Reserve System, for years the
very embodiment of fiscal integrity to the business world.

For most of Eisenhower's eight years, the Democrats had complained about Martin: as head of the U. S. central banking system, his decisions on money supply and interest rates were crucial. And in the Democratic view, his tight money policy,
acquiesced in by Eisenhower, had led to three recessions, heavy
unemployment, and billions of added interest charges on the
federal debt.

At the 1960 Democratic convention in Los Angeles, Kennedy's
most intimate advisers—some of whom became key White
House staff members—said plainly that Martin would have to
be "fired," or his policy-making power somehow boxed in, if he
balked at Kennedy's plan to pursue a more liberal program.
Thus, the question of the "independence" of the Federal Reserve was dragged into the campaign.

The so-called independence of the Federal Reserve is an
emotionally charged and somewhat synthetic issue, but it packs
a punch. In reality, the Federal Reserve cannot be truly independent of the wishes of any national administration, and no
one knows this better than the earnest and determined chairman of the Federal Reserve.

But as a rallying cry for conservatives, the "independence" of
the Federal Reserve ranks with budget balancing and motherhood. James Tobin, the gentle and brilliant Yale professor who
was a member of the Kennedy Council of Economic Advisers
for its first 18 months, puts it well: "The Federal Reserve to
some is the last citadel protecting the dollar and the country
from disaster." [9]

Midway during the campaign, Kennedy realized that his
strident emphasis on tight money, and the questions being
raised about Martin's and the Federal Reserve's future, needed
to be toned down. In the somber men's clubs where high corporate officials meet for lunch, in Wall Street board rooms—and
in Wall Street market letters—the notion that Kennedy was a
dangerous radical was gaining currency.

Kennedy never withdrew the charge that tight money had
been the main cause of the Eisenhower recessions. But he began

to stress that the FRB and the President had to work together, and then—an entirely new theme—the need to protect the U. S. dollar and correct the serious balance of payments deficit.

Late in September, as election day drew near, Kennedy outlined his evolving policy this way: "The Board of Governors of the Federal Reserve System is given a degree of independence by the Federal Reserve Act, but it cannot be considered a fourth branch of government. It must bear in mind the economic objectives of the Administration, and I am confident that it would respond to leadership by the Administration.

"In some instances, this will mean a reduction in interest rates; at all times, the Board and the President should work together to achieve national economic goals." [10]

This was temperate enough, and Martin was increasingly pleased by the mounting Kennedy assurances on the balance of payments question. It has never been revealed, but Martin flatly turned down a feeler from the Nixon camp for a speech supporting the Republican candidate. (It almost would have been worth it. How then would the Republicans have treated the subject of an "independent FRB"?)

A cordial and fruitful relationship between Kennedy and Martin was actually in the making, although they never met until after Kennedy was installed in the White House. It was a source of some concern to liberal Democrats that Kennedy and Martin hit it off so well. Instead of trying to force his resignation, as was recommended in the first flush of post-nomination excitement at Los Angeles, the upshot was that Kennedy reappointed Martin in 1962 for a new four-year term as chairman of the Board.

In addition to his attack on tight money, Kennedy seized upon the recession in the economy—whose very existence was denied by the Eisenhower Administration—as the underpinning for his famous theme that he "would get the country moving again." And he would do it by a forthright program of stimulating the economy by increased government spending, especially for housing, hospitals, education, urban renewal, and other needed social welfare programs.

Before the Urban Affairs Conference in Pittsburgh, Pennsylvania, on October 10, 1960, Kennedy said: "What stands between our people and the good life of which Aristotle spoke is not any lack of ability to produce consumer goods. That problem, for America, has been solved. What have not been solved are those problems which lie largely in the realm of public action—bad housing, poverty, recessions, unemployment, discrimination, crowded and obsolete schools and hospitals and libraries, inadequate recreation, the breakdown of mass transportation, polluted air and water, juvenile delinquency. . . .

"Some may say that all these things will cost too much. But the cost to the taxpayer will be far less than the present enormous cost of slums, traffic jams, crime and delinquency, and the economic decline of downtown areas. And the entire Federal share will actually be less than just one item in the present Federal budget—the excessive interest costs on the national debt that have been added by the high-interest policies of the Republican administration."

This indeed was a bold blueprint, and something for business to think about. To the American businessman, there is no nerve so sensitive as the one that sends out signals when spending, debts, and deficits are mentioned (unless it is the one titillated when the magic word profits comes up). It is useless to observe that the growth of the United States, since its Day of Independence, has been founded on debt and the reliability of its credit.

What the business world foresaw, in speeches such as Kennedy's at Pittsburgh, was the certain prospect of a bigger Federal Government, looming ever more important, involving bigger budgets and bigger deficits. Kennedy's frank espousal of the need for a larger public sector was merely an extension of the Eisenhower Administration's tacit recognition of the larger role of government in modern society. The difference was that Eisenhower had reluctantly embraced a larger role for government, whereas Kennedy said he welcomed it.

His specific views on an enlarged role for the Federal Government were outlined in an NBC interview on October 1, 1960:

Q. One of your advisers, Professor Galbraith, has an idea that has caught the attention of a lot of people, and it is that the American people are spending too much money for private comfort and luxury, and too little for such public facilities as schools, parks, libraries, and so on. What do you think of that?

KENNEDY: Well, I think that Professor Galbraith and others are anxious to concentrate as much attention as we can on the public needs of our time, and [we need] . . . the best schools and the best teachers. We are in the most competitive struggle that any free society has ever been engaged in. The individual can't build a school. The individual can't build a library. Professor Galbraith seeks to remind us that we have private and public responsibility, and if we don't recognize it we are not going to endure.

Q. Do you think the White House can change this emphasis from private luxury to public services?

KENNEDY: Roosevelt did an awful lot in his day. There was an awful lot of people in public life in the mid-twenties and thirties that came because of Theodore Roosevelt, and I think Woodrow Wilson did the same. . . . There is a strong sense of public responsibility in the United States, and I think the President is the one man to strike the chord.

Q. Then you are saying, Senator, that when we come to this matter of economic growth, that we cannot depend on the production and consumption of electric can openers, and gum massagers, and drink stirrers, and what not for economic growth?

KENNEDY: No, I think that all of those examples may be somewhat extreme, but I do think we . . . want to improve private comfort. After all, washing machines are essential and not a luxury, and automobiles, and all the rest. I think that the only thing we want to do is to remember the necessity of educating our children . . . I think the President [in] the pursuit of excellence in all phases of our national life . . . can do a good deal in setting the tone. Of course, we depend on individual effort, individual taste, individual judgment.

Such answers suggested a reasonable enough position, but Nixon's strategy was to paint Kennedy as an extremist, an economic radical. The Vice-President made that decision back in May, 1960, when he guessed, correctly, Kennedy would get the Democratic nomination. Before a closed-door session of the Republican-oriented, blue ribbon Business Advisory Council meeting at the Homestead in Hot Springs, Virginia, Nixon analyzed the situation this way: on international matters and on such domestic matters as civil rights, he could see few real differences between himself and Senator Kennedy; but the Senator was really the captive of the labor-left wing element of the Democratic Party, and would have to do labor's bidding once he got the nomination.

Therefore, Nixon said, he was staking out for himself the conservative side of economic issues where he could establish a clear-cut difference. Herb Klein, then Nixon's press aide, explained: "We've got something here that's clear cut, and we're going to hit it hard." It mattered little, of course, that to make the issue "clear cut," Nixon had to change some of his recorded views—that's acceptable procedure in American politics.

Soon after the historic Rockefeller Brothers' report appeared in 1957, Nixon happily jumped on the bandwagon with statements urging that the country "set as a goal not the present rate of growth of our economy of 3 percent, but the higher rate of 5 percent recommended by the Rockefeller Report." [11] But in June, 1960, Nixon, without so much as a blink of an eye, delivered a slashing attack on the "growthmanship" school of economics in a speech at St. Louis. He was after bigger game, now, than Rockefeller.

During the campaign, Nixon lost no opportunity to take the side opposite from Kennedy on economic issues. *He,* Nixon said firmly, would never tamper with the Federal Reserve System, or tinker with the oil depletion allowance. Nor would he withhold taxes, as Kennedy proposed, on dividends and interest payments. And he said: "I reject the idea that governmental spending should increase just to keep pace with total spending." [12]

Toward the end of the campaign, Kennedy's board of strategy decided that he had better set the economic issues straight. He did this in two key speeches, one to the Associated Business Publications Conference in New York on October 12, and the other in Philadelphia on October 31. Together, they were an amazingly prescient analysis of almost all the problems that lay ahead. Read closely, they show that the Kennedy approach would be to jab, not swing wildly; they foreshadowed that his pledge to get the "country moving again" would be tempered by a firm conservative instinct.

In his New York speech, Kennedy recognized and reported "the common assumption" that there was some sort of inevitable conflict between the business community and the Democratic Party. He rejected this as a carefully fostered political myth. His

Administration, he said, "will not be a businessman's administration, but neither will it be a labor administration, or a farmer's administration. It will be an administration representing, and seeking to serve, all Americans."

Kennedy pointed out that no President, Democratic or Republican, could countenance growing unemployment without doing something about it, and bracketed himself with Nixon as opposed to "excessive, unjustified, or unnecessary government intervention in the economy." He made what he considered a necessary obeisance to local and private effort, but insisted that the nation "must do better" in economic growth, jobs, the business cycle, price stability, and the balance of payments. Then, Kennedy developed what can be considered his own rewrite of the economic sections of the Los Angeles platform. In his own words:

"First, a Democratic Administration would use monetary policies more flexibly than the Republicans. . . . Without rejecting monetary stringency as a potential method of curbing extravagant booms, we would make more use of other tools.

"Secondly . . . we would use the budget as an instrument of economic stabilization. . . . In boom times we should run a surplus and retire the debt. When men and plant are unemployed in serious numbers, the opposite policies are in order. . . . But we must have a . . . coordinated monetary and fiscal policy. I do not advocate, let me make clear, any changes in the constitution of the Federal Reserve System. It is important to keep the day-to-day operations of the Federal Reserve removed from political pressures. The President's responsibility, if he is to lead, includes longer range coordination of economic policies. . . .

"Third, I believe that the next administration must work sympathetically and closely with labor and management to develop wage and price policies that are consistent with stability . . . the President of the United States must actively use the powers of leadership in pursuit of well-defined goals of price stability. . . .

"Fourth, we must make certain that there is proper encouragement to plant modernization . . . [through] tax revision, including accelerated depreciation.

"Fifth, . . . growth requires that we have the best trained

and best educated labor force in the world. Investment in manpower is just as important as investment in facilities.

". . . Finally, we must remember that in the long run, the public development of natural resources too vast for private capital—and federally encouraged research, especially basic research—are both sources of tremendous economic progress."

In Philadelphia, Kennedy turned in greater detail to the problem that would prove to be his overwhelming concern for at least three years ahead: the growing balance of payments deficit. One of the most complicated problems of our times, the balance of payments is little understood. Briefly, the United States, since the end of World War II, has been lending, investing, spending, and giving away more dollars to both the developed and backward nations of the world than it earns in world markets.

Our willingness to do this, a composite of generosity and self-interest, provided for the reconstruction and security of Europe after the war, and in a gradual improvement in the standard of living in the free world. By the same token, as the rest of the world—especially Europe—prospered, it accumulated a surplus of dollars. Where once dollars were scarce, and treasured more than many another nation's currency, they were worth less in the mid-fifties. Thus, those who had more dollars than they needed turned them back to us, and did what American nationals cannot do—cashed them in for gold.

As the campaign year of 1960 moved toward a close, the situation was growing worse. The deficit in the balance of payments was running at a rate of nearly $4 billion, and since January, U. S. gold reserves had been drawn down $800 million. Since U. S. gold hoards were not limitless, this drain couldn't go on forever.

In London, gold speculators, sensing and trying to create a dollar crisis, tried to make a killing: If the U. S. dollar could be devalued, then the price of gold, which the U. S. had fixed at $35 an ounce, would go up. Every ounce of gold would be worth more dollars—by the amount of the devaluation.

But the insidious thing, so far as Democratic prospects were concerned, was that much of the flurry in gold—the assumption that the dollar would be cheapened—was traced to the prospect of Kennedy's election. Europeans who took literally the Democratic platform attack on tight money, and others who were convinced by Nixon's assurances that Kennedy was a "big spender" concluded that the Kennedy era would be one of enormous inflation. In such a case, the United States could only pay off its international debts by devaluing the dollar. Almost desperately, the Kennedy strategists sensed the need to lay this question to rest—in a tight race, doubts on this point could cost Kennedy the election. The forum selected was the Philadelphia speech on October 31:

> The recent flurry of speculation on the London gold market has dramatized a problem which is not the product of this campaign, or even of the economic decline of the past year—America's adverse balance of payments. For the rise in the price of gold reflected the hope of a small number of speculators operating in a very thin market that the dollar will one day be devalued. Their hope is that this will be the necessary consequence of a continued shift in the balance of payments against the United States. . . .
>
> What would a new Democratic Administration do to reverse the present downward trend in our balance of payments?
>
> First, we pledge ourselves to maintain the current value of the dollar. If elected President I shall not devalue the dollar from its present rate. Rather, I shall defend the present value and its soundness.
>
> Secondly, we will begin immediate and vigorous negotiations to remove artificial barriers to the flow of American goods overseas, as well as restrictions on the flow of foreign capital to this country. We will ask our allies to share the increasing burden of building the military and economic strength of the free world. The nations of Western Europe, whose economies we have helped to restore, should now assume full partnership in the struggle against communism. . . .
>
> The remainder of our economic policies will have the broader goals of: (A) stimulating productivity and economic growth—(B) avoiding the periodic recessions which have caused a decline in business, a slowdown in our growth, and contributed to the more than $18 billion budget deficit of the last 8 years—and (C) halting the steady inflation which has brought the cost of living to the highest point in our history. Of course, to the extent that anti-inflationary policies are successful, they will increase our ability to compete in world markets and thus increase the flow of dollars to the United States.

What will those policies include? First, we are pledged to maintain a balanced budget except in times of national emergency or severe recession. . . .

Second, we will adopt a greater flexibility in the use of interest rates to control inflation. . . . We do not reject monetary policy as an instrument of controlling inflation. And we are also aware that sharp declines in the short-term interest rate could further aggravate the balance of payments problem. . . . But we do believe that monetary policy . . . must be used with full realization of the harmful effect that high-interest rates, especially on long-term obligations, can have on economic growth. . . .

Third, we must have a . . . coordinated monetary and fiscal policy. We do not, let me make it clear, advocate any changes in the constitution of the Federal Reserve System. . . .

Fourth, the Federal Government must work closely with labor and management to develop wage and price policies consistent with reasonable price stability. The erratic upward spiral of wages and prices . . . is one of the primary causes of inflation. . . . Without resorting to the compulsion of wage and price controls the President of the United States has a responsibility to exert the leadership of his office and the force of informed public opinion in the pursuit of reasonable price stability.

Fifth, we must stimulate plant modernization programs. . . . Wherever we are certain that tax revision—including accelerated depreciation—will stimulate investment . . . without damage to our principles of equity, we will proceed with such revision.

Sixth, we must develop . . . human and material resources. . . .

In his rather small, unpretentious office adjacent to the luxurious Federal Reserve board room, Martin breathed a sigh of relief when he read the Philadelphia speech. He felt then that Mr. Kennedy would be no threat to either the FRB or the free enterprise system—and that he would be able to work with him. Thus, even before Inaugural Day, the business world's No. 1 symbol of fiscal integrity—William McChesney Martin—knew that John F. Kennedy wasn't anti-business. But the business world hadn't yet caught up with the facts.

II | Coming to Grips With Recession

TAKING stock of President Kennedy a month after his brilliant inaugural address, the business community had every reason to be pleased. Like many a trip to the dentist, the voyage along the New Frontier was nowhere near as painful as advertised.

With verve and vigor, Kennedy and his aides had taken over an economy well into its fourth postwar recession. They stated a case for broad action to turn the economy upward, but kept their actions within the framework of "sound fiscal policies and relative price stability." These words were from a special Kennedy economic message to Congress, and they could have been said, as well, by Eisenhower.

Clearly, Kennedy had made a basic decision. His actions would be judicious, in keeping with the conclusion by a special task force headed by Professor Paul A. Samuelson that the economic dip would be relatively mild, and reversible without resort to a tax cut. He determined, on Dillon's advice, that it would be unwise to ask—as Samuelson had suggested, and Heller had urged—for discretionary authority to revise taxes. With 14 years of experience on the Hill behind him, President Kennedy knew that Congress is a jealous guardian of its prerogatives in the tax area.

He also decided, making good on a pledge in his "fiscal integrity" speech in Philadelphia, to ask for an 8 percent credit to stimulate business investment. This credit—ultimately set by

Congress at 7 percent—allows businessmen a straightaway deduction against taxes for investments in machinery and equipment used in the United States.[1] It was a source of bewilderment and annoyance to the Administration that this proposal, one of the cornerstones of its policy to help business modernize the means of production, was viewed by the business community with a jaundiced eye. At the same time, Kennedy's push for the investment credit represented a bitter defeat for the labor movement, which opposed it as a sheer giveaway, unnecessary in the face of a disturbingly large percentage of idle plant capacity. Labor fought it not only because it was one more tax cut for business, but because it added a new incentive to replace men with machines.

The proposal, as shaped in the Treasury under Assistant Secretary Stanley Surrey, was for a sliding credit for expenditures that exceeded current depreciation allowances. The idea, simply, was that it would encourage businessmen to undertake new investment. In effect, a company could buy a $1,000 machine for $930. Somewhat greedily, businessmen tried to discourage this device, preferring an across-the-board credit against investments they would be making in any event, or that had been made already.

Although the Administration promised that the credit wouldn't bar later changes in depreciation rules, business feared Surrey's idea would dull their long, insistent demands for more favorable treatment on this score. As it turned out, the investment credit was worth about $1 billion to American business in the first full year of its use—$1 billion that was lopped right off taxes, and retained in corporate coffers.

But at the time Kennedy was extending this luscious nugget, business shrugged it off, labor fought it, and the President was frustrated and furious with both. Oddly enough, the Heller Council of Economic Advisers was very much for the investment credit, convinced that the sluggish pace of investment was a key element making for general weakness in the economy.[2]

There were other signs, early in 1961, that began to worry labor and other liberal groups. The left-of-center wing of the Democratic party does not have a viable forum for the expression of its views. Such groups as the Americans for Democratic Action and the Conference on Economic Progress have been consistent, but not influential. The AFL-CIO, for reasons that we will examine closely later on, fenced, rather than fought, with President Kennedy. Some of the best pressure from the liberal wing of the Democratic Party originated in a few thought-provoking journals.

In any event, the cautious posture, the concern over the budget, the solicitation of business support, were elements of the Kennedy approach that began to be noticed. A conservative patina was much in evidence. Samuelson's task force report said flatly that "it is not realistic" to expect a sharp cut in unemployment too quickly. Kennedy was counseled to add only modestly to spending programs, and to take a "second look" in March to determine then the need for an emergency tax cut to choke off recession.[3] This would be a so-called second line of defense, and as events were to prove, not called on.

By the end of March, 1961, Kennedy's advisers knew that the recession was over* but wondered whether enough impetus had been supplied to soak up idle men and idle factories. The end of the final Eisenhower recession may have been the crucial time for Kennedy to drive the economy into high gear. As Heller observed in testimony before the Joint Economic Committee on March 6, 1961, "whenever it occurs, reversal of the recession is only the beginning, not the end of the task of restoring momentum to the American economy."[4] Unhappily, the Administration didn't rise to this challenge.

Such concerns were relayed to a Paris meeting of Western world economists by Kermit Gordon, then a member of the CEA, and now Director of the Budget. Gordon told the Europeans that the high rate of unemployment—6.8 percent—was the most disturbing thing about the U. S. economy. The official "interim" goal for full employment was to reduce the rate to 4 percent of unemployment. But at Paris—a meeting of the Organization for Economic Cooperation and Development—the economists talked straight and freely. What Gordon conceded was that the U. S. was unlikely to get below a 5 percent rate of

---

* In early March, Commerce Secretary Luther Hodges, moved by hopes, hunch, and a good instinct for what makes a headline, said, "We've hit bottom." The Administration was pained by Hodges' exuberance, since it still had a good deal of legislation to get through Congress. But Hodges was right. He told friends: "I can't prove it, but I've been feeling this way for two or three weeks."

unemployment without a more liberal spending and monetary policy than the Kennedy Administration felt able to pursue.

Kennedy's decision to move cautiously was not casually arrived at. Budget Director David Bell told a Washington meeting of the Business Advisory Council on April 4, 1961, that "many economists had raised the question whether the proposed federal deficit is large enough. The President's policy is clear. This is all he is prepared to recommend at the present time."

Secretary of Labor Arthur Goldberg, troubled by unemployment which had swelled from 5.1 percent of the labor force the previous May, 1960, to 6.8 percent in the spring of 1961, urged a more vigorous program. Even Samuelson, whose own mild prescription was being followed almost literally (except for discretionary authority on taxes) felt constrained to caution his academic friends that the plan being administered by the President was extremely limited. Samuelson wasn't critical, although he said that "we are in the midst of a 'placebo' program for recovery." But he was ready to concede that getting a tax cut in mid-1961 was out of the question: "The President had run on a platform that asked sacrifices of the American people," Samuelson wrote. "How then could he begin by giving them what many would regard as a 'handout?' " [5]

This was a period of low spirits for the group of liberal economists around Kennedy. His instincts daily proved to be more conservative than the tone of his campaign speeches. His acute sense of political realities persuaded him that he would have to dilute some of the goals he had brilliantly symbolized by the "getting the country moving again" theme. Moreover, it became apparent to those close to him that the political constraints weren't at all difficult for him to accept; they dovetailed rather neatly with his own real, basically middle-of-the-road views. If he didn't have to embark on a huge New Dealish spending orgy, that was a relief; John F. Kennedy was not a wild-eyed liberal. Just before he took office, he told one of his advisers-to-be that he wouldn't cotton to the idea of a tax cut, because it wouldn't mesh with the "What can you do for your country?" theme that would highlight the Inaugural Address.

Heller, the key man of the liberal group, wasn't "close in" at the start. The President had not even met him until October, 1960, after the first TV debate with Nixon. Heller's influence was no match for the President's own team—especially the Kitchen Cabinet headed by Ted Sorensen—most of whom had a relationship tested and steeled in the crucible of politics during and before the Presidential campaign. Moreover, just by instinct, Kennedy moved more easily along paths charted by Dillon, which were familiar and more to his liking. Early in the game, Kennedy found Heller a bit too professorial, and his memos discursive. But the President eventually got accustomed to Heller, and the economist—in the words of one of the White House insiders—"got acclimated to the White House and the needs of the President." Their relationship ripened into a good and close one.

There could be few complaints about the tone of Kennedy's first "State of the Union" message, delivered on January 30, 1961. It was like a refreshing breeze, after the Eisenhower years, to hear Kennedy honestly label the nation's economic problem for what it was, the product of a chronic slack whose end he could not and would not predict. Three days later, he sent his economic message to Congress. It was a potpourri of counter-recessionary measures, the product of excited day-and-night sessions in the White House, Labor Department, Treasury, and Department of Health, Education, and Welfare.

The economic message was prepared in such a fury of frantic effort that a press briefing on it was begun in the Fish Room of the White House before the full text was mimeographed. Typical of the frenetic state of affairs: when a reporter asked the briefing team a question on unemployment insurance, a White House official was dispatched to get the answer from Labor Secretary Arthur Goldberg, the one man who knew the answer.

But for all of the frenzy of action whipped up around the White House, there was but one really significant proposal: most of the other moves paralleled the makeshift, counter-punching type of anti-recession program Eisenhower had tried in 1958, keyed to a speed-up of spending already in the pipeline, especially military programs. But the one new thing was indeed important: in the field of monetary policy, the President and William McChesney Martin had evolved "Operation Nudge" (later called "Operation Twist")—an attempt to keep long-term interest rates from creeping too high while short-term rates were kept from falling too low.

This was a modest venture into new ground, and represented a notable victory for Kennedy. Until this time, the Federal Reserve policy had been to buy "bills only," or "bills usually": when operating in the securities market, the Federal Reserve would usually buy only very short-term obligations, rather than government issues of longer maturity. "Operation Nudge" was an accommodation to the pressures brought to bear by Heller and Council member James L. Tobin. Martin had to fight off some feeling within his own staff that he had "sold out" to Kennedy, but he was powerful enough to persevere in a determination to cooperate. But by and large, anything more dramatic was inhibited by the concern over the balance of payments crisis. As Representative Henry Reuss of Wisconsin has often said, "the $3 billion payments deficit 'tail' has been allowed to wag the $500 billion 'dog.'"

For the rest, the Kennedy economic proposals showed attention to human needs. There was a request for stopgap improvements in unemployment compensation; a cut in the Federal Housing Administration mortgage rate; an amendment to the Aid for Dependent Children Act so relief could be extended to children of unemployed persons who had exhausted their benefits; a demand for a Depressed Areas bill; and a program sponsored by Agriculture Secretary Orville Freeman to set up a half-dozen pilot food programs.

The President also proposed a five-part liberalization of the Social Security program; he planned a $258 million infusion into the consumer spending stream by instructing the Veterans Administration to pay at once dividends due through 1961; he asked for a two-stage boost in the minimum wage, first to $1.15 and then to $1.25 from the prevailing $1.00 level; he instructed all departments and agencies to comb through planned projects, with a view to expediting spending; Commerce Secretary Luther Hodges got specific orders to accelerate the highway program by making $724 million in federal funds available to the states at once instead of in dribbles throughout the year; he directed Goldberg to expand and improve the U. S. Employment Service, and to work with Defense Secretary McNamara to channel federal contracts into labor surplus areas.

Indeed, there was little that was left out. But apart from the "twist" on monetary policy, there was little really earth-shaking. Basically, business could be reassured, for Kennedy brushed aside the implication of the Samuelson report that budget deficits might have to be accepted for the first half of the decade, and reiterated instead his adherence to the principle of balancing the budget over the life of the business cycle.

"In harsh terms," said the Democratic majority of the Joint Economic Committee in the spring of 1961, "it could be said that since the late 1960 'gold rush,' our monetary policies have been shaped not solely by the needs of the domestic economy, but largely by the way European bankers are supposed to react to a given level of U. S. interest rates. Similarly, large or continuing deficits in the Federal budget must be avoided, it has been suggested, because such deficits alarm European bankers and tend to undermine confidence in the dollar."

The President left the decision on tax cuts to be made in 75 days—itself, the tip-off to waning possibilities; 75 days would bring the issue to April 15, past the Samuelson-suggested timetable. Wilfred Lewis observes, kindly, that Kennedy and Samuelson "appear to have been somewhat optimistic" in thinking that both the recession and the stagnation in the economy could have been handled without a tax cut.[6] There was more to it, of course, than wishful thinking: the President was afraid of going too fast—afraid that he might get tagged as some sort of radical, afraid that he would lose some of his popularity, afraid, simply, that he couldn't push through a more dramatic program even if he wanted to. There was plenty to support his purely political judgment; as temperate as his program was, Republicans like Charles Halleck, applying a minimum of economics and a maximum of politics, said that Kennedy's spending programs would cost billions and do nothing.

On March 6, 1961, Heller outlined to Congress the details of his theory of the economic "gap"—the vast difference in billions of dollars between the actual performance of the American economy and what it *could* turn out, operating near capacity.[7] He measured this gap at about 8 percent, or $40 billion of the then current Gross National Product. How much is $40 billion? It is, as Heller pointed out, about the size of another Pentagon budget, or twice the amount spent on public education—or about $500 per household.

The call by liberal friends of the President to "do more" is based on this "gap" in the economy, and the clear evidence from testimony by the Administration's own experts that the programs evolved were inadequate. "We face a problem of stubborn slack," Heller himself has said, "and the road to full recovery is a long one. The expansionary effects of government programs will be welcome even if they occur well after the recession has been reversed." [8]

In theory, at least, the business world should have been fairly content. Mr. Kennedy had talked fearlessly about the public sector and the public role during the campaign, but as President, he was breaking little new ground. "We will do what needs to be done to fulfill the high promise of the American economy," the President had told Congress in his special economic message. But he was willing, like Dillon, to drag his feet on the more venturesome ideas of his liberal economic claque.

To be sure, there were compelling reasons for any new President in early 1961 to move deliberately rather than dramatically. Kennedy had inherited not only a recession from Eisenhower, but a balance of payments crisis worsened by inept, panicky moves undertaken by Eisenhower's outgoing Treasury Secretary, Robert B. Anderson (who is a close personal friend of and adviser to President Johnson). It was necessary to create an image of the new Democratic President as a wise, careful, and prudent custodian of the dollar.

It was no easy task. Franklin D. Roosevelt, of course, had come into office faced with a terrible depression and a defeatist attitude that threatened to engulf not just the economy, but the democratic way of life. Happily, Kennedy did not face a real depression—among other reasons, New Deal reforms had made such an economic collapse all but impossible.

But Kennedy faced one problem even more ticklish than any confronting FDR. In fighting economic downturns, the President of the United States in the 1960's had to devote at least half of his attention to the international monetary situation. And the traditional methods of fighting recession at home, as refined since the passage of the Employment Act of 1946, were the precise ones that could affect the international crisis. These were easy money, tax cuts, heftier spending—every one of which, if successful, could deepen our balance of payments deficit, and accelerate the loss of gold.

Interest rates, if kept low enough to encourage businessmen to borrow, may lead to expansion of sales and job opportunities. But those who have funds to invest look for more advantageous interest rates abroad. Why take 3 percent in New York if you can get 4 percent in London or Amsterdam? This leads to an "export" of capital which builds up dollar balances held by other nations. Since the United States maintains the value of the dollar by willingly exchanging an ounce of gold for 35 U. S. dollars held by foreign central banks, excessive dollar balances abroad, if cashed in for gold, could exhaust our own reserves.

By the same token, tax and budget policies designed to prime the economic pump at home can be considered inflationary by the money markets of the world. If prices rise sharply as a result of a more active economy, then dollars held abroad are worth less—except in terms of one commodity whose price is fixed: gold. So inflation at home could speed gold losses, too.

Kennedy's dilemma was to bring about domestic recovery without accelerating the gold flow. Carrying water on both shoulders is always tricky, especially when one gets conflicting advice on the way the particular stunt can be performed. Heller (for expansion) and Dillon (for caution) jockeyed for position and influence. Dillon even set up his own committee of economic consultants in the Treasury under Seymour Harris, and lost few opportunities to suggest that Heller was an academic theorist. He likes to refer to Heller as "Professor" Heller.

The net result, by any objective standard, was that Kennedy's early actions on the economic front were less vigorous than were expected by eager Democrats. As Professor Henry C. Wallich, a respected conservative economist, once a member of Eisenhower's Economic Council, wrote in the *American Scholar:* "The discipline of the balance of payments . . . has kept many members of the new Administration chafing with impatience. They have wanted to take strong action to reduce unemployment and to stimulate growth. Fear of gold losses has reduced their original program to something not much more ambitious than the Republican might have been." [9]

Gardner Ackley, earnest member of the Council of Economic Advisers who joined the team in mid-1962 when Tobin returned to Yale, has stated the problem rather neatly. "Our continuing large payments deficit," he told an audience of economists at San Francisco State College, "has placed an obvious constraint upon our use of monetary policy. It has also furnished an additional excuse for those who oppose the use of fiscal policy to expand the domestic economy." [10]

When it came down to the gut issue of spending government money to infuse strength in what many thought was a stagnating economy, Kennedy felt obliged to turn the other way. In his special budget message on March 24, 1961, the President assured the business community that he was following sound fiscal practices. As Wilfred Lewis of the Brookings Institution wrote, Kennedy felt obliged to say that his new nondefense proposals "would not of and by themselves unbalance the budget submitted by President Eisenhower in January." [11]

Labor leaders were polite in public, but privately bitter. In June, 1961, Walter Reuther, head of the United Automobile Workers, delivered a blistering denunciation of Kennedy's economic policy behind the closed doors of the Labor Management Advisory Committee. He said bluntly that the Kennedy team had lost its sense of urgency, and told Walter Heller to his face that he was making public speeches that were excessively optimistic for a period blighted by heavy joblessness. The Administration did its best to hush the incident up.

Ted Sorensen, President Kennedy's most intimate adviser, explained to me that there were three key reasons for Kennedy's initial emphasis on a budget-balancing posture that smacked— to liberals at least—of something out of the Eisenhower era:

1. For eight long years, Eisenhower had been "chanting the virtues" of a balanced budget, and it had become an *idée fixe* in the minds of Congress and the public. To re-educate the nation would be a slow process—and risky. For example, if the budgeted outlays were heavily out of balance, Congress might balk at important legislative objectives.

2. The President himself really believed in the idea that the budget should be balanced in periods of relative prosperity.

3. It hardly jibed with his pleas for national sacrifice to present a budget out of balance because of heavy new civilian programs. Defense spending could be justified—guns were all right, but too much butter could easily be attacked.

Kennedy thus put the lid on spending. "Often," recalls David E. Bell from his period as Budget Director, "the President would tell me to go back and cut something in half. He's a very tight man with a dollar." [12] What resulted was a limp-along program. It is true that Kennedy freely acknowledged the need to war upon a recession Eisenhower ignored. But the fear of international repercussions dominated his strategy. A massive report on the balance of payments situation by the Brookings Institution in 1963 made this summary comment:

> The U. S. Government has not, on the whole, compromised its basic foreign policy and defense objectives because of balance of payments considerations. These considerations, however, have led to some undesirable policies. They have played an important role in failure to achieve the Employment Act's objective of maximum production and employment. The expansionary fiscal policy needed to restore high employment has been delayed and made more difficult to achieve by fears that expansion would make the balance of payments worse. . . . For balance of payments reasons, policies have been adopted tying economic aid to procurement in the United States and requiring military expenditures to be made in the United States rather than abroad. Such policies, aside from adding considerable cost to the taxpayer and arousing resentment in the rest of the Free World, protect high-cost U. S. industries from the spur of foreign competition and foster poor allocation of resources.

The conflict between moves to expand the economy and produce jobs at home, and policies which might narrow the payments deficit was a constant dilemma for Kennedy. The attempt to resolve it was the central motif of his Administration from the very beginning. Almost without exception, Kennedy leaned on the "conventional wisdom" when making a choice. From the first attempts in 1961 to squeeze down the budget, to the dramatic action in July, 1963, approving an increase in the Federal Reserve discount rate in order to block short-term capital losses, the Kennedy Administration took positions that were traditional, classical, and essentially pro-business.

Look at the orthodoxy of Kennedy's attempts to meet the balance of payments crisis: he cut overseas spending, kept our foreign aid money (so far as possible) at home, raised short-term interest rates, insisted that the dollar would not be devalued, called for heroic efforts to boost American exports, and limited foreign borrowings of long-term capital. All very prudent. But he might have decided, early on, that the way to protect the American balance of payments was to expand the American economy. Essentially, a strong economy, rather than an artificial balancing of accounts, is the best security for the nation.

I cannot fault President Kennedy all of the way. Given the Babbittish level of the Congress, and the sterility of some of the leadership of his own party on the Hill, it would have called for exceptional courage to set out upon other than the conventional path. But it is necessary to record that the Kennedy government did not take the initiatives to find new solutions—either for its problems at home, or with the balance of payments. It was less daring than the conservative government of Macmillan in Britain, which in April, 1963, cut taxes, increased spending, boosted its deficit, and started its economy up (and its balance of payments deficit down) in a way which seems to be adding luster to a continuing boom in Europe.

Tax Reform, First Stage: It's Still Deductible

IT STRIKES me as ironic that Mr. Kennedy, elected as a liberal, should have staked so much of his initial tax proposals on the investment credit. It was the heart of his first tax message, and as originally designed, would have cost the Treasury exactly the total to be recouped from plugged loopholes.

The rationale he offered for it—to counter the argument that the nation already had excess idle capacity—was the need for modernization of American factories, which had fallen behind Europe's wholesale rebuilding program after World War II. This sales pitch tied neatly, too, into balance of payments objectives: better and more efficient plants could help us compete in world markets.

But basically, Kennedy's reason for pushing the investment credit was a desire to do something for business in line with his Philadelphia speech. To support it, the Council of Economic Advisers and the Treasury looked at statistics, and decided that the slow rate of growth could be blamed on a relative reduction in spending by business for new plant and equipment. The figures cited to prove it were that from 1949 through 1957, expenditures on such business fixed investment averaged close to 11 percent of the gross national product, whereas in more recent years, the percentage had fallen to about 9 percent.[1]

How, then, to stimulate increased business investment? The Kennedy Administration's decision was to tempt business with the carrot of tax incentives, although many economists believe

46

that the basic inspiration for expanding or improving plant capacity develops when businessmen are pressed to meet demand for their products. In other words, consumption—as the Administration itself has argued in other situations—may be the more important determining factor.

The Kennedy Administration's tax policy was nevertheless directed to the investment side—a process that continues what went on during the Eisenhower Administration. The effect of tax changes made in 1954 during the Eisenhower Administration, according to estimates made by Senator Paul Douglas, has been to reduce the average annual tax burdens of American business by about $3 billion. The 1962 investment credit, and changes in Bulletin F depreciation timetables added more than another $2.5 billion annually to corporate cash flow.

Thus, even before the Administration's $11 billion tax program is considered (see Chapter XII) the combined decisions of the Eisenhower and Kennedy Administrations through 1962 had the effect of cutting corporate tax rates in excess of $5 billion annually—with no personal tax cuts to stimulate the consumption side of the economy. This is doubtless one major reason for sustained high unemployment, since the effect has been to swell private savings to an excessive level. Cash lying idle in corporate bank accounts doesn't create jobs.

In the spring of 1964, Walter Heller pointed with pride to the results of the higher "priority" given to the stimulation of private investment. In speeches calling attention to the new record levels of profit achieved under the Kennedy-Johnson banner, Heller estimated that in addition to the generous additions to depreciation put through in 1962, the results of the Revenue Act of 1964 would be to reduce the corporate tax burden by yet another $2.5 billion. In contrast to the complaints of the 40's and 50's that profits were overstated because of inadequate depreciation, Heller observed to a Minneapolis audience, the "benign" influence of the Kennedy tax program had been to hide billions in real profits under the heading of depreciation allowances.

When the President first proposed the investment credit, Stanley Ruttenberg, then research director for the AFL-CIO and now economic adviser to Labor Secretary W. Willard Wirtz, said: "If you look at the big corporations of America—

General Electric, General Motors—or you name them, and what I am going to say will be more or less true in 90 percent of the cases—they have invested in recent years less than the total amount of cash which they have available to them. In other words, their profits plus their current depreciation allowances are more than enough to cover their existing levels of investment. And I think any further incentive to expand this is not wise." [2]

Ruttenberg's point about the enormity of corporate cash flow has been well substantiated. As a matter of fact, the *Wall Street Journal* on September 9, 1963, reported that some corporations are embarrassed by their unwieldy bank accounts. According to the *Journal*, the availability of money doesn't necessarily touch off an investment boom. Howard B. Speyer, vice-president and treasurer of Champion Spark Plug Co., is reported to have looked up from his corporation balance sheet showing $48.8 million in cash and marketable securities—an almost unbelievable 48.6 percent of 1962 sales—and asked: "What are we running—a spark plug company or a bank?" Incidentally, the Detroit gag about General Motors, which in mid-1963 had $2.3 billion in cash and securities (more than the assessed property valuations in 18 of the 50 states) is that GM is saving its cash in order to buy up the Federal Government.

Taking it as a whole, corporations in 1962 had an internal cash flow—retained profits, depletion allowances, amounts charged off for depreciation, and other bookkeeping deductions —of $38.9 billion, or $7.4 billion more than in 1957. But corporate outlays for plant and equipment in 1962 were only about the same—$37 billion—as they were in 1957.

Thus, corporations accumulated extra cash and reserves in 1962, and weren't motivated to accelerate the expansion of plant capacity to any significant degree. This has an important bearing on the argument that Ruttenberg was making against the investment credit. And the latest government figures show that 1962's $37 billion plant spending figure was exceeded by only a bare 5 percent in 1963, even though 1963's internal cash flow was again very heavy, a record $41.7 billion. [3]

As a matter of fact, although the Treasury attributes a substantial share of the 5 percent gain in 1963 spending to the investment credit, it based the argument for a reduction in the corporate rate to 48 percent, and for reductions in capital gains and upper-bracket income taxes on the need for "a strong additional stimulus to business investment." [4]

But back in 1961, it was the investment credit that was going to do the job. It had a high priority among the speechmakers. Even Arthur Goldberg, while some of his friends raised eyebrows, joined in. To a National Press Club audience, Goldberg announced that "around $75 to $90 billion of our plant and equipment is obsolete. . . . We must regain our pre-eminence in this field, using the tax system if necessary." Privately, Goldberg complained that labor's opposition to the investment credit was parochial.

The Administration argument was that by giving businessmen a flat credit against taxes for investments that exceeded current depreciation allowances, it would encourage projects that wouldn't otherwise have been considered. Hence, national growth would be stimulated. Businessmen themselves weren't sure this was probable. Even more important, if there was to be tax action in this general field, what they preferred was accelerated depreciation that would dramatically reduce their reportable profits.

Meanwhile, Kennedy directed the Internal Revenue Service to review the depreciation guidelines for textile machinery and equipment. Depreciation deductions permit a business to charge off, over a period of years, the cost of equipment and other assets. Thus, the loss of value due to wear and tear and obsolescence is recovered—and, presumably, replacements purchased. These guidelines, in Treasury Bulletin F, set out the average useful lives of equipment.

Under pressure from the textile industry to permit more rapid depreciation, the Kennedy Administration shortened the average useful lives figure—and then proceeded to do much the same thing in the summer of 1962 for the auto, aircraft, electrical equipment, machine tool, railroad, and steel industries. Not only did the new rules provide a more rapid write-off of assets, but the red tape was simplified to allow a businessman to apply a single depreciation figure to broad classes of assets, rather than to each item of depreciable property.[5]

This was a boon to businessmen—one of the greatest steps in a generation, said Commerce Secretary Luther Hodges—and significantly, one that the business community had been trying to wheedle out of the Eisenhower Administration for eight long years.

The investment credit—a separate matter—was coupled, in the 1961 tax message, with a number of reforms designed to correct inequities and to recoup the revenue loss involved in the investment credit. The reforms included elimination of some of the special tax privileges that had been developed abroad by corporations and individuals, a withholding tax on dividends and interest, and an attack on "expense account living." [6]

Of all of Kennedy's early Presidential messages and speeches, the one that came nearest to matching the image of the New Frontier that had been projected during the campaign was the reforms section of his tax message in April, 1961. His Inaugural Address may have been loftier on a broader plane, but the tax message was bold and specific. Sadly, the high hopes that it generated were eroded bit by bit over the next two and one-half years.

To his credit, having decided to appoint Surrey as an Assistant Treasury Secretary, Kennedy wasn't dissuaded when conservative Democrats found Surrey's ideas too advanced. But Dillon had to promise Senator Harry Byrd that Surrey wouldn't make policy before Byrd withdrew his opposition.

Surrey had been an almost obvious choice when, after the election in 1960, eager New Frontiersmen tagged tax reform as one of the fields to conquer. He was co-editor with Dean Warren of Columbia University of the standard casebook on income taxes—a McGuffey in its field.

When Wilbur Mills in 1959 put together a 2,382-page "compendium" on tax reform possibilities, he called on the handsome, bushy-browed Surrey to write the key article on what was wrong with tax law. After Kennedy's election, Archibald Cox (now Solicitor General) suggested that Surrey act as chairman of the "task force" committee on tax changes. Among other members was Mortimer M. Caplin, who later was named Commissioner of Internal Revenue.

Opposition to Surrey was based on his long-standing criticism of tax loopholes, including that all-time favorite sacred cow, the oil depletion allowance. Surrey had also said such things as: "Congress has . . . allowed its capital gains policy to get out of control and become enmeshed in lobbying pressures." With a list of these gems at hand (dug out by Congressional tax expert Colin Stam), Finance Committee Chairman Harry Byrd and the late Senator Robert S. Kerr subjected Surrey to a bristling cross-examination. Byrd snapped at one point: "You don't have a very high opinion of the Congress."

Surrey, an honors graduate of the City College of New York, threw himself completely into the Administration's tax program. Surrey worked hard, but with limited results. As Senator Paul Douglas observed when Treasury Secretary Dillon testified October 16, 1963, before the Senate Finance Committee, the Administration talked loud and handsomely about tax reform in 1961, and promised results in 1962. When it got few results in 1962, it promised thoroughgoing reform in 1963. But when the House Ways and Means Committee in the summer of 1963 knocked out most of the attacks on privilege, the Administration confessed it was helpless, and stood ready to take a tax cut—regardless of reform, and regardless of the manner in which it extended large new benefits to upper-bracket taxpayers. To all intents and purposes, major tax reform, which once was a high-priority goal of John Kennedy's, never was accomplished during his 34 months in office. The glistening hopes of the tax-reforming liberals have faded away.

At least, there is the memory of the initial tax program, stressing equity and fairness. It recognized as basic the idea that if two persons have the same income, they should pay the same tax. "The standard of equity or fairness, must, of course, be applied in the light of infinite variations," Surrey observed. "But the standard of fairness is real and compelling."

This simple and compelling idea, which long had been urged by Surrey, Heller, Caplin and others when they were academic theorists, had now ostensibly become part of the working Administration philosophy, with all three of these men in key positions on the New Frontier. Surrey pointed out that nothing does more to create an image of business as a favored, specially privileged sector of the economy than loopholes and expense-account living. Wage earners and men on salary correctly assume that others have ways of getting preferential tax treatment. "The professional man," Surrey said, ". . . is disturbed by his inescapable tax burden when he compares himself with the executive favored by stock options, generous pensions, and other fringe benefits. The businessman or executive in turn is always wondering whether his tax advisers have obtained for him the latest thing in capital gain deals, or real estate shelters, or life insurance packages, or foreign tax havens.

"Proper tax planning in our complicated society is sensible and necessary—but proper planning is far removed from the frantic chase for the latest and hottest tax deal gimmick." Even the casual drugstore book shopper is aware of the plethora of "Tax Guide" paperbacks, which usually boil down to ways of cutting corners on one's tax return. And the most popular annual series of one of the leading business columnists each year is a quickie guide to the latest tax wrinkles—all perfectly legal, to be sure.

In his first tax message, Kennedy addressed himself to the question of morality in getting tax reform and compliance. To add about $1.7 billion in revenues—which roughly balanced out the original estimates of what the investment credit would be worth to U. S. business—Kennedy proposed to tighten up on individual income earned abroad; elimination of the most notorious aspects of tax "havens" overseas; a flat ban on "pseudo-business" deductions and other expense account rackets; repeal of the 4 percent dividend credit and $50 exclusion—a provision of especial importance to high-income families; abandonment of special tax privileges for insurance companies, savings and loan associations, and co-ops; and legislation to plug certain loopholes in the capital gains tax structure.

Finally, Kennedy proposed what should have been easy for any honest and well-ordered society to accept: not a new tax, but a system of withholding on dividend and interest income, to make sure that those who receive such income pay taxes. The record has been unbelievably bad; the revenue service estimates that about $3.3 billion in dividends and interest—much of it paid to wealthy families—goes scot-free of taxation in the most blatant kind of cheating operation. The cost to the Government in tax revenue is somewhere between $800 million and $1 billion a year.

Withholding is not a new principle: it is accepted as a way of life by millions of wage earners who, incidentally, are taxed at higher-than-necessary rates to make up for the taxes that go unpaid on somebody else's dividends and interest.

These, then, were the promised tax reforms—the first install-ment. The second batch would wait, as it turned out, until 1963 before being proposed as part of Kennedy's major tax cut pro-gram. The 1961 package was quite modest, but it looked to be a reasonable start. Representative Wilbur D. Mills, "Mr. Taxes" in Congress, was committed to the principle of tax reform; at least, he had a reputation as a tax reformer, having supervised extensive hearings on every phase of the hodge-podge tax law. But until 1961, no national administration had lent its prestige to basic reform of the complicated tax code, nor tested Mr. Mills' real ability to push a big chunk of reforms through the Ways and Means Committee of the House.

Increasingly, the average taxpayer began to understand that his taxes had to be higher than a fair share, to make up for the privileges granted a few. "Whenever one taxpayer is permitted to pay less," President Kennedy pointed out, "someone else must be asked to pay more." [6] Take the expense account matter, for example. It was difficult for Kennedy to understand how anyone could disagree with his conclusion that expense account abuses were not only a charge on national revenues, but a weak-ness in the nation's moral fiber as well.

"The time has come," he said in his message, "when our tax laws should cease their encouragement of luxury spending as a charge on the Federal Treasury. The slogan—'It's deductible' —should pass from the scene." Just as logical was the need to erase the fine print in the tax law which permitted some Ameri-can companies and individuals to escape the bulk of their obli-gations by going abroad.

It may have semed logical, but those affected didn't think so. The furious battle that bankers and businessmen—men who traditionally complain about unbalanced budgets—fought against the recoupment of justly due taxes on interest and divi-dends was incomprehensible to Kennedy. In the midst of the battle, Dillon, whose language is usually restrained, said that "the campaign has set new records for distortion of the facts and has created widespread public misunderstanding." [7] Even as the billions in dividends and interest poured into their bank accounts and pockets, untaxed, the business world fought with-holding.

The argument—that withholding was difficult to understand

and administer, cumbersome, unfair—was reminiscent of the major fight waged many years ago against the pay-as-you-go system of taxing wages and salaries. Yet this system has worked perfectly well, and most salaried persons today probably wouldn't know how to cope with their annual tax bills if there were no withholding system.

Kennedy, in congratulating Mills on reporting the 1962 bill, observed that the proposed withholding tax on dividends and interest was not new, but "makes certain that taxes now due are in fact paid. . . . Why should those whose income is received in dividends or interest be treated differently, permitting an escape from taxes by a deliberate or neglectful failure to report such income?" [8]

There was no real answer to the President's question. Irrational fears defeated the proposal. One corporate officer explained that some of the company's dividend recipients might mistakenly think that their dividends had been cut and sell their stock! Although the Ways and Means Committee approved withholding, the mail campaign inspired by businessmen, bankers, and savings and loan associations ultimately defeated the proposal. Congress' susceptibility to this kind of pressure is a sad commentary on the American legislative process. The lobbies are more powerful than the people.

I find it hard to excuse the stubborn fight made by the business and banking community against withholding taxes. Certainly, the trumped-up complaints about mechanical difficulties are but a minor matter for the banks, companies, and individual recipients. They could have been handled with suitable regulations and exemptions. And even if annoyance to some was real, it hardly compared with the fantastic loss of revenue to the American people as a whole.

The prospect that widows and elderly persons might somehow starve for their groceries if Uncle Sam nipped off 20 percent as a withholding tax on their investment income was sheer nonsense. But the campaign worked, proving once again that a well-heeled pressure group fighting to keep intact a tax benefit is a dangerous contender. I think that those who twist and turn to preserve special privileges for the few shake the American system to its very core. I can't take seriously those business leaders—pillars of their communities—who have two standards, one reserved for themselves, the other by which to judge a Jimmy Hoffa or Dave Beck.

In emasculated form, the 1961 proposals finally wound up as the Revenue Bill of 1962. First honors for a job badly done should go to the Senate Finance Committee, under the right-wing leadership of Senator Harry Byrd of Virginia. Byrd has been on the Finance Committee of the Senate for 30 years, and he prefers the pace, temper, mood, and answers of 30 years ago. But it should not be forgotten that the Administration showed a weak spine, too: the Treasury bargained and compromised until there was little left. As for Mr. Mills, the Kennedy Administration discovered for itself what old-timers on Capitol Hill could have predicted. Wilbur D. Mills, the man from Arkansas, wants to keep everybody happy, and get legislation passed. It is the real art of the possible, with Mills. He is not consumed by a burning desire for tax reform; he is a politician who makes a shrewd assessment of what is possible. He sets no extravagant goals.

But the basic award, as I have said, should go to Byrd for the 1962 results. He abandoned the withholding proposal, and substituted a requirement that institutions paying more than $10 a year in dividends and interest must report the payments to the Internal Revenue Service. This will help, but it is not the same as withholding.

Over-all, in contrast to the modest goals of Kennedy's message, a pale product was concocted. It made the expense account racket a bit more difficult to operate by requiring substantiation of various forms of allowable excess eating and drinking, and instituted a few other reforms, including minor inroads into mutual thrift institutions, cooperatives, and insurance companies, which until then had escaped taxation altogether. And it was only a light hand that touched foreign income earned abroad by individuals or corporations, compared to the clampdown that the Administration had demanded.

The barrage that greeted the Revenue Service's attempts to put the new expense account law into the form of a regulation is peculiarly illustrative of a tenacious spirit in some sectors of

American industry. Well-entrenched and legalized forms of tax avoidance are not easily yielded up, and somehow, the attempts to preserve such rights can be cheeky and blatant without arousing too much public resentment.

Caplin, a mild-mannered man, although he was a top-rated amateur boxer in his college days, was made to look like an unreasonable ogre when he published the first set of more stringent rules called for by Congress. The 1962 law called for limits on expense account deductions. For many years, the problem of excessive deductions for travel and entertainment had been a special problem for the Government. Back in 1952, the then Commissioner, John B. Dunlap, expressed concern, and told agents to check travel, entertainment, and gift deductions carefully.[9] Expense-account padding was an All-American game. Everybody, it seemed, participated; lavish restaurants flourished, the credit card business boomed. Among a certain business elite, the use of cash went out of style. Expense account living was, in effect, the individual counterpart to the industrial game of antitrust violations: if you could get away with it, it was all right.

The 1962 Revenue Act imposed strict record-keeping requirements; put a $25 ceiling on gifts to an individual within a year; set out new rules for travel expense, and new rules to assure that a claimed deduction is really related to a person's business, trade, or profession. This attempt to enforce a return to an aura of legitimacy was made because even a Congress resistant to reform could not ignore IRS statistics showing that 48 percent of returns claiming expense account deductions were faulty, and two-thirds of the deductions disallowed were actually personal expenses and not bona fide business items.[10] The "expense account lunch" was becoming a way of life, and even more serious offenses were hard to bring to justice under the existing, vague statutory concept of what was "ordinary and necessary." Life for the revenue agents was complicated by the "Cohan rule" (named for the famous entertainer) which permitted deductions based on estimates, even without corroboration, of what might have been spent.[11] Cohan won a decision on this issue in a famous case argued before Judge Learned Hand in 1930.

As one horrible example, Caplin reported that a corporation paid the complete costs of a Caribbean vacation for the president of the company and his wife, for the installation of a dishwasher in his home, and a TV set given as a gift to one of his relatives.[12] This taxpayer was, happily, convicted of fraud. But the burden of proof for establishing fraud has been on the Government, and sometimes this has been difficult to do where the taxpayer was excused from furnishing full substantiation.

The objective of the 1962 tax law with respect to travel and entertainment expenses (T & E, to the trade) was to curb abuses that had plagued revenue commissioners for 10 years. Congress made it clear that it did not intend to put a brake on legitimate business activity: businessmen can still make deductions for necessary expenses that can be substantiated.

The basic change made by the 1962 act was to place the burden of proof for entertainment, travel, and gift deductions on the taxpayer. And herein lay much of the fuss; for the statute made this change effective by requiring the taxpayer to substantiate "by adequate records" or other evidence the various elements of his T & E account. "In the old days," a Washington IRS executive said, "an agent had to gnash his teeth and allow some share of a ridiculous estimate. Now, he can say: 'The party's over, chum!' "

The second goal of the new legislation was to deny deductions for items which essentially are social or living expenses. To give effect to this objective, the law required the showing of a much closer relationship between the taxpayer's trade or business and the actual expenditure.

These simple objectives brought down on Caplin's head the denunciation of the restaurant industry, and some sections of the entertainment world. If the anti-Caplin campaign is taken at face value, then most of the posh restaurants in the big cities and half of the theatres and night clubs are supported by illegitimate business expenses: the purchase of meals and tickets by businessmen who intend to charge their companies—and eventually Uncle Sam—for food, drink, and entertainment *not* connected with their business or profession.

One would have guessed that some of the associations who howled the loudest would have been embarrassed, because the regulations were so basically permissive. They provided that so long as any T & E expenditure met the old standard of being "ordinary and necessary" it would be deductible:

1. If there was an active, legitimate business discussion during the entertainment period; or

2. If goodwill entertainment (like a night club show) was being provided either just before or just after a bona fide business discussion; or

3. If a goodwill lunch or dinner is provided in a typical restaurant or hotel—even if there is no business discussion. This is the so-called "quiet business meal." [13]

This range is so broad, covering all kinds of courtesy entertainment commonly provided by many businessmen currying goodwill among customers, that it is hard to take the complaints seriously. Criticism should be directed, instead, to the excessive liberality of Caplin's interpretations of the law.

The Commissioner observed that he had been asked whether the guest being entertained must actually be a customer. "The answer," said Caplin, "is 'No.' In referring to this type of business guest, he is sometimes described as 'the natural object of business attention.' Included here would be legitimate business prospects, as well as customers. The fact that repeated contacts might be needed to culminate the business transaction would not defeat the deduction. Nor is it necessary to show that the efforts were successful." [14]

The one really meaningful change in expense account rules requires receipts for meals or entertainment that exceed $25. This does not place a $25 limit on allowable expenditures, which are subject only to the test of "reasonableness." But the generous entertainer, if he intends to claim a deduction, say, for a $60 dinner at the Four Seasons in New York, must get a receipt from the restaurant or hotel. If he doesn't, then he or his company will have to foot the whole bill. Completely fictionalized "swindle sheets" thus are eliminated—to the extent that they carry items exceeding $25. Presumably, imagination can still run rampant under the $25 figure. Internal Revenue Service experience is that many business firms now require some sort of verification from their employees for all expense account items, even those under the $25 level. This helps them cut down on kited expense accounts—while blaming the austerity program on Mortimer Caplin.

Another change is a rule disallowing some travel deductions when a taxpayer's business trip is combined with a personal vacation. But the Revenue Service, smarting under the barrage of criticism of its preliminary set of regulations, backed away from a strict interpretation of the law. Originally, Caplin planned to require that a taxpayer pick up a proper share of travel expenses if as much as 25 percent of the time away from home was devoted to nonbusiness purposes.

But the new, so-called "tight" regulations on allocation of travel expense are a joke; the final regulation lets a taxpayer get away with substantially the same free ride if he had no control over arranging a combined business-pleasure trip, or if the personal part of it was not a major consideration in deciding to go. A few of the most glaring violations of the law's intent will be caught. For example, the big businessman who decides to go to a one-day meeting in London, then tools off for the Grand Tour of the Continent, will no longer be able to charge off the New York–London round-trip air fare, as was the case before.

Business gifts are limited, generally, to $25 annually per recipient. This is a net gain in the law. On the other hand, after Caplin's plan to get tough about the deductibility of country club dues was publicized, the IRS retreated, and adopted a rule which lets a taxpayer deduct part of such dues, provided he uses the club more than half the time for business purposes.

Adding it all up, Mr. Caplin himself made the right assessment when he said that the new regulations "reflect a liberal approach." [15] For example, under the language of the law, it would have been easy (and justifiable) to bar "lavish and extravagant" entertainment by placing some dollar limit on business entertainment, even if it otherwise qualified as legitimate. There is no such limit in the new regulations.

What happened was that the Administration backwatered in the face of strong opposition to the expense account regulations. Through Caplin, Mr. Kennedy tried to get the business community to restrict the most gross abuses, while leaving unfettered most of the privileges of the cocktail set. But even this generous attitude wasn't enough for some. The National Restaurant Association complained to Treasury Secretary Dillon that "the essence of our problem in our judgment is that the law is too complicated for businessmen to understand." As Al Smith would have said, this is sheer baloney.

If the man on a salary, working on his Form 1040, can understand what he's supposed to do, then the National Restaurant Association, with its lawyers and accountants, can understand the law, too. Chicago restaurant operators appeared to have no difficulty, for example. The Chicago & Illinois Restaurant Association, in combination with the Chicago Association of Commerce and Industry, said so after a conference with Caplin on August 27, 1963. Lawrence C. Buckmaster, executive director of the restaurant group, observed that the new law "is not directed at curtailing legitimate business entertainment. . . . The clampdown is directed at abuses."

The real fact, for all of the petty complaints and newspaper headlines, is that the IRS is today only slightly less soft than it was on the expense account racket. The slogan "It's deductible" that Kennedy said he wanted to banish from the American scene is still very much with us. All one needs, living it up on the expense account, is a receipt.

Out of the first stage of Kennedy's planned tax reforms, then, came a juicy investment stimulus to business—hardly what the loophole pluggers had in mind back in 1960 during the campaign. To go along with it, there were a few reforms and improvements, plus the spectacle of the business world battling against withholding taxes on certain kinds of income, and an enormous flap created by the restaurant industry to preserve a swindle-sheet economy. It was hardly an edifying note on which to close the first go-around on taxes.

The Business Advisory Council: Divorce and Remarriage

SECRETARY OF COMMERCE Luther Hartwell Hodges, courtly former governor of North Carolina, points out that he was the Kennedy Administration's "only tie with the nineteenth century." Hodges, now sixty-six, was sixty-three when appointed, eleven years the senior of Dean Rusk and Arthur Goldberg.

But Hodges, a successful businessman before entering politics, was determined to keep up, physically and in spirit, with the younger New Frontiersmen. He told a National Press Club audience that his department, though "primarily concerned" with business and industry, would not be "its tool and not its automatic spokesman." With pointed reference to a businessman-Cabinet member of the Eisenhower Administration, Charles (E. for Engine) Wilson, Hodges said firmly: "You will never hear from me that this country should do this or that simply because business wants it. What is good for General Motors may, or may not, be good for the country."

Hodges' conviction that the Commerce Department ought to be something more than a mouthpiece for the business community brought him into conflict almost immediately with the Business Advisory Council, an exclusive and self-perpetuating club of top corporate executives that had enjoyed a private and special relationship with the Government since 1933.

The conflict between Hodges and the BAC generated a spectacular power struggle in Washington, and until overshadowed a year later by Kennedy's controversy with Roger M. Blough and the steel industry, was the chief basis for complaints that the President and the Administration were anti-business.

Although the BAC had been operating under every national administration since the first Roosevelt term in 1933, there was little public awareness of its privileged status until *Harper's Magazine* published an article of mine called "America's Most Powerful Club" in September, 1960.[1] This article suggested that the BAC was "a tightly run fraternity" that met privately with top government officials, had access to information not available to other private groups, and said that "from Administration to Administration, this elite group has had a continuous privilege to participate in government decisions with no public record or review."

The article revealed, also, that the BAC picked up the check for government officials who consulted with the Council during spring and fall "work-and-play" sessions each year at some of the country's best-known resort hotels, and had obtained favorable rulings from the Internal Revenue Service permitting deductions of the annual membership dues which covered the cost of Council meetings.

The Council maintained a wall of secrecy around its meetings, keeping newsmen out of its actual sessions—and at arm's length when they insisted on trying to find out what was going on. In addition to the two "work-and-play" sessions (meetings in the morning; golf, tennis and riding in the afternoon; banquets and receptions in the evening) the Council met four times a year in Washington for streamlined business sessions.

In Washington, the *Harper's* story was read with interest and annoyance by the outgoing Eisenhower Administration, which not only had worked closely with the BAC, but had used it as a recruiting agency for filling top executive posts, including Cabinet posts.* Typical was the reaction of Joseph P. Hall, president

---

* After the 1952 election, the BAC was having its work-and-play meeting at the Cloister, a short distance from Augusta, where Eisenhower was alternating his golf with Cabinet planning. Council members Sidney J. Weinberg and Lucius Clay, both personal friends of Ike, shuttled between the Cloister and Augusta, after which Ike selected three prominent members of the Council, all political novices, to be members of his Cabinet: George Humphrey of the M. A. Hanna Co. as Secretary of the Treasury; Charles E. Wilson of General Motors as Defense Secretary; and Robert T. Stevens of J. P. Stevens & Co. as Secretary of the Army.

of the Kroger Co. and a big wheel in the BAC, who was asked by the Indianapolis, Indiana, *News* to comment on the *Harper's* article. Charles Vaughan, business editor of the *News*, wrote as follows in his column:

> Hall was among a group of businessmen discussed in a recent article in *Harper's Magazine*. . . . The article charged that this semi-social club—the Business Advisory Council of the Commerce Department—is shielded from the press and the public yet wields great influence in Washington affairs.
>
> Asked for his reaction, Hall smiled and said officials of the Commerce Department were greatly upset by the article and were considering some reply. Since it appeared in a high type "literary" magazine it was not too widely read and Hall advised them to keep quiet.
>
> "Why bring it to the attention of more of the public?" Hall asked. The Commerce Department kept quiet.[2]

But Candidate John F. Kennedy and his team of New Frontier managers read "high type 'literary' magazines," among others. It was stored away by the Kennedy team for future reference. Almost as soon as Kennedy took office, the question of the BAC and the role it performed came to a head by reason of a special circumstance: Ralph J. Cordiner, chairman of the BAC, was also chairman of the General Electric Co., largest of the 29 firms that had pleaded guilty to criminal charges of price fixing and bid rigging on electrical equipment. Administration officials—White House staff as well as Commerce—felt that the top corporate executive of a firm so deeply embarrassed as G.E. should not head a group advising the Government.[3]

Entirely apart from the special problem with Cordiner, Hodges disapproved the whole BAC concept. In a private conversation with me soon after he took office (which he has consented to my reporting here for the first time) he said candidly that no group ought to have the special channel to government thinking available to the BAC. Moreover, he was concerned about the composition of the BAC: it was made up exclusively of the very biggest U. S. businessmen—all presidents or board chairmen (with a few exceptions) of major companies.

And, Hodges said bluntly, the element of secrecy so cherished by the BAC could not be justified when government officials were present. It was clear to me also that the Secretary of Commerce was offended by the custom cultivated by the BAC during the prior 28 years, according to which he would have to approve, automatically, new members selected by the BAC's Executive Committee. Hodges had the not-so-strange notion that he ought to have something to say about who his advisers were to be. For my part, I gave Mr. Hodges at his request a summary of my experiences covering the BAC for *Newsweek* over a 10-year period.

I knew after that meeting with Hodges that his strong views would collide with the BAC's way of conducting its affairs. It was only a question of time. Hodges decided to put new "ground rules" into effect, postponing his first scheduled encounter with the BAC until March. By then, he hoped, the BAC and Cordiner would do the "right thing." At first, he didn't expect the BAC to turn down a demand that the secret nature of the meetings be abandoned, and the membership broadened a little bit. He wrote with beautiful understatement in a recent book:

> I was already having some difficulties with this group [the BAC] which didn't take eagerly to my suggestion that it accept representatives of small business and open up to the press all its meetings involving participation by federal officials. I was reluctant to add to the existing friction by demanding that the G.E. executive relinquish the chairmanship, although I certainly thought he should.[4]

Hodges told his very first press conference on February 14, 1961, that "the people who put him in, they and Mr. Cordiner will have to settle [the situation]." They did, just two weeks later: Cordiner resigned as chairman, remaining a member of the BAC, and was succeeded by Roger M. Blough, chief executive officer of the United States Steel Corporation. This relieved the tension, and a meeting with Hodges was set for March 14.

But before that meeting took place, Hodges set out to deflate the BAC to what he considered to be a reasonable role for it. As he told a Congressional hearing, he decided against appointment of new BAC members "unless I approve them . . . or select them." He added: "If a Government official, including the Secretary of Commerce or anyone else in Government, makes talks or reports, it will be made public. In other words,

I will not have it a closed situation so far as Government people are concerned." [5]

In direct conversation with Blough, and occasionally using Undersecretary of Commerce Edward C. Gudeman, a former Sears, Roebuck & Co. executive, as an intermediary, Hodges made it clear he would ditch the BAC altogether unless it broadened the base of membership, allowed the Government a role in naming new members, and agreed to the presence of a government representative at all meetings of the Council. Hodges' attitude was unmistakable: he was quite willing to do without the BAC altogether—so the businessmen had better agree to some changes.

To be sure, Hodges added, the Kennedy Administration wanted to keep open the channels of communication with the business world, but it didn't feel bound to any of the BAC customs or habits. The BAC, which was an upper-crust private club, more like a social fraternity than anything else, was not about to let its bars down easily. Election to the BAC was the ultimate tribute by big businessmen to their fellows who had *really* arrived. Having long had the privilege of cozy, intimate, off-the-record meetings among themselves and with invited government officials at the posh Homestead at Hot Springs, at the Del Monte Lodge at Pebble Beach, California, or at the Cloister at Sea Island, Georgia, the men who ran the Business Council —60 actives and about 100 associates—were appalled at the idea of a slight democratization. The executive committee met in New York, and refused Hodges' conditions.

The rejoinder of the pink-cheeked, white-haired Commerce Secretary was to the point. After consultation with Kennedy, he canceled the March 14 meeting that had been arranged after Cordiner's resignation.

Blough once again met with the key members of the BAC executive board, including Sidney J. Weinberg, senior partner of Goldman, Sachs, & Co.—a power in the BAC since its inception—and Leonard F. McCollum, president of the Continental Oil Co. This time, the result was capitulation to Hodges, but as was soon evident, it was an uneasy peace. Weinberg later told me that many BAC members, resisting Blough's peacemaking, said angrily: "To hell with the whole thing—let's not be pushed around." But the impassive, unemotional Blough put down the insurrection. His view was that the Council ought to maintain some kind of a relationship with the Government. A meeting with Hodges was rescheduled for April 4, at the Willard Hotel in Washington, at which time the membership approved Hodges' "suggestions."

These covered five main points:

1. The BAC would be broadened from 60 to 65 active members to permit the addition of some "small" businessmen. Proposals for new membership would have to include half again as many names as openings, so that Hodges would not be "rubber-stamping" BAC nominations.

2. The Secretary of Commerce would become "General Chairman" of the BAC, superimposed on the regular chairman of the BAC, with the power to call meetings and arrange the agendas.

3. All meetings at which a government man spoke or reported would be open to the press. (Breaking new ground, the luncheon session of the April 4 meeting featured an on-the-record talk by David E. Bell, then Director of the Bureau of the Budget.)

4. Minutes of the meetings would be kept (although not necessarily made public) and the Government would pay routinely for the expenses of anyone sent on official business to a BAC meeting.

5. To underscore the reduction in rank of the BAC, in contrast to its old quasi-official status, the BAC's staff director and secretaries would be required to move out of the two rooms they had occupied in the Commerce Department for many years.

Sitting stiffly with Hodges at a press conference at the Commerce Department, Blough explained that the BAC had agreed to Hodges' suggestions because "the business community feels a real desire to accommodate its operations to suit the Secretary's feelings and his needs." But there was a hint, even as the truce was declared, that there would be trouble ahead: the way Hodges understood the agreement, the BAC wouldn't hold a meeting unless requested to do so by the Government, and would always have a government official present. Blough observed at the press conference: "I'm not quite sure that we are understanding each other with respect to that." [6]

Most of the BAC members found it hard to contain their bitterness. Others, like Weinberg, shrugged it off. "We'll see how this works," he told me after Bell's talk. "We've been used to one system, but we're businessmen, and we've got to work with the Government. We want the Kennedy Administration to be successful, because that means we'll all be successful. As for the BAC meetings, they can get a hell of a lot more out of us than we can get out of them. I've never gotten any inside dope at a BAC meeting that I couldn't have got out of *The New York Times* or *Newsweek*. So I'm content."

So, the spring work-and-play meeting was convoked, as usual, at the Homestead—and it was a disaster. Except for Hodges, not a single prominent New Frontiersman showed up, an acute signal that the BAC had been seriously downgraded. The Secretary, attending an out-of-town BAC meeting for the first time, was dismayed: the agenda was dull, and the "advice" offered the Government was minimal. "It was little better than a local Chamber of Commerce meeting," said one government man present. "They were just talking to each other about their own problems."

The superficiality of the formal BAC discussions was often evident to reporters who attempted to cover the meetings. For example, in May, 1961, at the Homestead, Roswell Magill, a New York tax lawyer who for years headed the BAC's tax subcommittee, delivered what purported to be an analysis of the Kennedy tax program after freely admitting that he had read only summary versions of Treasury Secretary Dillon's statement, and none of the elaborate supporting papers. Magill nevertheless launched into an attack on the proposals.

Charles Bartlett, Washington correspondent and friend of the President, observed that the BAC "imposed some rather insensitive treatment" on Hodges and his aides by allowing Magill to proceed. "There were snickers as . . . [they] sat listening to it." [7] Then, at the banquet, crusty old George Humphrey, strong man of the Eisenhower Cabinet, took the rostrum to make a bitter attack on Hodges' plans for revamping the BAC.

Hodges left what he later referred to as his "tryst" with the BAC convinced that the Government got precious little advice from the BAC that was worthwhile—and whatever might be gleaned from the elite corps could be obtained in Washington, and not at a luxury spa. My own observation, covering that meeting for *Newsweek,* was that the situation was fast deteriorating. Hodges had submitted a list of 10 "small" businessmen to the BAC, and asked them to name five. But the BAC would agree to three only: Alphonsus J. Donahue, president of the Donahue Sales Corp. of New York; Alvin Howard, partner of the New Orleans investment firm of Howard, Weil, Labouisse, Friedricks & Co.; and Justin Kingson, president of Millburn Mills, Quidnick, Rhode Island.[8]

Above all other things, the BAC cherished its "right" to meet privately, without messy intrusions by reporters. They were certain that the give and take among the membership, as they discussed plans and problems of their own companies and industries, would dry up if there were outsiders present. Moreover, the BAC members could sense from Hodges' first specific assignment to it—a study of the maritime industry—that it would be asked for technical advice of somewhat limited importance. That spring at the Homestead, it was a far cry from the high-level, cozy tête-à-têtes with the cream of the Cabinet, as in earlier years.

On May 16, three days after the spring meeting had concluded, Hodges was asked at his regular press conference in Washington if he thought the meeting had been useful. He answered:

> Well, let me say this about the Business Advisory Council meeting at Hot Springs. It is a lovely place, lovely weather, and fine people, really. Men and women individually, just high grade. I would say this, and I said it to Mr. Blough: I think the program was far too crowded, left little time for discussion, and there was not enough in my book, not enough actually tying it together with the Department of Commerce.

The BAC got the message—both from the press conference, and in a brusque letter from Hodges to Blough, in which the Secretary returned to his insistence on at least helping to shape the agenda, and holding the meetings in the more businesslike atmosphere of Washington. Moreover, Hodges said, the BAC would have to conform strictly to Justice Department regulations governing all federal advisory meetings.

In New York, Blough and his executive committee huddled again and decided to cut loose from the Government. Rather than hold meetings under the Hodges' rules, they would resign the connection with the Commerce Department, assume an entirely private status, and offer "consultation" to any government agency that wanted it. At Blough's request, IBM Chairman Thomas J. Watson, Jr., a personal friend of Kennedy's and a member of the BAC (but not at that time on the BAC executive committee) arranged an appointment for Blough and a small delegation to see Kennedy on July 5.

Hodges, who was away on a fishing trip, got a phone call from Kennedy telling him of the date. The President planned, an aide said later, "to mollify Blough, and tell him what a great bunch of guys they were." But Kennedy didn't get a chance. In a scene that was to be nearly duplicated the following April, Blough walked into the White House and laid a letter and memorandum on Kennedy's desk, advising him that the BAC was divorcing itself from its official ties. The BAC plan, like the steel price hike a year later, was both a surprise and a *fait accompli*. Politely, the President told Mr. Blough that he had no objections to what the BAC termed "broadening the base" of its activities, a euphemism for emancipation from the clutches of Secretary Hodges. As Blough went before TV cameras outside the White House West Wing, Gudeman, tight-lipped, said only: "We're satisfied." But William C. Ruder, then in charge of Commerce Department public relations, told the Blough group as they left the President's office: "Gentlemen, you have just murdered yourselves."

Two days later, with the President's approval, Gudeman wrote Blough that if he and his associates wished to "disaffiliate" with the Department, they were free to do so—but Commerce would keep the BAC structure itself. In other words, Blough & Co. could depart, but they had to leave the name behind. This was unexpected, but the businessmen accommodated to it quickly. At a meeting in the University Club in New York on June 10, 1961, they dropped the word "advisory," and became the Business Council—the BC instead of the BAC.[9]

And so, after 28 years of existence as a Commerce Department adjunct, the Council became strictly "private." In Washington, the plain intention was to let the Business Council wither on the vine. Hodges drew plans for a new BAC, one that would include a broad cross section of American business—big, medium, and small-sized. It would include representatives as well of labor, agriculture, and education.

But these plans were soon put aside, and never revived. Instead, a campaign was undertaken to restore communications with the Business Council. Kennedy and Hodges had misassessed public reaction. Bartlett, a few days after Blough and the others met with Kennedy, wrote as follows, obviously reflecting the Presidential view:

> The causes and consequences of the Business Advisory Council's break with the Commerce Department are regarded in informed circles here as less than significant and even somewhat amusing. . . .
>
> In their present mood, top administration officials will be inclined to ignore Roger Blough's group . . . and so the old BAC, deprived of its quasi-official status, will be left to hold its conventions in much the same manner as any private association. . . .
>
> It is in fact difficult to see how the emancipated BAC will manage to retain its luster in the new circumstances. It is now simply another of the groups which exist in Washington to float unsolicited advice upon the Federal waters. . . .[10]

Such a reduced status might well have been the new BC's lot. But the BC regained its old luster—and more—because Mr. Kennedy did an about-face. What the Administration hadn't foreseen when it acquiesced in Blough's divorce decree was the "anti-business" scare that would come out of it, at the very time any and all "bridges" to the business community were desperately needed. In the summer of 1961, the world was in upheaval: there was crisis in Berlin, in Laos, in Vietnam. There was a steady increase in defense spending, necessitating a growth in the federal budget and the resultant deficit. The balance of payments problem was still present, and the Administration wanted business's help in stimulating exports. Moreover, a basic change in trade policy was in the making, too, and this was another area where Kennedy knew business support was essential.

In Wall Street, the almost daily uptick of prices mirrored the traders' view that inflation was certain. For the first time, there were rumors in Washington and Pittsburgh that the steel industry, if it felt it could get away with it, would raise prices that October, after paying the final round of wage increases under the contract that had settled the 1959-60 strike. Labor was restive because of Kennedy's insistence that wage advances be limited—and unemployment was still an unsolved problem.

With this myriad of problems facing him, and sensitive to the growing insistence that he was "anti-business," the President turned full circle from his earlier, firm and bold posture toward the Business Advisory Council. He didn't like being called anti-business. He allowed himself to be pressured into a major campaign to woo the business community, and especially to restore relationships with the new Business Council. To a considerable degree, he was influenced in this by Robert Kennedy's concern, and by some of his friends in business, notably Thomas Watson. Watson, one of the nation's biggest businessmen, is also one of the most forward-looking. Until Blough asked him to arrange the October 5 appointment with Kennedy, Watson had not been prominent in Council activities. But Watson, after playing his peacemaker role between Kennedy and the Council, became a vice-chairman, and is in line—if he wants it—for the chairmanship within a few years.

Prominent roles in effecting the patch-up at this point were also played by Heller and White House aide Ralph Dungan, who kept in touch with Blough; and by Myer Feldman, the President's Deputy Special Counsel who, as the White House expert on textile matters, was in close contact with Robert T. Stevens, a former chairman of the BAC and an influential member.

Blough and Dungan arranged for small committees of the BC to be assigned to each of several important government departments and agencies—and to the White House itself. For example, Blough headed the liaison group assigned to the Council of Economic Advisers, and soon struck up a "Walter" and "Roger" relationship with Heller. He also persuaded Heller himself to confer periodically with the BC's committee of economists, which up to then had met only with technicians of lower government rank. Logically enough, Watson headed the "liaison" with the White House as chief of a three-man delegation including Henry Ford II and Juan T. Trippe, president of Pan American World Airways. Washington, sensitive to status symbols, could see that the BC was making a strong comeback.

Secretary Hodges has never made a single public observation on Kennedy's resurrection of the Business Council. But it is safe to guess that he privately feels that Kennedy let him down. It is certainly clear that during the renewal of diplomatic relationships with the BC, Hodges was carefully kept out of the picture, and delegated, instead, to approach other sectors of the business community. For example, it was Hodges who arranged a session on August 21, 1961, in Kennedy's office for the presidents of the Chamber of Commerce, the NAM, and the CED. The President opened the conversation with a general comment on the Berlin crisis, and then said: "Gentlemen, I understand that we're labeled anti-business. Why is that?"

Taken by surprise, the business leaders found it difficult to articulate their complaints. Kennedy took hold of the conversation again, pointing out that there were prominent businessmen in the Kennedy Administration. He singled out Hodges, Dillon, Gudeman, and Robert V. Roosa, Undersecretary of the Treasury. Then, the President added, he guessed that his aid to education program wasn't popular with business, but he felt it was impossible to keep up with the Russians without a federal education program.

Finally, the businessmen found their tongues. They brought up the tax reform bill, and complained about the investment credit proposal. The President answered that the investment credit had been designed to achieve the maximum stimulus to the economy with the minimum revenue loss to the Treasury. Furthermore, were it not for the Berlin crisis, he said, he would be thinking in terms of a general tax cut in 1962.

He then made a big point of the need to get businessmen to help administer the foreign aid program. He conceded that it was a great financial sacrifice for top-income men in business to take a government post, and said he hoped to do something about it. Finally, Chamber President Richard Wagner, a Chicago oil investment executive, taking advantage of the opportunity, invited the President to address the Chamber meeting the following April. The invitation was confirmed in writing, and accepted.

This meeting, and a few others like it, served to impress participating business leaders with Kennedy's knowledge in depth of economic problems, and his earnestness in seeking rapport with the business community. What baffled Kennedy, as he came out of these sessions, was the rigidity of the business viewpoint.

Meanwhile, the rapprochement with the Business Council was moving along exceptionally well. Blough told Dungan that the BC planned a two-day session at the Mayflower Hotel in Washington in September. Would the Administration cooperate? The answer was affirmative. Not only would President Kennedy send a big delegation of the most prominent New Frontiersmen, headed by McGeorge Bundy, but after the meeting, the whole Council was invited to the White House for cocktails with the President at 6 P.M. on September 21.

The White House entourage worked hard on this one. The prospective budget deficit was now calculated at about $7 billion, instead of about $3 billion, and even if most of it could be laid at Khrushchev's door, Kennedy was still being sharply criticized by some businessmen and Republican politicians as a spender. Labor leaders complained about the Kennedy campaign against "inflationary wage increases," itself part of Kennedy's assurance to business that he was playing no favorites. But the President wanted to restore a good working relationship with the Business Council, regardless of labor's concerns.

Dungan, in charge of the White House task force to make peace with the BC, arranged "a good show." He produced, as speakers, Bundy, Acting Secretary of Labor W. Willard Wirtz, and Ambassador Arthur H. Dean—all of whom were instructed to provide texts of their speeches to the press. (Bundy and Wirtz did, but there was a slipup on Dean's.) In addition, guests for dinner or cocktails included Dungan himself, Acting Treasury Secretary Henry H. Fowler, Deputy Defense Secretary Roswell Gilpatric, and Hodges.

Promptly at 6 P.M. on September 21, six black Cadillacs and several taxis wheeled into the main driveway of the White House, and delivered more than 40 members of the Council to the front door. In the Oval Room, a beaming John F. Kennedy, with Luther Hodges at his side, welcomed them with drinks, cigars, and reassuring conversation. Among those present was Ralph Cordiner of G.E., whose resignation as BAC chairman had been forced only a few months back. The Administration, Kennedy said firmly, had no hostility to business. He recalled

the theme of a speech he had made early in his Administration
to the National Industrial Conference Board, in which he
talked of the "interdependence of business and government."
And he restated his determination to have a balanced budget in
1963. It was a graceful performance. "If it all sounds like kiss
and make up," said a White House aide, "that's just what it is."

For the Council members, the overture was acceptable. They
hadn't relished being on the outside looking in, and now sensed
they could have the upper hand; after all, Kennedy needed a
good relationship with the BC, and as a "general" adviser to the
Government, it could carve out a role more important than its
old one of "advising" just the Commerce Department. If Kennedy wanted to cultivate a relationship, it was willing to be
cultivated. After all, it never had enjoyed any social entrée to
the White House before kicking up its heels.

Happily walking out of the White House on his way back to
the Mayflower to hear Bundy at dinner, Sidney Weinberg
summed it up in a phrase: "We're back in business." The work-
and-play meetings at Hot Springs could go on again, complete
with cocktail parties, golf tournaments, and—given Kennedy's
willingness to be clubby—there was the chance to rub elbows,
socially, with important government brass. Above all, the Business Council loves to socialize.

That night, at the Mayflower, Bundy was at his brilliant best
in summing up the Administration's position:

> . . . The whole notion of drawing a line between anything as
> large and varied as the business community of the United
> States, and anything as complex and multifarious in its ma-
> chinery as the Government of the United States is foolishness.
> You know that it's foolishness—we know that it's foolishness.
> You know and we know that when you come to the serious
> questions of judgment and action which face the Government
> of the United States, the simple headline question—for busi-
> ness or anti-business—doesn't make much sense. . . . It is not
> the way problems pose themselves. It is not the way most of
> you gentlemen think. . . . The questions which come up day
> in and day out between thousands of men of affairs and hun-
> dreds of men in the varying departments of government simply
> do not yield to these easy slogans. You know it and we know it.
> And it's a game that we ought to stop. And it's a game which
> I assure you this Administration will not play unless it is forced

on us. . . . It is important to us that we give up the easy contests between the business interest and the wicked Administration which have been part of our folklore before.

. . . We are required as a society, to pull together not for one of these objects: the military, the ideological, the economic, but for all three. That's the real Troika, if you want to put it that way. This problem of our society is a problem which stands and falls together. Your profit rates are of no great interest if very large numbers of megatons have been dropped on your plants. Our position in temporary political power is of no great importance if in fact the power of the United States ceases to avail. . . . We are together in this thing." [11]

The next step was to convince labor as well as management that the President's many appeals for wage restraint as well as price restraint were to be taken seriously. On September 14, 1961, Kennedy had written steel union president David J. McDonald that the wage increase to be negotiated in 1962 should be "within the limits of advances in productivity." Business leaders were frankly skeptical that Kennedy would really apply the heat.

To make the Administration's position clear, Economic Council member James Tobin delivered a brief lecture to more than 50 top economists and research experts affiliated with the AFL-CIO early in October. Tobin, whose own credentials as a brilliant economic theorist had long since been established, laid it on the line. He said that wage increases had to be kept within productivity gains, primarily because the U. S. had to guard against an inflation which could worsen the balance of payments deficit. He conceded that there had been times, before he took his office, that he felt high employment and an expanding economy might justify a mild, creeping inflation. But now, he saw the other side of the picture. Tobin denied that he was pressuring the steel workers' union. But in his account of the meeting, Joseph A. Loftus of *The New York Times* said that Tobin's remarks "generated an hour of questions and comments that at times took on hostile tones."

Union officials were seriously concerned by the policy implications of Tobin's speech. They felt, first of all, that productivity gains should not be the sole basis for wage increases. For example, if the cost of living goes up, the labor view is that workers' pay should be adjusted upward. Or if there are serious cases of inequity in wages, labor believes they should go up—even if the increases exceed productivity. And how about situations where an industry's productivity is sharply higher than the national average? If wages in such cases were to be held to the national average of productivity gains, would prices be reduced?

Stanley Ruttenberg, high regarded economist and special assistant to Secretary of Labor W. Willard Wirtz, was then research director of the AFL-CIO, and one of the economists at the meeting with Tobin. He observed later: "If you could get price reductions in the industries whose productivity advance is greater . . . and increases in the others whose productivity is less than the economy as a whole, you'll get relative price stability." In other words, labor was chary about being tied to a rigid formula, and didn't like the handwriting on the wall: Uncle Sam would be looking over the shoulders at the bargaining table to influence "noninflationary settlements."

Of course, labor's discomfort on this issue was a source of cheer to the business community. They still didn't think that Kennedy could keep wages stable, but they were coming around to a belief that he would try. And with the memory of their September reception at the White House fresh in mind, the Business Council members were in a happy frame of mind as they prepared for their October meeting at the Homestead.

As they arrived in Hot Springs by car, train, and private plane, the Council members knew that the Hodges' "reforms" had been abandoned. There would be no minutes; there was no need to have a government man present; they would choose their own agenda; they would meet, as before, behind closed doors. Government officials would provide texts of their prepared addresses, but no transcript of questions and answers.

To underscore and cement the new working relationship, Kennedy sent an all-star team of seven Cabinet or near-Cabinet officials to the meeting: Secretary of the Treasury Douglas Dillon; Undersecretary Henry H. Fowler; Economic Council Chairman Walter W. Heller; International Development Administrator Fowler Hamilton; Deputy Secretary of Defense Roswell Gilpatric; and Hodges and Gudeman. (Hodges developed a sudden case of flu and didn't make it.)

Charles H. Percy, young chairman of the Bell & Howell Co., now Republican candidate for Governor of Illinois, surveyed the government brass mingling with BC members and their wives in the enormous Victorian lobby of the Homestead, and said with a broad smile: "What talent! We've never had that many important people down here before." It may have been a slight exaggeration, but the contrast with the spring meeting, a bare five months before, when Hodges alone held the fort for the Government, was lost on no one. In essence, the BAC had been revived. "Only the name has been changed," one member smiled.

The BC had indeed become the very symbol of the larger business establishment in the United States. And in those sad first moment after President Kennedy's death, when President Johnson needed to establish contact with the business world, he called not the head of the Chamber of Commerce, nor the President of the NAM, but Frederick R. Kappel, chairman of the BC in 1963.

Kennedy had hoped that conciliatory gestures would bring a response from the BC that would damp down the image of his Administration as anti-business. Dillon and Fowler outlined in great detail the Treasury's plans for more generous depreciation allowances, and Blough responded that this would be "on the helpful side." Heller, meanwhile, concentrated on the Administration's determination to curb wage-price inflation. Kennedy would insist, Heller assured the October 1961 meeting, that labor do its part. Blough observed, cautiously, that Heller's plea for price restraint was "provocative of thought." Then he added: "There are more and more people in Washington who understand what business needs to stay in business."

Administration men came away from Hot Springs convinced that they had made real progress in achieving a better working relationship with the business community. The businessmen were more than pleased to be dealing with Dillon and even with Heller than with Hodges, now *persona non grata*. (The earlier unpleasantness was now referred to only as "the Hodges incident.") Heller went out of his way to demonstrate to the Council that he had no horns, and assiduously cultivated the BC members' goodwill, in Washington and in later meetings at Hot Springs. He wanted to dissipate the notion that he was a way-out theorist or that his economics were too liberal, and apparently succeeded; at a recent BC meeting, one member remarked: "Walter, either you've changed some of your views or we've changed ours."

By the end of 1961, Kappel, president of the American Telephone & Telegraph Co., summed up the situation this way:

> President Kennedy has taken pains to emphasize that he and his Administration are not anti-business. The force and sincerity of this position seem perfectly clear to me, for as the President has also brought out, the Government is dependent on business progress for the realization of national objectives. It is certain, for example, that the goal of a balanced budget in fiscal 1963 depends on a further rise in industrial activity; and beyond this the general theory of this Administration, as I interpret it, looks to the power of enterprise to develop ever-expanding national resources. In such circumstances, I am sure the Administration has no wish or reason to defeat its own purpose.
>
> . . . I say, let government get *with* private enterprise, heart and soul, and give it the room to drive ahead. I am confident the results will be good for the nation.
>
> I am the more confident when I reflect that the goals of industry, labor, and government are not basically different. What is it we all want? Economic growth. Wider markets. Rising employment. National prosperity and strength. And all these in freedom, well short of the yoke of wage and price controls— that spectre in the wings, or around the corner, which I have heard Mr. Heller say, with the ring of conviction, that he and his associates in the Council of Economic Advisers detest and abhor.[12]

So the dividends were coming in: Kappel was certifying that Kennedy was not anti-business, and Heller was gaining a certain acceptability. But a close reading of the results of the council meeting, and of the Kappel speech, would have shown that sharp divergences remained. Despite his generally favorable conclusions, Kappel spoke out sharply against the theory that "increasing productivity" justifies higher wages. And above all, Kappel warned that the Government had to give more attention to "diminishing" and "seriously deteriorated" corporate profits.

The Kennedy Administration, as has been observed, was determined to hold wage increases down, or within reasonable limits. This was also the goal of the business community. But the Administration's rationale was a different one. In part, Kennedy simply wanted to take an even-handed approach—or, as Heller put it, symmetrical: he felt obliged to prevent wage excesses as much as price excesses. But the key to the Administration approach, as Tobin had indicated to the union economists, was the need to prevent a wage-push inflation that would worsen the balance of payments deficit. For businessmen, this was but a tangential concern. Their main worry was much closer to home: the so-called profits squeeze. And what was foreshadowed here was the great struggle in 1962 over steel prices.

Blough soberly warned, as the council meeting ended, that despite Heller's assurance that the economy was moving upward, and Dillon's promise of new tax depreciation help, profits were painfully low.[13] They are "alarmingly low, alarmingly low," he repeated.

Behind his cold exterior, Blough enjoyed his new role as a communicator between the business world and President Kennedy. He had received the accolades of his fellow members for his part in the new relationships. (Said Weinberg: "Roger is the greatest chairman we've ever had. No one else has had such a difficult situation to bridge.")[14] And Blough decided to use his status to convince the New Frontier that it had to give more attention to profits.

"Take a look at the trend of profits since 1955," he told reporters at the conclusion of the October 1961 BC meeting. "Then compare it with any other index you want. You'll find that the portion of the sales dollar going to industry is alarmingly low.

"Then find the percentage of the gross national product devoted to the improvement of facilities and installation of new equipment in France and Germany, and compare that with what you have here. If you do that, you'll get some impression of what is really wrong with this country in terms of growth. The trend here has been down, and in the other countries, up. If you want more growth here, some new way has to be found to put more into new facilities."

What Blough didn't make explicit until the following April was that the "way" he had in mind for his own company was a price rise in steel.

V | Business Ethics

ONE casualty of Kennedy's itching desire to mend fences with the business community was Luther Hodges' worthy but naïve effort to raise the standards of business ethics. It deserved a better fate.

The origins of Hodges' sincere attempt to elevate business morality were in the Philadelphia electrical cases. On February 7, 1961, just days after Kennedy took office, Federal Judge J. Cullen Ganey, sitting in Philadelphia, had imposed jail sentences on seven high officers of companies that conspired to rig bids, fix prices on, and divide the markets for heavy electrical equipment worth $1,750,000,000.

It was a landmark in antitrust history and litigation, and not simply because of the prison terms he meted out. Before Judge Ganey was through sentencing the corporation executives (some of whom in their spare time were church deacons, Little League organizers, and Chamber of Commerce presidents) he laid the blame right where it belonged, at the doorsteps of the corporations themselves, and those who direct their policies.

Said Judge Ganey:

"What is at stake here is the survival of the kind of economy under which America has grown to greatness, the free enterprise system. The conduct of the corporate and individual defendants alike has flagrantly mocked that image and destroyed the model we offer today as a free world alternative to state control or socialism and eventual dictatorship. "

It might be said at this point that the Philadelphia electrical cases—left over from the Eisenhower Administration—were the high-water mark of the Kennedy Administration's antitrust accomplishments. For under Robert Kennedy, the Justice Department has been timid rather than bold or adventuresome in antitrust activities.

Robert Kennedy should get plus marks for his slowly maturing attitudes and attacks on racial discrimination. But whatever businessmen puffing on cigars in the Duquesne and University Clubs prefer to believe, Bobby doesn't rate better than "C's" on antitrust. As former Assistant Attorney General Lee Loevinger (now a Federal Communications commissioner) told a reporter: "It is probably true that we are affected by business uncertainties to the point where we are holding up cases with a novel or uncertain legal approach. We are sticking pretty much to the predictable, to the established lines." [1]

But it didn't affect any uncertainties to be offended by the electrical cases. What shocked Washington officialdom as well as those of the public aware of it was the admission by the two biggest companies involved—General Electric and Westinghouse—that their top employees were guilty. This was something new; the usual pattern of antitrust suits is accusation, denial, and a fine. But in the Philadelphia electrical cases, started by Assistant Attorney General Robert A. Bicks in a Republican Administration, top management men confessed to the baldest kind of price-fixing and conspiracy, spiced with some of the sordid trappings of a cheap novel. And what's more, they were about to go to jail for it.

Hodges felt that the electrical conspiracy cases might "make the country feel that it was an indictment of the whole business structure. . . . I think we should be very careful not to say that all business and all industry is bad because of . . . these incidents. . . . I very definitely feel we ought to do something on a national basis to express what I think is the point of view of the great majority of American businessmen—namely, that they want to do their manufacturing and their selling on an honest basis." [2]

Even before the first indictments were handed down, G.E. announced that some of their guilty employees would be disciplined. Westinghouse, for its part, said the accusations spelled out in the indictments were a "shock to management." There could be no pretense of innocence, even though the Government stopped short of charging that the president or members of the boards of the companies involved shared the guilt of their slightly lower-ranked subordinates. But Judge Ganey said bluntly that "one would be most naïve indeed to believe that these violations of the law, so long persisted in, affecting so large a segment of the industry and finally, involving so many millions upon millions of dollars, were facts unknown to those responsible for the conduct of the corporation."

As Miriam Ottenberg wrote in the Washington *Evening Star:* "In effect, he was asking what has puzzled a lot of other people: How could subordinates conspire on the grand scale to fix prices and slice up the business without the big bosses knowing about it?" [3]

I was told in confidence by a member of the Business Council in May, 1961, that when the Justice Department first broke its criminal case against the companies, at least one company board of directors ran its own quiet investigation of the chief executive officer. They concluded that he had told the truth when he had said he didn't know of the illegal meetings with competitors.

"The next question was obvious," this insider reported. "How efficient was he if he didn't know what was going on?" This question was also resolved in favor of the executive after a "searching" study, because the operations in question were only a relatively small part of this giant company's business.

In Washington, the Kennedy Administration proceeded on two fronts. It made it clear that it no longer wanted Ralph J. Cordiner, chairman of the board of General Electric, as chairman of the Business Advisory Council. G.E. had been fined $437,000—the largest chunk of the nearly $2 million in total fines assessed against 29 companies—and three of its high officials had been sentenced to 30 days in jail. Moreover, all the companies faced heavy damage suits from the purchasers of their equipment.[4]

No charges had been levied against Cordiner, nor against Robert Paxton, G.E. president. But on February 28, Paxton resigned, with ill health assigned as the reason, and Cordiner resigned the BAC post because "my time and attention must be devoted solely to the affairs of the company."

That removed an immediate irritant. But the Administration felt that it ought to move in another, and broader direction to bolster what it considered the sagging morality of business. What bothered Hodges and Attorney General Kennedy was the bland, unspoken assumption that price-fixing was a routine tool of business. It was hardly immoral or unethical—and illegal only in a technical sense. If one was caught at the game, well, a fine couldn't be too much. It might even be worth the price, like a parking ticket during rush hour.

Fortune Magazine's classic two-part series on "The Incredible Electrical Conspiracy" [5] quoted a G.E. man who said: "Sure, collusion was illegal, but it wasn't unethical. It wasn't any more unethical than if the companies had a summit conference the way Russia and the West meet. These competitor meetings were just attended by a group of distressed individuals who wanted to know where they were going."

In Washington, few believed that the men at the top—who got there, presumably, by knowing where the bodies are buried at every rung of the American corporate ladder of success—didn't know what was going on in their own companies. They were especially bothered by Cordiner's refusal to accept any vestige of corporate culpability, in contrast to the more realistic statement made immediately by the late Mark W. Cresap, Jr., president of Westinghouse: "I don't take the position that I can wash my hands of it. My viewpoint is that this is a management failure." Some months later, Cresap added that at Westinghouse it was recognized that strong policy directives to comply with the antitrust laws were not enough. "It is essential, in plain words," he said, "that the head man impress on the organization his personal determination that he will tolerate no improper conduct." [6] G.E., which had a strict company policy demanding adherence to the antitrust laws, fired its jailed officials and let it go at that.

But some American business leaders were not complacent. One was Henry Ford II who said: "There is really only one thing for top executives to do at such a time as this. That is, to forget the alibis and the explanations and have the fortitude

—the plain guts—to stand up and say: 'This is our failure. We are chagrined and sorry. It will not happen again.' "

The day after Judge Ganey's denunciation of the top corporate managers, President Kennedy was asked at his press conference if a code of ethics would be useful. "I think it would be very beneficial," he answered, "if business groups today would consider what they could do to protect themselves from charges of conflict of interest of the kind that we have recently seen . . . and also of the effort made by these large electrical companies to defraud the public. . . . I must say I would be interested to watch what progress they can make in that area."

Hodges' public relations man, William C. Ruder, stimulated by the Kennedy response, suggested that Hodges form a study group to produce a code of ethics for business, and the Commerce Secretary got a green light from the President to do so, and designated it the Business Ethics Advisory Council.

He selected as members 26 businessmen, clergymen, educators and a few journalists, and called them to a meeting in Washington on May 17, 1961, to explore the problem. In his letter of invitation, Hodges spelled out his hope that the meeting would be a "first, small start in re-establishing public faith in business morality—and in helping conscientious management to find effective ways of coping with their internal problems." [7]

With this step, Hodges incurred the unspoken enmity of a large segment of American business. These businessmen not only didn't solicit Hodges' aid in coping with their internal problems, but felt that they were being unnecessarily condemned for the sins of a few. Their bitterness increased when they read a speech prepared for a North Carolina audience in which the Secretary said "we would be completely unrealistic unless we recognize that business is under an indictment" because of the electrical conspiracy cases.

Himself a businessman for 30 years before entering North Carolina politics, Hodges was determined. He felt that the Philadelphia case was only the most recent and glaring illustration of deteriorating morality in the business world. He ticked off the fall from grace of the president of the Chrysler Corporation in a conflict of interest situation; the Goldfine favors to Sherman Adams in the Eisenhower Administration; the ease with which the television industry countenanced corrupt quiz shows; the reports by a Senate committee of business connivance with certain labor unions.

Others doubted the real use of a code of ethics. The tough-minded chairman of the House Judiciary Committee, Representative Emanuel Celler of New York, said bluntly: "A general code of ethics, without binding sanctions, hortatory in sense, has little value in accomplishing the objectives sought." Celler favored stricter application of existing antitrust laws, and less reliance by the Justice Department on consent decrees.

Labor Secretary Arthur Goldberg, who years before as chairman of the ethical practices committee of the AFL-CIO drew up a code for the federation, also had reservations. Goldberg said: "Codes are worthless when they're general, but valuable if detailed and specific." For example, the AFL-CIO code barred any union official from accepting compensation for acting as a welfare fund trustee. A comparable requirement for industry, Goldberg felt, would be to bar a corporate official from owning an interest in any company dealing with the corporation. Such a code, if in effect and observed, would have protected the Chrysler company from its embarrassment relating to Mr. Newberg.

"If codes are detailed," Goldberg told me, "they perform a great educational function at the top and down the line. They focus attention on the problem. You'd be amazed if you knew how many union officials would call me up and ask: 'Under the code, can I do this or that?' But if the code just says: 'Don't get caught,' then it isn't worth anything."

Although Hodges knew that he couldn't develop anything that detailed, he determined to press ahead. Behind his massive desk in the Commerce Secretary's richly paneled office, Hodges spoke soberly. "The thing that worries me," he said, "is that the public may get an unfavorable image of business. And nothing could be worse for business than a public impression that business is taking advantage of people." Most businessmen *do* conduct themselves properly, he said, but he felt that the impact of the Philadelphia cases would be overwhelming. "When you had those good, big company names involved," Hodges said, "you had a shadow thrown on everything."

Hodges put the Business Ethics Advisory Council to work on the formulation of a code of ethics. He felt that once promulgated, a code would and should receive broad sponsorship from business organizations and trade associations, and serious attention from companies aware that self-policing would be a policy of wisdom. It was a dreamy-eyed vision, and the attempt produced some admirable rhetoric, but nothing in the way of new ethical standards. It did, however, sharpen business hostility. One member of the Business Council said: "Luther Hodges is an old fool, and we'd all like to tell him to go to hell. This whole business is a lot of nonsense."

Hodges was aware of the BC's attitude, but he pressed ahead. He called in as consultants Professor George Albert Smith of the Harvard Business School and Edwin Morris, managing partner of the Cleveland office of Booz, Allen, and Hamilton, along with an assortment of other businessmen and educators, to get the ball rolling. As a starting point, he said that an ethical business philosophy calls for "a substantial degree of self-restraint, self-discipline and self-policing by businessmen in order to function consistently in the public's welfare."

Hodges had a broad concept in mind. He was not so much concerned with personal or petty problems, as with the more significant relationship of the business world to the rest of society. "The ethical question of business enterprise," Professor Arthur S. Miller observed, "is not so much that of the personal peccadilloes of a few errant businessmen. It is the larger matter of the relationships that the dominating corporations have with other segments of the nation." [8]

The following are examples of potential ethical problems that Hodges cited:

> Closing a plant. What to do for the workers you want to keep; you can't keep or move.
> Installing labor-saving equipment (automation). What to do with the "labor saved."
> Expense accounts; entertaining—giving and receiving gifts.
> Pressure of competition—when conflict with the law seems minor.
> Conflicts of interest.
> Value to society of a product or a service.
> Sales promotion—pressure selling; appeals to emotions and neglect of logical considerations.
> Advertising—truthfulness (technical—implications); taste.

Pricing of successful products to carry their own costs plus costs of unsuccessful products.

Pursuit of preferential treatment (tariffs, quotas, taxes, exemptions).

Prejudice—race, color, religion; in business, in the community with business participation.

Stockholder relations—the problem of telling the whole truth.

The small town's major employer—does the corporate responsibility stop at the factory door; if it doesn't, where does it?

Taking a position; when does management have an obligation to speak out on a public issue?

What developed out of this, under the direction of William C. Decker, board chairman of the Corning Glass works, as head of the Business Ethics Advisory Council, was a statement of principles and a "Call to Action" produced in January, 1962.

The statement itself was not a code of ethics for the business community as a whole. Instead it called on businessmen for a "continuing pursuit" of the highest standards, and laid the responsibility for such standards and methods of enforcement squarely on the shoulders of the "policy-making body" in each enterprise—the boards of directors and top management. And it wound up with a number of questions for businessmen to ask themselves. The underlying theme of the questions suggested, among other things, that businessmen had social responsibilities "concurrent" with making a profit.

Late in March, 1962, Hodges and Decker met with the Business Council to explain the Call for Action. Hodges relates that they got a very chilly reaction. Two or three argued against the whole idea, suggesting that the mere issuance of the document would tend to make the public feel that all business is unethical. "Not a solitary soul stood up to support the proposed program," Hodges writes in his *Business Conscience*. He shouldn't have been surprised: the special privileges that both Presidents Kennedy and Johnson have conferred on the Council have encouraged some of its members to be imperious. On occasion, these free-enterprise aristocrats have shown bad manners; once, in the troubled summer of 1963, when invited to the White House to hear Kennedy plead for their help in desegregation, all but two members of the Council (Roger Blough and Frederick Kappel) remained seated when the President entered the East Room where they had assembled. This crude offense to protocol annoyed the President and infuriated his aides.

Hodges really expected that his effort to stimulate the business conscience would produce results. He was disappointed in this, just as he was disappointed to see the changes he enforced in the old BAC go down the drain. He had a right, perhaps, to expect more; the President, when he took office, insisted on a high code of conduct along the New Frontier. Officials, for example, were barred from accepting lecturing or writing fees, and Cabinet officers were discouraged from taking wives along on official missions (if they do, they must pay for them). But the spring and summer of 1962 were to witness the eruption of the great fight over steel, and the second attempt to patch things up with the business community. In this atmosphere, the drive for better business ethics was quietly laid to rest.

VI | The Big Steel Crisis: Kennedy vs. Blough

THE New York headquarters of the giant United States Steel Corporation are at 71 Broadway, overlooking the historic Trinity Church graveyard, peaceful and incongruous in the midst of the busy skyscrapers. On Wednesday afternoon, April 11, 1962, U. S. Steel Chairman Roger Miles Blough turned on the television set in his private 20th-floor office, and waited for President Kennedy's press conference to come on.

He knew that Kennedy was angry. That was clear enough after Blough had walked into the President's office the night before with the surprise announcement that U. S. Steel was raising prices $6 a ton. Several other big steel producers had since followed suit.

But he didn't realize just how infuriated the President was until he watched and listened to Kennedy, his voice taut with emotion, denounce in bitter language the willful group of men who had displayed "irresponsible defiance" of the public interest.[1]

It was an experience that comes to but few men. "Some time ago," said the President (in a reference to his Inaugural Address), "I asked each American to consider what he would do for his country, and I asked the steel companies. In the last 24 hours, we have had their answer."

Blough listened as Kennedy continued the tongue-lashing:

The simultaneous and identical actions . . . constitute a wholly unjustifiable and irresponsible defiance of the public interest.

89

In this serious hour in our nation's history, with grave crises in Berlin and Southeast Asia, when . . . restraint and sacrifice are being asked of every citizen, the American people will find it hard, as I do, to accept a situation in which a tiny handful of steel executives, whose pursuit of private power and profit exceeds their sense of public responsibility, can show such utter contempt for the interest of 185 million Americans.

It was an awesome indictment, unparalleled in bitterness and scope. As Blough watched the televised press conference—alone in his 20th-floor office—I was just one floor below with a dozen lesser steel corporation officials grouped around another TV set. They sat in grim silence, totally unprepared for—as one put it —the President's "barnburner." As the picture tube showed Kennedy leaving the State Department auditorium stage, a company official snapped off the set and said: "Well, I thought he would have viewed the situation more in sorrow than in anger."

I had flown up to New York from Washington after phoning Blough and making a date for an interview that afternoon. It had been apparent that Kennedy, stunned by the steel price increase, would blast back, and I wanted to get Blough's story directly from him. I had suggested that we wait until after the JFK press conference, and Blough invited me to watch it in the company offices, then come up to see him.

For the real beginning of the fateful confrontation between Kennedy and Blough in the spring of 1962, one must go back to the devastating 116-day steel strike of 1959. This developed into the longest and costliest steel labor dispute on record because President Eisenhower pursued an incredible, nineteenth-century, hands-off attitude. It was ended only when Eisenhower's Secretary of Labor, James P. Mitchell, and Vice-President Nixon secretly—so that Eisenhower wouldn't find out—mediated the dispute.

During the 1960 campaign, and soon after he took office, Kennedy made it clear that *he* would not sit idly by, as Eisenhower had, and watch the economy slowly strangulate in the bind of a management-labor dispute. He adopted the philosophy of Arthur J. Goldberg, Mitchell's successor as Secretary of Labor, that there was a public interest to be considered as well. Goldberg, former counsel to the Steelworkers Union, assumed his new role with a determination to force a revision of old concepts of collective bargaining.

All too often, collective bargaining operated according to jungle law; the parties fought, struck a bargain determined by which side was stronger at the moment. And under the pattern established for years, where the Government did intervene to force a settlement, it usually was on the understanding that higher wage costs would simply be passed on to the consumer. "Ten years ago," Goldberg mused in a private conversation as he ended his term as Secretary of Labor, "I never even heard the term 'balance of payments.' Today, it has to be a consideration at every bargaining table." Indeed this was something new! To be "free," Goldberg liked to say, collective bargaining had to be responsible. This not only meant that the Kennedy Administration would not tolerate anything like the 1959 steel strike, but it would try to anticipate and head off such power struggles before they started.

On September 6, 1961, when rumors in the trade hinted at a steel price increase coincident with the final stage of the wage boost negotiated by Nixon and Mitchell, Kennedy wrote steel company presidents asking that they "forego a price increase," in which case it would "clearly then be the turn of the labor representatives to limit wage demands to a level consistent with continued price stability." On September 14, he wrote in the same vein to McDonald: "The Steelworkers Union can make a significant contribution to the public interest. . . . This implies a labor settlement within the limits of advances in productivity and price stability."

This was the "symmetrical" approach worked out by Goldberg and Economic Council Chairman Walter Heller. The plain meaning of Kennedy's letter to the steel companies was that if they played ball, he—the President—would turn the heat on labor. Of McDonald, he demanded statesmanship, and gave him a measure—productivity limits—of how far he could go. The companies did, in fact, pass up a price increase in the fall of 1961, but most of the executives resented the Kennedy letter and doubted that Kennedy would or could pressure McDonald.

Some of the responses to the Kennedy letter were unbelievably blunt, even rude. One dispensed with the usual "Dear Mr. President" salutation, and started out, simply: "Sir." [2]

Nevertheless, the Administration was encouraged by the fact that prices had not been advanced, and Arthur Goldberg was put to work that fall and winter to apply the same heat to the union. Kennedy really was trying to make good on the "symmetrical" approach, but most observers weren't sanguine. Others were derisive: after all, wasn't Arthur Goldberg a former paid hand of the McDonald union?

The doubters didn't know Goldberg very well. Once the graying ex-labor lawyer stepped into the Kennedy Cabinet, he had only one client—John F. Kennedy. Day in and out, he insisted on "the greater exercise of government responsibility in the area of collective bargaining." In countless speeches and interviews Goldberg hammered away at the theme that the Government must more and more "provide guidelines to the parties to insure that settlements reached are right settlements—not only in the interests of the parties themselves, but which also take into account the public interest." [3]

This was strong medicine for the ex-plumber who heads the AFL-CIO, burly George Meany. In Bal Harbour, Florida, where the AFL-CIO Executive Committee was enjoying a sundrenched session, President Meany exploded that Goldberg was "infringing on the rights of a free people and a free society." But Goldberg's message came through loud and clear to his old boss, Dave McDonald, President of the United Steelworkers of America: Kennedy wouldn't help him get an excessive wage settlement.

In private talks with McDonald, Goldberg—for years the brains behind the steelworkers' many bargaining achievements —urged McDonald to agree to an unprecedented, ahead-of-schedule start on negotiations. If the situation deteriorated into a strike, Goldberg warned McDonald, the Kennedy Administration wouldn't hesitate to throw the book at the union.

On January 23, 1962, the President himself met secretly with Blough and McDonald at the White House, and urged that they start talking early and come up with a noninflationary pact. The upshot of this meeting, after further conversations in Pittsburgh, was agreement to start the talks on a new contract at the end of February, four months ahead of the June 30 expiration date. This seemed to be a victory for the President's public plea for "industrial statesmanship." [4] The negotiations, between teams headed by McDonald for the union, and R. Conrad Cooper of U. S. Steel for the industry, broke down rather quickly, but Kennedy threw his personal prestige into the breach, and talks were resumed March 14.

During this hectic period, Goldberg kept up an unremitting pressure on both Blough and McDonald. In his Economic Message in January, Kennedy had said that the nation "must rely on the good sense and public spirit of our business and labor leaders to hold the line on the price level in 1962." [5] In tougher phrases, Goldberg kept returning to that thought. He pointed to the productivity guidelines in the 1962 Economic Report, which implied a wage boost of no more than 3 percent (see Chapter X), and said bluntly that a settlement in that framework was what the President wanted to see. And he wanted the matter settled quickly, to avoid the twist and pull on the economy occasioned by an inventory buildup in anticipation of a strike, followed by liquidation of excessive stocks later.

One of the secrets of Arthur Goldberg's success as Secretary of Labor was that having the President's full confidence, he never hesitated to speak in the name of the President. And if he felt it necessary to speak in the President's name, and let him know about it later, that was all right with Mr. Kennedy. Thus, Goldberg could and did express Kennedy's concerns and views in vigorous terms.

Kennedy's economists were convinced that if the possibility of a steel strike were out of the way without an inflationary settlement, it would be a tonic extending economic recovery. Thus, when word came that a new contract had been signed on March 31, three months ahead of schedule, for a modest 10-cent wage package, there was rejoicing in Washington. Kennedy himself hastened to arrange a special telephonic hookup to the Penn-Sheraton Hotel in Pittsburgh to congratulate McDonald, Cooper, and their aides.

It was an amazingly cheap settlement, so much so that McDonald gruffly refused to put an official value on the package. And none of it was in actual hourly wage rates; all of the 10 cents—the industry's estimate, verified quietly by union lawyers —was in fringe benefits designed to improve pensions and to ameliorate the pain of the growing unemployment in the steel mills. The notion that the union needed government help to win such a limited settlement from the industry bothered some of the labor "pros." Just before the new contract was initialed, one grumbled: "I sure wish Kennedy had put Goldberg on the Court instead of White." [6] He got his wish to have Goldberg removed from the labor scene a few months later.

It was true, of course, that the economic climate was exactly suited to Goldberg's drive for a quick and noninflationary settlement. Rising unemployment and competition from other products for steel's markets provided neither the union nor the industry with strong bargaining weapons. Common sense thus dictated a harmonious settlement. But in the steel industry, there has been a singular lack of common sense; as Cooper pointed out, the 1962 contract was the first that had been signed since 1954 without a strike.

And since it was the first time that the Government had plunged into a steel collective bargaining situation, before a crisis, Kennedy was entitled to feel that he had risked the prestige of the Presidency and won a great home-front victory. In the week that followed, the contract was universally hailed as "noninflationary," and the nation settled down to assess the new influence the Kennedy Administration had brought to bear by asserting "the public interest."

And then the bomb dropped. It was dropped by Roger Blough.

On Tuesday, April 10, 1962, or as soon as the last union had signed the basic agreement of March 31, the Board of Directors of U. S. Steel met in New York, and decided to raise prices an average of $6 a ton, an increase of 3.5 percent, billed as a boost to enable the company to "catch up" with earlier cost pressures.

Blough had a secretary call Presidential aide Kenny O'Donnell, and request an appointment with Kennedy for about 5:45 P.M. Blough took a company plane (one of the fleet U. S. Steel maintains) to Washington and proceeded to the White House.[7]

Kennedy wondered what Blough had on his mind (as a matter of fact, when he saw his name on the calendar, he checked with his secretary, Mrs. Evelyn Lincoln, to see if someone hadn't made a mistake). He didn't have to wait long to find out.

Ushered into the President's oval study, Blough said: "Perhaps the easiest way I can explain why I am here is to give you this and let you read it." Whereupon, Blough handed the President a 4-page mimeographed statement which at the very moment was being given to the press in New York and Pittsburgh for A.M. release, Wednesday, April 11.

The President skimmed the mimeographed sheets, and his expression became grim. He reread the release slowly. "I think you have made a terrible mistake," he told Blough. The President rose, went to the door of his office and told Mrs. Lincoln to get Arthur Goldberg "immediately." Within minutes, the Secretary of Labor, who had been in his wood-paneled departmental office, was at the White House. The President told Goldberg that Blough had raised prices. It took a moment for it to sink in. Infuriated, Goldberg turned on Blough, and asked:

"Why did you bother to come, if the price increase is already decided on?"

Fiddling with his bifocals, Blough responded that it was a matter of courtesy. Scornfully, Goldberg said that it was hardly courteous to confront the President of the United States with a *fait accompli*. It was, Goldberg said, more like a double cross.

A few weeks before, on his way to a meeting in Washington's Sheraton-Park Hotel with Walter Heller and the Business Council's economists, Blough had told me that he saw a rough similarity between his job and the President's. "The President has a tough job," he said sympathetically. "He can't be liked by everybody." And, he continued, broadening the reference to include himself: "Sometimes, we have to take positions that are not quite popular."

That tense evening in the White House, lectured by Goldberg as the President sat by, silent and angry, Blough knew that he had taken a position that was "not quite popular" along the New Frontier. But he didn't yet know what he had touched off.

As soon as Blough left, a Presidential aide said later, Kennedy and Goldberg decided that "this is war." They sent for Heller, Special Counsel Ted Sorensen, brother Bobby, Council member Kermit Gordon, and O'Donnell. They were joined later by a few others, including Assistant Press Secretary Andrew Hatcher.

His fury slowly rising, the President strode up and down his office, blasting the stupidity and cupidity of Roger Blough and the U. S. Steel Corporation. It was then that he got off a bitter observation:

"My father always told me that all businessmen were sons of bitches, but I never believed it until now!" * This explosive bit of frustration, when it became public a few days later, helped to convince many that he was really anti-business, deep down. Businessmen, of course, often applied the same term, and worse, to the late President.

By the time Kennedy left his office that Tuesday evening to dress for a Congressional reception, some of the lines of attack were settled, and work was begun on a draft of a Presidential statement. The mood was one of gloom; no one was really hopeful of upending the price increase. But the President's order, meeting the challenge thrown down by Blough, was to mobilize every force within the Government. Truly, it was a cold-blooded campaign—the U. S. Government vs. U. S. Steel—and Cabinet officers, Congressmen, and personal friends were thrown into the battle. Among the weapons were antitrust subpoenas, a grand jury investigation, diversion of Pentagon business, threats of hostile legislation, personal appeals to smaller steel companies, and above all—the unique power of the Presidency.

As I walked the flight of stairs to Blough's private office in New York that Wednesday afternoon, I wondered how a man just excoriated by the President of the United States before the entire nation would react. I was prepared for almost anything except Blough's unbelievable aplomb.

A high government official once described Blough to me as a "cold fish." This may be unkind, but it is accurate. Calm and unruffled, Blough walked into the board room adjoining his

---

* The version quoted here was published by *The New York Times* on April 23, 1962. The first published version was reported by *Newsweek*, some days ahead of the *Times* story, without reference to the phrase "sons of bitches." It is the recollection of some who were present that the President said "S.O.B.'s." In any event, at a later press conference, when asked about the *Times* version, the President didn't deny he had used the phrase, but smilingly noted that he was talking about steel executives, not all businessmen.

Kennedy was annoyed that this story had leaked out of his private conference with his advisers. He tried to track down the source of the "leak" to *Newsweek*, whose version was on the newsstands (and read at the White House) on Monday, April 16.

own office, and sat down with me and Phelps Adams, U. S. Steel
vice-president for public relations. His greeting was matter-of-
fact, and while he clearly didn't like the idea of being condemned as a power-hungry tycoon, he wasn't visibly upset. This
was a tough, unemotional businessman, insensitive, I think, to
public reaction.

The basic justification for a price increase, Blough said, was
that U. S. Steel, like any other company, must have enough
revenues to continue in business. "The President feels that we
acted contrary to the public interest," he said in a monotone.
"Well, I feel that a lack of proper cost and price relationships is
one of the most damaging things to the public interest."

This was the essence of the case: steel was caught in a cost-
price squeeze. The industry needed extensive modernization
that could be financed only by building up internal reserves.
Blough claimed that with no price increase in four years, U. S.
Steel's profits as a percentage of sales had slipped from 9.5 percent in 1957 to 5.7 percent in 1961. And even though the 1962
wage agreement was conceded to be modest, the industry felt
that it exceeded productivity gains, and thus would accentuate
the squeeze on profits.

Blough scoffed at the idea that Kennedy had been double-
crossed. He cited his September 13 response to the President's
September 6, 1961, letter requesting that the steel companies
hold the price line. "If anybody thought that U. S. Steel would
not at some time raise prices, they must not have been reading
the English language," he told me.

The Blough letter—which U. S. Steel proudly had printed up
as a classic explanation of its case—said that "the pressures of
the market place are inexorable, and cannot be disregarded by a
steel company or any other company, or for that matter, cannot be disregarded by any nation which wishes to maintain its
position in a competitive world."

This kind of generality didn't answer the double-cross charge.
It was quite true, as Blough reiterated, that he had made "no
commitment" to anyone with respect to prices. But this was a
thin semantic reed. The fact was that Blough had also done
nothing to counter the impression that there was a quid pro
quo: no inflationary wage boost, no price increase.

I put it to Blough directly. Didn't you, I asked, let this impression get around? Blough offers the world an impassive expression most of the time, and his voice is restrained. But he summoned some feeling to say: "Certainly not!"

Why was it assumed in Pittsburgh, in Washington, in business circles everywhere, that there would be no steel price increase? Tapping a yellow pencil on a conference table, Blough answered: "That didn't result from anything I've said. I suspect, perhaps, that the impression was a by-product of the Government's economic guidelines, which led some people to think that all past [wage] increases might just be forgotten."

But that was not the general belief then—or now, in retrospect. As the London *Economist* observed: "Earlier . . . the steel companies . . . had welcomed the Administration's help in bringing the steel workers to the bargaining table to negotiate a new labour contract well in advance of the expiry of the old one, and in pressing them to moderate their demands. But as soon as the contract was signed, Mr. Blough broke what everyone had presumed, although it had not been stated specifically, was his side of a bargain." [8]

Mr. Kennedy may have overreacted—but if he did, it was because he felt he had been deceived, or "sandbagged." (A year later, when the steel companies announced selected price increases on some products, it was on the anniversary of the 1962 imbroglio. It may have been a coincidence of dates, but Kennedy didn't think so.) To complicate things, the trickery, as JFK saw it, deprived him of a substantial achievement that he had staked much to win. And no Kennedy has ever liked to lose, or to see the fruits of victory vaporize.

Bobby Kennedy later put it this way: "Mr. Blough sat in on a number of conferences with the President, and with Secretary of Labor Goldberg where efforts were made—which he applauded—to keep David McDonald and the steel union from asking for a large increase in wages. That effort was made on the basis that there wouldn't be any rise in the price of steel. Mr. Blough never said during that time: 'Well, no matter what happens, I'm going to have to raise the price of steel.' . . . So when the rise was announced, it came as a complete surprise to us." [9]

What Blough didn't sense was that many business and financial experts would conclude that he pulled a boner. Typical was the feeling of Per Jacobsson, late Managing Director of the International Monetary Fund. Returning to Washington on the Eastern Airlines shuttle, I had the good fortune to bump into this financial wizard, confidant of statesmen. It soon became apparent that Jacobsson, on the last lap of a trip back to Washington from Switzerland, hadn't heard of the steel news.

"Mr. Jacobsson," I asked, "did you know that Roger Blough raised steel prices six dollars a ton last night?"

A big, friendly bear of a man, Jacobsson was stunned. "He did what?"

I repeated the news, and filled him in on the day's developments, including the President's denunciation of Blough, and the beginnings of the rollback effort.

"But that's incredible," Jacobsson finally said. "Why, I've just been all over Europe, and they were happy with the wage settlement because they assumed that it meant there would be no price increase. And I told them they were right!"

That was the assumption here, too, coupled with a belief that a new interpretation of the "national interest" was taking hold —one that would somehow temper the demands of labor or management. But such a broad interpretation of the national interest isn't accepted by Blough. He told me, during that private session in April 1962, that steel should not be considered a bellwether industry. "You hear the argument," he continued, "that steel is different because we have more impact on the economy. I just don't agree with that. We must have enough profit to do the things that have to be done."

But what Blough had difficulty in explaining then or later was how a price increase would help the domestic steel industry meet already vigorous inroads being made by cheaper foreign steel, or competition from other materials like aluminum, concrete, and plastics. He conceded that a higher price for domestic steel might temporarily add to the competitive problem, but insisted: "If we're going to be able to compete in the long run, we need better plants, and to get those, we need higher profits that will permit reinvestment of capital. That's why we raised prices."

The Administration's position, of course, was that the higher-price route was neither a necessary nor desirable way of financing capital improvements. An analysis by Walter Heller's Council observed on this point: "Neither economic principle nor the actual experience of the steel companies affords a justification for the view that prices should be set at levels permitting 100 percent internal financing of investment capital. Capital improvements increase the value of the assets owned by stockholders; increasing prices to pay for them amounts to taxing steel users for the benefit of the stockholders." [10]

But neither the Administration's counterarguments nor its over-all concern about the economy carried much weight with Roger Blough. What came through very clearly was that the President of the United States had his job to do, and Roger Blough had his own to do, and he didn't understand why people just couldn't see it that way. I asked: "In making a difficult decision like a price increase in steel, what weight would you say you gave to the Administration's reiteration of the need for price stability?"

His answer, in measured tones, was most revealing: "Against the background of thinking in terms of costs—which is the background I think in—the Government's position was one of the factors that was weighed very heavily, along with all the others we have to contend with."

Thus, Roger Blough, as he put it so well himself, is a man who thinks "in terms of costs." To such a man, the national urgency, as expressed by the President of the United States, was only "one of the factors" that received consideration. But it was just *one* factor, weighed along with others—say, the cost of scrap or pig iron. In the world of the Roger Bloughs, costs and prices and profits are the big determinants. Something as fuzzy as a sense of responsibility—the Goldbergian "national interest" concept—is not very high on the list. After all, how do you show the "national interest" on a balance sheet?

Blough's bid for a price increase was at once bold and imprudent, worsened by overtones of bad faith. It betrayed an insensitivity to the larger issues involved. The company was aware that the President had a press conference scheduled the next day, and didn't even think its timing was bad, in a public relations sense. The fact is that Blough expected fully to get away with it. At worst, he expected a slap on the wrist, not a sock on the jaw. His misassessment of how Kennedy would respond was an incredible gaffe, which could be made only by a man who thinks exclusively in terms of costs and prices. Now, he had been labeled profit-and-power hungry by a popular young President, and the question was, as that event-packed Wednesday came to a close, could Blough resist the Presidential onslaught?

He couldn't, as it turned out, but at that juncture, the results were not visible. The Presidential press conference blast over, Blough, unruffled and unmoved, didn't think his price increase was at all jeopardized.

On Wednesday morning Bethlehem Steel, No. 2 in the industry, announced a price increase. So did the other big companies: Republic, Youngstown, Jones and Laughlin, and some smaller ones like Wheeling. By the time the President strode into the State Department auditorium at 3:30 P.M. to deliver his blistering denunciation, the follow-the-leader bandwagon, so typical of the steel industry, seemed to have begun, inexorably, to roll over the Kennedy Administration.

However, as night fell in Washington that Wednesday, there were still five small companies, representing 14 percent of the industry's capacity, that had not raised prices. These were Inland Steel, Armco, Kaiser Steel, Colorado Fuel & Iron, and McLouth Steel. Immediately, the Administration pursued a "divide and conquer" strategy.

Perhaps the key role, ultimately, was played by Joseph L. Block, Inland Steel Co. chairman, who at the time was vacationing in Japan. Block was no stranger to Washington: during the early 1940's, he was one of the heads of the War Production Board Steel Division. More recently, he had accepted membership on Kennedy's 21-man Labor-Management Advisory Committee created at Goldberg's suggestion.

When George Meany a few months before denounced Goldberg's insistence that the public interest had to be considered paramount, it was Block who came to his defense with this public statement: "A contest of strength where the stronger side wins doesn't prove a thing. Each side has to represent its own interest, but neither side must be unmindful of the needs of the nation. Who else can point out those needs but the Government?" So the Administration's ploy was obvious: try to get the Chicago-based Inland to hold off. That might firm the spine of the other smaller companies, and in a steel market already pressed by competition, it might tumble the leaders off their price perch.

But would the strategy work? In respect to Inland, there were two things "going" for Kennedy. First, Block was friendly to the Administration, close to Goldberg, and was known to feel that Blough was not the most effective spokesman for the business community. This was his view long before the 1962 fracas over prices. Second, Inland's business was good.

And so, what might be called "the telephone campaign of 1962" got under way, much of it directed by Undersecretary of Commerce Edward C. Gudeman, a former Sears, Roebuck executive from Chicago. On Wednesday morning, back from an emergency White House meeting on steel, Commerce Secretary Luther Hodges called in Gudeman and said:

"Eddie, get on the phone!"

Hodges didn't know that Gudeman, a boyhood chum of Inland vice-president P. D. Block, had phoned him at 7:45 A.M. on his own initiative. Gudeman's approach was low-pressure, with no threats. Had P.D. thought through all of the implications of an industry-wide price boost? Gudeman wanted to know. Later, Gudeman reached Gene Trefethen, No. 2 man at Kaiser, and appealed to him to hold the line. Meanwhile, Goldberg phoned Leigh B. Block, Inland vice-president for purchasing, and Treasury Undersecretary Henry H. Fowler reached Inland President John F. Smith, Jr.

The theme of all the calls followed the Gudeman line: Don't take precipitate action—the President is right—Big Steel is wrong—at least, wait a bit and think it through. "Anybody who knew anybody else got on the horn," explained one participant later. "We called friends, and the people we called called their friends," Gudeman said. The response was at least mildly encouraging. P. D. Block admitted to Gudeman that he had been surprised by Blough's action, and promised that Inland would not make a price boost announcement immediately; instead, the company would think things over carefully. On Thursday, P.D. reached Joe Block in Japan, and after a long conversation, they agreed that Inland would not raise prices. The announcement was made this way by Joe Block on Friday from Kyoto: "We did not feel that it was in the national interest to raise prices at this time. We felt this very strongly." [11]

In Washington, the Kennedy team could hardly believe the good news. In a calmer moment later on, Goldberg told me: "I never doubted that Joe Block would be shocked by Blough's decision. But you had to have guts to buck Big Steel, and Block had the guts." It was only a battle, and not the war; it would take more than Inland to win, and the telephone campaign was redoubled. Defense Secretary Robert S. McNamara, Undersecretary of State George Ball, White House aide Ralph Dungan, joined Gudeman, Heller, and Fowler in their long-distance efforts. President Kennedy himself phoned Edgar Kaiser of the Kaiser Steel Co.

The real hope for forcing a price rollback rested on dividing Bethlehem Steel Co. from U. S. Steel. But so far as is known, the Administration could devise no personal appeal to Bethlehem. It therefore embarked on a different approach to the No. 2 company, one that brought the FBI into play, and helped to establish the image of a Kennedy Government strong-arming its way through the economy.

From start to finish, there were strange elements to the role played by Bethlehem in the 1962 crisis. Just the day before Big Steel's decision to raise prices, Edmund F. Martin, Bethlehem Vice-President, had told a stockholders' meeting in Wilmington, Delaware, that "there shouldn't be a price rise." He added: "We shouldn't do anything to increase our costs if we are to survive. We have more competition both domestically and from foreign firms."

But as soon as Roger Blough raised prices, Bethlehem dutifully fell in line. Was this collusion? The contradiction between Martin's speech to stockholders and the company action in the space of little more than a day wasn't lost on the Kennedys. After Martin claimed he had been misquoted, Bobby Kennedy set out to get the facts, and the way he did it was typically brash.

At 3 A.M. Thursday morning, an FBI agent phoned Lee Linder, a Philadelphia reporter with the Associated Press who had covered the Bethlehem stockholders' meeting. Although Linder suggested that the matter wait till morning, two agents arrived at his home at 4 A.M., and questioned Linder on Martin's precise words. Another newsman, John Lawrence of the *Wall Street Journal*, was awakened at 5 A.M.[12] At 6:30 A.M. in Wilmington, two other agents were waiting for James L. Parks, Jr., of the

Wilmington *Evening Journal,* another reporter who had covered the Bethlehem stockholders' meeting, when he arrived at his office for work.

Parks reported that the agents were polite, and that he—like the others—confirmed the original version: Martin had indeed said there shouldn't be a price increase. But not surprisingly, the Administration was criticized for sending FBI men around in the middle of the night. To the Republicans, it smacked of "gestapo tactics," and they said so loudly.[13] The Administration's tactics were offensive to others, too. For example, columnist Joseph A. Livingston, generally friendly to Kennedy, wrote: "Persons who regard themselves as 'liberals' and even New Dealers had reason to resent U. S. Steel's insensitivity in raising prices. But they also have reason to recoil from the relentless use of power by the President." [14]

Bobby Kennedy's inflexible attitudes helped to shape business's judgment of his brother. For example, in trying to run to earth the rumors of price collusion, Bobby dug deep—even into personal expense account reports by some corporate heads. When one such situation was brought to President Kennedy's attention, he agreed that Bobby had gone too far, and took steps to call him off.

However one assesses the Justice Department tactics—my own view is that the industry was playing a rough game, for keeps, too—they paid off in terms of Bethlehem. The company was caught in a public exposure of its conflicting statements. Coincident with this, McNamara announced that Pentagon policy would be to shift contracts where possible "to those companies which have not increased prices." He added that he would also study the possibilities for substituting other materials for steel. (This was more meaningful than a rather wild estimate by McNamara that the $6 steel increase would increase national defense costs by $1 billion a year.) To drive the point home to Bethlehem—the nation's largest ship-steel supplier—the Pentagon awarded a $5,000,000 armor plate contract to the Lukens Steel Co., which had not raised prices.

Meanwhile, close on the Joe Block announcement from Kyoto, Edgar Kaiser in Oakland, California, said that the Kaiser Steel Corp. "will not raise its mill prices at this time." Armco made no move one way or the other, and the Colorado Fuel and

Iron Corp. said it was studying the possibility of selective price changes. So the bandwagon was stalling, and the Administration pressed its advantage. Bobby Kennedy announced a grand jury probe of events, and said that subpoenas for documents had already been served on Bethlehem and other company officials.

On Thursday, April 12, with the outcome far from clear, it was Kennedy's turn to watch Blough handle a televised press conference. His opening statement defended the price increase and denied that there had been "any commitment of any kind" not to raise prices. But the President and his aides got their first inkling of victory when Blough said it would be "very difficult" for Big Steel if some other major producer did not also raise prices. "It would definitely affect us, and I don't know how long we could maintain our position," Blough told a questioner.[15]

By this time, the maneuvering took on an Ian Fleming-ish aspect. Late Thursday night, lawyer Clark Clifford went out to Washington National Airport, where he met secretly aboard one of the U. S. Steel fleet of private planes with Vice-President Robert Tyson. This rendezvous was arranged by Kennedy's newsman-friend, Charles Bartlett. Goldberg had already had several fruitless talks with Tyson, and Kennedy was persuaded that he should try a fresh negotiator. The Clifford-Tyson huddle appeared to have come to a dead end also, but on Friday morning, Blough passed on word that he thought conversations should continue.

Sensing a turning point, Kennedy packed both Goldberg and Clifford onto a military transport plane to meet Blough, Tyson, and other U. S. Steel executives in New York. En route, Goldberg got a radio-phone message: Armco had joined with Inland and Kaiser in standing athwart Big Steel's price boost. In a comfortable suite at the fashionable Carlyle Hotel, the gray-haired Goldberg, his own reputation very much on the line, reviewed all the arguments on the Administration side. The phone rang, for Blough, and then for Goldberg. For both, it was the same message, feared by the one and hoped for by the other: Bethlehem had thrown in the sponge "in order to remain competitive" with Inland, Kaiser, and Armco. According to a participant at the Carlyle denouement, Blough appeared to be "pale and shaken."

Goldberg didn't let up. He listed for Blough some forthcoming ammunition: In a few hours the White House would release a Heller "White Paper," tearing apart the economic justifications Blough had offered in his Thursday statement. Then, on Saturday, Treasury Secretary Douglas Dillon, who had been vacationing at his Hobe Sound, Florida, home, would call in reporters to suggest that the industry was greedy; it could recoup $40 to $45 million in the tax credit and depreciation Kennedy was proposing—or nearly as much as raising prices might yield. The barrage would be continued with an Orville Freeman press conference, in which the Agriculture Secretary would charge that the price increase would cost American farmers $45 million a year. And there would be Congressional harassment, including new hearings under the industry's archfoe, the late Estes Kefauver of Tennessee.

But it was the Bethlehem pullout that did it. Just why Bethlehem backed off as it did and when it did is not completely known even now. It is a reasonable assumption, however, that Bethlehem was embarrassed by its contradictory position on prices, and entertained real worries about competition from Inland and Armco. And it had no taste for any further antitrust matters.

Around 5 P.M., Blough caved in at the Carlyle, and a happy Arthur Goldberg got on the phone to give Kennedy the message. At exactly 5.28 P.M., wire service news tickers clattered with a bulletin, taken from this corporation handout: "The United States Steel Corp. today announced it had rescinded the 3½ percent price increase made on Wednesday, April 11."

Leslie B. Worthington, U. S. Steel president, explained that "the price decision was made in the light of the competitive developments today, and all other current circumstances, including the removal of a serious obstacle to proper relations between government and business." It was a roundabout way for saying the company felt it was under pressure, and had no alternative.

It was a stunning turnabout. The companies that had followed U. S. Steel and Bethlehem up, followed them down. In Washington, after Goldberg's call, Kennedy told Heller to bury the "White Paper," the Cabinet press conferences were canceled, and a date was made for Blough to meet with Kennedy early the following week, prior to the regular Presidential press conference. The President sensed that he would face a difficult period of repairing and restoring relationships, and he told one aide to find areas "where everybody can now work together."

So once again, just a week after he dropped his bomb, Blough walked into the President's office, and this time they talked alone. The victor—a President who had blasted a big steel tycoon while the nation listened in, and then forced him to backtrack on his decision—assured Blough that he held no grudges. He said, also, that he recognized the industry's need to modernize plant facilities, that the Government would help it in this process, and that he would tell the nation so at his next press conference.

They talked for 45 minutes, an uncomfortable session for both men. Kennedy had never been overly impressed with Blough. It was a mystery to him how a man with such a pale personality had become a leading business spokesman. But Blough had been useful in 1961 in re-establishing contact with the Business Council, when Kennedy desperately tried to shuck the "anti-business" tag. And now, for whatever internal turmoil he felt, Blough was willing to keep open a channel of communication to the upper-crust segment of the business world.

Thus, Kennedy happily and sincerely assured Blough that there would be no anti-business vendetta. He promised Blough that he would make this clear to the nation, and that a suitable collection of high Administration officials would be dispatched to the May meeting of the Business Council at Hot Springs. In addition, the Administration would press forward with its plans for a White House Conference on National Economic Issues later in the month, at which JFK would be the principal speaker.

At his next press conference, April 19, Kennedy tried to damp the fires of controversy. He said: ". . . Nothing is to be gained from further public recriminations." He added that he believed firmly in "holding the role of the Government to the minimum level needed to protect the public interest." And without ever suggesting that he had any regrets about his tough attitude and efforts of the preceding week, he promised that his Administration would not proceed from there to engage in broad wage and price fixing. The main thought Kennedy attempted to leave: steel was a very special case, not a guideline for the future.

Kennedy's attempt to bury the hatchet was well received by

some. The astute Sidney J. Weinberg, senior partner of Goldman, Sachs, and Co., for 30 years a power in the big business
world (and a vice-chairman and founder of the Business Council), told me after the press conference: "Kennedy said exactly
what was needed. That's the way a chief executive ought to be—
magnanimous at a time of victory. And it's right for the country,
very beneficial. Of course, there are scars left, because a lot of
people in the business world think that he blew his top a week
ago, but his new attitude helps. Believe me, the country would
have been in trouble if he hadn't taken steps to smooth things
over."

The business community at large, however, was still in a state
of shock. It was stunned by the awesome display of Presidential
power, embittered by the crack about sons-of-bitches, the use of
FBI agents, the rearrangement of Pentagon orders. And it was
fearful of the implications of Kennedy's successful intrusion
into a basic private decision-making area—the setting of prices.
Businessmen who privately confided that Blough's move was
"inept" or "bush-league" or "dumb" felt that Kennedy's intervention was hard to justify, even if he did feel that Blough
double-crossed him.

Above all, what businessmen wondered was: Can it happen
again? Through businessmen he liked and trusted—such as
Thomas J. Watson, Jr., of IBM and Robert A. Lovett, former
Secretary of Defense—and in private conversations with friends
and newsmen, Kennedy passed the word along that the unique
combination of circumstances was highly unlikely to come up
again. For example, there was this exchange in what amounted
to a semiofficial interview that Heller gave *Newsweek:*

Q. In what situations or circumstances would the Administration again bring to bear the same weapons it employed in
the steel price case?

A. It's hard to conceive of any situation that would call forth
the same response. First, steel is a bellwether in its basic
role in the economy and as a pace-setter. Second, there were
special circumstances, as you well know: there had been a
wage settlement in conformity with the national interest,
as spelled out in our guidelines for noninflationary wage
increases. So steel was a special situation. This is not to
deny that the Government will express and assert the pub-

lic interest in other wage and price decisions having a broad impact on the economy.[16]

To the degree that this word got through, it was encouraging to businessmen. If Blough had been inept, they argued, Kennedy had overreacted. Kennedy may have felt the same way, but—to the end—he never would admit it, even if some members of his team privately concede he went too far. Late in 1962, when he was asked in a television interview by American Broadcasting Co. correspondent William H. Lawrence for a retrospective appraisal, the President said:

> . . . Though I don't like to rake over old fires, I think it would have been a serious situation if I had not attempted with all my influence to try to get a rollback, because there was an issue of good faith involved. . . . If I had not attempted, after asking the unions to accept the noninflationary settlement, if I had not attempted to use my influence to have the companies hold their prices stable, I think the union could have rightfully felt that they had been misled. In my opinion it would have endangered the whole bargaining between labor and management, would have made it impossible for us to exert any influence . . . in the future . . . on these great labor-management disputes. So I have no regrets. The fact is, we were successful. . . .
>
> I just think, looking back on it, that I would not change it at all. There is no sense in raising hell, and then not being successful. There is no sense in putting the office of the Presidency on the line on an issue and then being defeated. . . . Given the problem that I had on that Tuesday night, I must say I think we had to do everything we could to get it reversed.[17]

Blough's own backward reflection was that Kennedy's "vehement" reaction did not really stem from fears of inflation, but in order to keep his standing with the labor movement. "His earlier stand against a 35-hour work week had displeased the labor unions," Blough said. "I believe that he and Secretary Goldberg felt an increase in steel prices . . . would be viewed as evidence that the Administration's policies were adverse to labor's interests. . . . It is my opinion that the price increase would not have hurt, but would have helped the American economy. . . . Pricing by political pressure . . . weakens the industrial strength upon which America's very survival may depend in time of crisis." [18]

The truce after battle, in the spring of 1962, left a host of problems. Kennedy's display of power would bring forth the demand that he exert similar pressure on labor unions if they got out of line, and this would be tougher to do. For the steel industry, there was still the problem of finding the right time and the right way to raise steel prices. (As it developed, it was a full year away.) For the President, there was that residue of bitterness, never eradicated.

The widely read *Kiplinger Letter,* for example, said after prices were rescinded that "many businessmen now feel sure that Kennedy is anti-business, even those who have wondered about it in the past or argued against it. Now they tell us that they know it. This even comes from those who feel that the steel companies bungled the whole thing." [19]

Actually, the reaction of the business world was somewhat more subtle. True, the sheer flexing of Presidential muscle was a spectacle. But that was just the external symbol of something that ran deeper. In board rooms and over dinner tables, what businessmen told each other was that the President had abridged a basic right, the right to make business decisions. If business makes the wrong decisions, they feel, those decisions should fall of their own weight, without government intrusion.

In his televised rebuttal to President Kennedy, Blough had stressed that ". . . each individual company in our competitive society has a responsibility to the public, as well as to its employees and stockholders, to do the things that are necessary, price-wise, however unpopular that may be at times, to keep in the competitive race."

But was competition truly the only factor, as Blough suggested, in establishing prices? The initial grand jury investigation came to an end on March 19, 1963, without arriving at a specific conclusion. This was in the middle of an era, it might be noted, when the Kennedy Administration was still trying hard to eradicate the anti-business stigma. Then in April 1963, the steel industry announced a "selective" price increase, just as the antitrust division began a study of "leads" turned up by the dissolved grand jury.

On October 16, 1963—a month after a second set of increases by the steel industry—a new grand jury was convened in New York, and the major companies were subpoenaed for information on steel sheet, strip, plate, bars, and tin mill products. This panel on April 7, 1964, returned an indictment against eight major companies and two officials accused of illegally conspiring over a six-year period to fix prices for "extras" in the $3.6 billion sheet steel industry. ("Extras" are additional charges for particular sizes, gauges, or quality content of the steel.)

A real shocker in the six-page indictment was the accusation that the huge, supposedly sophisticated steel industry had stooped to the same device that had sent officials in the electrical equipment industry to jail: secret price-fixing sessions in hotel rooms. The Biltmore and the Sheraton-East in New York were specifically named.

The outcome of this indictment—the seventh in two years against various companies—won't be known for perhaps another year or two. But in the public mind, it raises basic questions about steel prices and how they are established. "It's also worth remembering," the New York *Herald Tribune* said in an editorial after the grand jury indictment, "that during the whole steel price hullabaloo [of 1962], one of the companies' principal arguments was that the price rise couldn't have been rigged because competition within the industry was so cutthroat . . . If indeed, steel executives had been meeting clandestinely in hidden hotel rooms to rig the prices of those 'extras' that figure so largely in their intra-industry competition, then what happens to their argument?"

Just after the companies rescinded the $6 price boost in 1962, the *Wall Street Journal* said: "Let us first of all be clear about just what the Government did. It said that a private company could not change the price of its product, a property right which is obviously basic to a free economy. In other words, the Government set the price. And it did this by the pressure of fear— by naked power, by threats, by agents of the state security police." [20]

This conclusion certainly overstates the facts, but it is typical of the real sense of business jitters that prevailed. When Commerce Secretary Hodges, for example, made a passing reference to aluminum prices, aluminum stocks fell on the New York Stock Exchange. The *Wall Street Journal* notwithstanding, Kennedy had no grand design to change the price mechanisms of American industry. The *Journal* didn't mention the companion pressure that had been brought to bear against the United Steelworkers. And it made no effort to judge whether, in reality, the weakness in the steel marketplace itself was not the dominant reason for the collapse of Blough's attempted push on prices.

The significance of the post-steel-crisis months lies not in the reality of Kennedy's mood—whether he was anti-business or not —but in the fact that much of the business community concluded that he was. Soon, special "S.O.B." buttons showed up in Wall Street, and even Sidney Weinberg sported one on his lapel at the May Business Council meeting at Hot Springs, Virginia. ("It means Sons of Brooklyn," Weinberg joked.)

Kennedy, of course, knew that the business community was hostile, and planned to use a speech scheduled for April 30 to the United States Chamber of Commerce for conciliatory gestures. But business confidence was to prove an elusive goal. The stock market was slipping badly, and historically business has an especially snappish regard for Washington when the bears ride in Wall Street. No one knew it then, but Black Monday's market crash was only a month off, and fair or not, this record-breaking slide would be blamed on the steel flap—and on Kennedy.

VII | Rapprochement, Second Phase

THE year before, in 1961, President Kennedy had ducked an invitation to speak to the U. S. Chamber of Commerce, that paragon of middle-class America. As the official spokesman for 3,800 assorted big and little businessmen, the Chamber is one of Washington's most powerful and prolific lobbies. From its handsome offices, facing the White House across Lafayette Park, the Chamber operates a dignified propaganda mill that keeps pace with the output of the AFL-CIO's mimeograph machines just down the block.[1]

Kennedy's rejection of his first chance to address the Chamber in 1961 didn't slip by unnoticed by the business community. Inasmuch as Eisenhower had addressed either a Chamber dinner or general session in each of the prior three years—and, in fact, had made an appearance in six out of his eight years as President—Mr. Kennedy's absence was one of the facts carefully toted up in the accounting of those who rated him anti-business.[2] In the patch-up process after the fight over the Business Advisory Council, Mr. Kennedy therefore accepted Chamber President Richard Wagner's bid to address the Chamber's 50th Anniversary convention on April 30, 1962.

With the steel crisis just days behind, this offered Mr. Kennedy the opportunity to launch a new effort at rapprochement. The White House speech-writing establishment, headed by Ted Sorensen, worked over the draft of Kennedy's speech as carefully as if it were an inaugural address. The tone that Kennedy wanted to strike was one of conciliation and moderation. He would say, specifically, that he opposed price and wage control, and believed strongly in the freedom of decision making within the private economy.

Facing the Chamber audience in Washington's staid old Constitution Hall, home of the Daughters of the American Revolution, Kennedy developed the theme of mutuality of purpose among government, business, and labor. "If American business does not earn sufficient revenues to earn a profit," the President told the Chamber, "this Government cannot earn sufficient revenues to cover its outlays. If American business does not prosper and expand, this Government cannot make good its pledges of economic growth."

Then, he got to the steel crisis: "It is easy to charge an Administration is anti-business, but it is more difficult to show how an Administration, composed—we hope—of rational men, can possibly feel they can survive without business, or how the nation can survive unless the Government and business and all other groups in our country are exerting their best effort in an atmosphere of understanding, and I hope cooperation."

He made a strong case for price stability, the ultimate goal because of the troublesome balance of payments deficit. With great feeling, Kennedy continued: "It costs the United States $3 billion a year to maintain our troops and our defense establishment and security commitments abroad. If the balance of trade is not sufficiently in our favor to finance this burden, we have two alternatives. One, to lose gold, as we have been doing. And two, to begin to withdraw our security commitments." Since neither was acceptable, the problem had to be approached the other way around, that is, by keeping wages and prices stable. This, Kennedy said, would enable the United States to build a larger export surplus as an offset to its international expenditures.

"In short," Kennedy declared, "our primary challenge is not how to divide the economic pie, but how to enlarge it. To fight now over large slices of the existing pie, by seeking higher margins on lower volume, or higher wages ahead of productivity, can only weaken our effort to expand the economy of the United States."

He didn't talk defensively about his crackdown on Roger

Blough and the steel companies, but he repeated earlier assurances that he was not heading toward price controls: "We have many burdens in Washington—we do not want the added burden of determining individual prices for individual products. We seek instead an economic climate in which an expanding concept of business and labor responsibility, and increasing awareness of world commerce and the free forces of domestic competition will keep the price level stable and keep the Government out of price-setting." He ended with a Biblical quotation: ". . . There is a time for every purpose under the heaven . . . a time to cast away stones and a time to gather stones together." Now was the time, Kennedy said, "for us all to gather stones together to build this country as it must be built in the coming years."

It should have been reassuring: the tone was friendly, the economic rationale soundly rooted in conservative dogma.[3] There was plenty of evidence at hand to suggest that the President was to the right of many elements in his own party, which felt that the economy needed a stronger stimulus. But the olive branch that Kennedy tried to extend to the business world had no official takers at Constitution Hall. He was followed to the rostrum by Chamber President Wagner, a Chicago oil man, who said coldly that there had been "an erosion" of the traditional governmental checks and balances, and that "we should remember dictators in other lands usually come to power under accepted constitutional procedures." [4]

This pompous touch was out of keeping with reality—not even the United States Chamber of Commerce was seriously concerned with Mr. Kennedy's propensities toward dictatorship. But the President did fail to convince the Chamberites that he would wield the powers of his office with an even hand. What it came down to, in essence, was a feeling that Kennedy was "tougher" on business than he had been or would be on labor. The President's own assurances that he would demand equal restraint from labor were simply not believed. In one carefully drafted section of his address, he had said: "Union leaders' interests lie in the rate of return on labor for their members. To the extent that their efforts are devoted to securing equitable wages for their workers, our interests are identical. . . . To the extent that their efforts take the form of demands which will not upset the balance which thus far has stemmed inflation, our interests are in concert. Those areas where conflict exists between what I would call private interests and the general welfare must be met, and it seems to me by assumption of responsibility by all who care for our country."

This was a broad hint that labor had better not push him too hard, couched, to be sure, in terribly vague language. But the following couldn't be mistaken:

"And may I add at this point that when an Administration has not hesitated to seek Taft-Hartley injunction for national emergencies, has successfully urged moderation on the steel-workers and other unions, has expressed a firm and continuing opposition to the twenty-five-hour week, or anything less than the forty-hour week, and has gone on record against feather-bedding and racketeering and roadblocks to automation, it surely need not to be asked whether it will invoke the national interest wherever it believes it to be threatened."

That was pretty plain talk—the unions could understand it even if the Chamber chose not to. What the Chamber wanted to hear Mr. Kennedy say was that he would crack heads among the union leaders, if he found it necessary. One small business-man from Idaho expressed it this way: "I feel that the President has been harder on industry than on labor in applying his standards. If he is going to prohibit increases in prices, then he must do something like that with wages."

Businessmen were ready, however, to accept assurances by President Johnson that he would be even-handed in dealing with business and labor. On April 27, 1964, Johnson got a rous-ing reception from the Chamber, which interrupted a rambling, friendly address scores of times with applause and laughter, even though he needled them with the observation: "All of you have a martyr complex, and all of you think you are mistreated." And when President Johnson bracketed warnings at a dinner for businessmen on the need to hold the price line with the assur-ance he would say the same thing about wages to labor leaders, the promise was taken at face value. "He is to be commended for this," Blough said. "And I think he is sincere."

But in April 1962 it was different; events had reawakened the whole complex of traditional complaints and resentments that had been subsurface for nearly a year: taxes were high, deficits too big, and the squeeze on profits continued. These complaints, indigenous to the business mind, came rushing forward again in the wake of the steel crisis. One of the top leaders of the Chamber gave me this private view of Kennedy: "I think the fundamental trouble is that the President just doesn't understand business too well. His experience is in politics, not business, and although he's glib and can talk the language, I don't think he has a full comprehension of what goes into making a business decision."

H. Ladd Plumley, who succeeded Wagner as Chamber president for 1962-63, pinpointed "uncertainty" as the element most bothersome to business. At a luncheon for Washington correspondents shortly after visiting Mr. Kennedy in July, Plumley said that businessmen must operate under conditions that are "predictable and plottable, so they can plan their own moves." Since Kennedy's rollback of steel prices, Plumley insisted, businessmen felt that Kennedy wanted to "steer" the economy— and where he would direct it next, they didn't know.[5]

Seemingly, there was a tensional release in wrapping up all frustrations about profit, taxes, sagging stock values—and depositing them on the White House doorstep. Even as sophisticated an economist as Gabriel Hauge, former Eisenhower aide and now president of the Manufacturers Hanover Trust Co. of New York, said during early May: "There is a good deal of concern in the business community over its relation to Government. . . . As business looks down the road, it wonders what all this portends for the area of private-decision making. . . . Does this mean that the Government is going to define the public interest and achieve it in supervising wage negotiations and in controlling prices?"[6]

Digs less subtle, but enjoyed even more, were the crude "jokes" growing up around the Kennedy-business relationship. In Wall Street, the most popular line was: "When Eisenhower had a heart attack, the market broke. But gosh, if Kennedy could have a heart attack—the market would go up!" During the Chamber meeting, a right-wing weekly newspaper, the *Washington World,* made a hit by gathering together the latest anti-Kennedy "humor." Most pertinent story: The President told the NAM that he would keep prices up and wages down, then went to the AFL-CIO, and said he would hold prices down, but let wages go up. Then, according to the story, he turned to Arthur Goldberg and said: "Take care of it, kid!"

President Kennedy was greatly disappointed in the results of his speech to the Chamber. He thought he had gone a long way toward giving business the kind of assurance it wanted—and had been rebuffed. A top-notch, veteran reporter considered that his reception was courteous, but not cordial.[7] I talked to a substantial number of the Chamber delegates myself who scoffed at the notion that Mr. Kennedy was anti-business, and to at least a few who thought he was "right" on steel. But Kennedy, with a politician's keen sensitivity to audience reaction, evaluated the reception by the Chamber as frosty—although it was not the kind of chill given him by the NAM in December, 1961. In the twenty-minute speech to the Chamber, there was applause only once—when he said that the Government has "a large stake in your profits." The President viewed it this way: a reasoned appeal for better understanding had failed in re-opening any significant channels of communication—at least to the Chamber of Commerce mentality. Afterwards, he invited Plumley in for talks a few times, but these didn't produce any changes in attitude. Kennedy sensed that there was a grudging acknowledgment by a few businessmen that he had been provoked by the steel companies, but this was based on a feeling that Roger Blough's tactics were poor, not that Big Steel had been on the wrong side of a basic issue.

What came through loud and clear to Kennedy was the "Let's have a real crackdown on labor" attitude. Here, we get close to the heart of the matter: for many businessmen, their gripe was not really that Kennedy was anti-business, but rather that he was *not* anti-labor. This was the real dimension of the problem —this was the crux of the debate.

At a press conference in the fall of 1962, Kennedy spoke forcefully in favor of the union shop. To some businessmen, this was an offense ranking with the crackdown on steel. An impartial board headed by mediator George Taylor, studying a dispute in the aircraft industry, had recommended a union shop provided two-thirds of the affected workers voted for it. Asked for his reaction, Kennedy said: "Well, in the first place, most major industrial companies or industries in the United States have accepted the union shop many years ago. . . . This [has] been acceptable for many years to many companies which are even larger than the ones involved. . . . I would hope the company would accept it [the Taylor recommendations] because if a strike comes . . . the responsibility would be very clear, I think, to the American people for the—for such an action."

Although some 75 percent of American union labor works under union shop contracts, many American businessmen were shocked that it received this specific Presidential blessing. To them, it was part of a total unpleasant picture of growing labor power, coupled with Administration demands for price restraints, but no wage freeze.

The Kennedy goal of a stable price level, as Gabriel Hauge must have known, contemplated neither a freeze of all prices nor a freeze of all wages. As Walter Heller observed, "over-all price stability does not . . . rule out individual price changes in a market economy. Some of these changes will be down, as witness electronics, electrical machinery, chemicals, paper, and aluminum in the past year. Some will go up, as have heavy machinery, farm machinery, and many services. The important thing is that price changes should be the result of competitive forces that guide our resources into their most productive uses." [8]

This was true of wages, as well: some wages might go up *more* than the increase in average productivity, and some *less*. The objective was to hold the *average* increase within the bounds of average productivity gain.[9] Some had interpreted the guidelines to mean that no wage increase should go beyond the *average* increase in productivity—and this was unrealistic. So was the thought of any absolute freeze on wages. As much as some businessmen may have yearned for this, it would have negated all tradition and sense. Instead of a continued expansion of the economy, with rising standards of living and broader consumer markets, a wage freeze would insure contraction and probably depression.

In the private councils of the White House, however, it was recognized after the Chamber speech that business had a fixed image of the Kennedy Administration. The business community insisted that *it* was in the doghouse—and that labor held the upper hand. Kennedy's problem was to try to deal with this appraisal of his Administration, whether it was right or wrong.

At the very same time, the labor movement was becoming increasingly concerned by pressures to hold wage gains within the scope of the Economic Council's wage-price guidelines. Walter Reuther, fiery leader of the United Automobile Workers of America (AFL-CIO), broke into print early in May, 1962, with a statement warning the Government not to apply the guidelines to forthcoming negotiations in the aircraft and missile industries (organized by the UAW). What Reuther perceived, correctly, was that the main thrust of the wage-price guidelines, as set out in the 1962 Economic Report, was directed to wages rather than prices. (Even in steel, the Kennedy case rested wholly on the precondition of a noninflationary wage increase.)

Kennedy's wage-price program, evolved in the Council of Economic Advisers and in the Labor Department, was designed to prevent prices from spiraling *by attacking wage inflation.* Or, to put it another way, Kennedy was trying to ground the wage-price spiral by making sure that wages, in the first place, didn't take off into the wild blue yonder.

This didn't mean, Kennedy's economists hastened to explain, that the Administration had lost interest in holding prices down —Roger Blough could testify on that score. Moreover, the ultimate aim was to achieve price stability. But inasmuch as there was no "demand-pull" inflation in 1962 (too many dollars chasing too few goods), the only real worry was "cost-push" inflation (where wages and prices chase each other up).

Business leaders found this hard to grasp, but labor understood it only too well: there were two key guidelines spelled out, one covering wages, the other, prices. For "noninflationary wage behavior," the guideline would allow a wage increase "equal to the trend rate of over-all productivity increase." [10] This was easy to determine in key industries by examining the collective bargaining proposals, and matching wage demands against productivity. (Even where there was disagreement on actual percentages, the basic trends could be determined easily.)

But the general guideline for noninflationary price behavior was a more complex concept. It called for price reductions when the industry's rate of productivity exceeds an over-all measure;

for an increase in prices when the opposite relationship pre
vails; and stable prices if the two rates of productivity are equal.
Since there are—literally—hundreds of thousands of items with
separate prices in the enormous U. S. economy, the Administration couldn't possible identify all of them, even if it wanted to.
Obviously, the Administration could be interested only in a few
big pace-setter industries like steel (and actually was hard
pressed to name another).

For all practical purposes, therefore, the Kennedy team believed it only logical to make its effort to handle cost-push inflation by concentrating efforts on the wage side. And that was
precisely what made Reuther and other labor leaders restive.
The President tried to ease some labor fears by assuring at one
press conference that the Administration was not going "from
city to city" to set labor rates. And Walter Heller persuaded
Reuther to soften his public challenge to the guidelines.

Then there was a chance for the President to come face to
face with Reuther at the UAW convention in Atlantic City on
May 8, and the business community eagerly awaited the confrontation. What sort of an exposition of Kennedy views would
be laid before a large labor audience? How would it dovetail
with his speech to the Chamber of Commerce?

When Mr. Kennedy walked into the Atlantic City convention
hall, packed with UAW delegates, he received an ovation. He
grinned and said: "Last week, after speaking to the Chamber of
Commerce and the presidents of the American Medical Association, I began to wonder how I got elected. And now I remember." [11] But Kennedy put the banter aside immediately.
After repeating, in almost the same words he used before the
Chamber, that "this Administration has not undertaken and
will not undertake to fix prices and wages in this country," the
President delivered this warning:

"The same responsibility for a noninflationary and peaceful
settlement applies both to you and to management in your
forthcoming negotiations in the aircraft and missile industries.
I am confident that you will meet that obligation, exercising
the restraint and responsibility which will, in the end, reward
you as it rewards the country."

And he went on, in a section which, it seems to me, is such a compound of the conservative wisdom that Gabriel Hauge might have written it:

> What good is it to get an increase in wages if it is taken away by an increase in prices?
>
> What counts is the real increase in wages, which comes from increased productivity and technology. And that, I am glad to see, has been recognized for many years by this union.
>
> We have two tasks in economic policy, to create demands so that we will have a market for all that we can produce, and to avoid inflation.
>
> To return to a policy of halting inflation by curbing demand, would be self-defeating; but to expand the forces of demand by feeding the fires of inflation, would be equally dangerous and delusive.
>
> While individual adjustments may have to be made to fit the previous patterns in individual industries, in general a wage policy which seeks its gains out of the fruits of technology instead of the pockets of the consumers, is the one basic approach that can help every segment of the economy.
>
> . . . It is a simple, inescapable, economic truth that increases in productivity—in output per man hour—they set the outer limits of our economic progress. . . . No financial sleight of hand can raise real wages and profits faster than productivity without defeating their own purpose through inflation.

Meanwhile, at the Homestead in Hot Springs, the Business Council was trying to enjoy its spring meeting, but had more than half an eye cocked toward the Dow-Jones ticker tape in the writing lounge. The stock market was still going through a serious shake-out, and many of the BC men with investment company connections were nervous—with good reason, as it turned out in a few days. News accounts of the President's speech to the UAW had been read with interest, but were considered to be of little significance. "We need deeds, not words," snapped a testy BC member.

Of all of the business leaders present, Blough, who had been Council chairman since Cordiner was dumped in 1961, was the most affable and relaxed, despite the relative freshness of his battle with Kennedy over steel prices. "There should not be any areas of misunderstanding between business and government," he confided. "I am hopeful that the climate will improve." Approvingly, he noted that the President had sent a dis-

tinguished group of government officials to the meeting, including Treasury Undersecretary Henry H. (Joe) Fowler; Walter
Heller; Undersecretary of State George Ball; Howard Petersen,
special assistant in charge of the trade program; and William C.
Foster, head of the Arms Control agency. Fowler, as a matter of
fact, brought a special peace offering: a detailed account of the
progress being made by the Treasury's staff on new tax-write-off
schedules, long demanded by the business community, but
never delivered by a Republican Administration. (As promised
by Fowler, the new write-off schedules, worth more than $1
billion a year in new depreciation allowances, were issued that
summer.)

Blough seemed willing to resume diplomatic relations with
the Administration, despite Kennedy's crackdown on U.S. Steel,
and Kennedy was grateful to Blough for this attitude. But conciliation wasn't the general mood of the Business Council. First,
there was a tendency, within the BC, to be critical of Blough's
poor judgment in precipitating the crisis. Then, the weakness
in the stock market was a pervasive concern, and most of the
business leaders found it perfectly easy to attribute this directly
to a "crisis of confidence" composed of general mistrust of
Kennedy, early signs of recession in the economy, and the Government's investigation of the securities markets.

Keith Funston, President of the New York Stock Exchange
and a Business Council member, said during the meeting:
"There is a serious question about a decline in investor confidence. There are other factors in the market, of course—the
high price-earnings ratio for some stocks, increasing yields in
savings banks and loan associations, the discrepancy between
stock and bond yields—but although you can't prove it, there
seems to be a diminishing of investor confidence."

You couldn't prove it then, as Funston said, and it never has
been proven. But it certainly has become part of the mythology
of the times that a hostile feeling between Kennedy and the
business community played a role in the May 28-31 break in the
market. (See Chapter VIII.) In a research report published in
March, 1963, the Stock Exchange attempted to give the "anti-
business" feeling an official place in history by listing among
explanations for the crash: "Uncertainty about the national
Government's attitudes toward the business community, height-

ened by the mid-April steel price controversy and the Securities
and Exchange Commission's investigation of the securities markets." [12]

In mid-May of 1962, the business community was jittery,
resentful, hostile, and worried about its relations with Mr. Kennedy. Some few thoughtful leaders were concerned that business would get itself frozen into an anti-Kennedy attitude, comparable to the hate-Roosevelt feeling that dominated business
thinking in New Deal days.

Marion B. Folsom of the Eastman Kodak Co., a Republican
who had served President Eisenhower as Secretary of Health,
Education, and Welfare, and also as Undersecretary of the
Treasury, was one who openly expressed this concern. Folsom, a
progressive businessman who directed postwar planning studies
for a special House committee from 1944 to 1946, was worried
by the mood he detected at the May Business Council meeting
and elsewhere. He felt that if suspicions between business and
Government hardened, there would be—eventually—no communication at all. Folsom contends that a Chief Executive of
the United States, Democrat or Republican, must be strong to
be effective. He must not, of course, be a dictator—but Folsom
feels, in contradistinction to the Chamber's Richard Wagner—
that the checks and balances in the U. S. system are adequate.

But not very many leaders of the U. S. business community
were ready to accept the Folsom view. Kennedy's approach to
peacemaking was foolishly being rejected by the business world.
Blough, for his part, was ready to give up the sniping, and to
accept at face value the President's assurances that he was interested in being neither "anti" nor "pro" business or labor.
Others were not, and among them was Henry Ford II, one of
the seven industry members of the President's Labor-Management Advisory Committee.

In the course of recommending changes in the Taft-Hartley
labor law, the 21-man advisory committee suddenly got itself
embroiled, after the steel crisis, in the question of monopoly
power. Ford, who refused to go along with other members of
the committee in recommending broader power for the President to settle key strikes, wrote this separate opinion: "The increasing tendency of Government to involve itself in collective

bargaining situations, demonstrates, I am convinced, that present policy toward collective bargaining grants excessive power to labor unions." Joseph L. Block, Inland Steel chairman, hero of the steel crisis a few weeks before, joined in with a denunciation of the "monopoly power which enables a single union (or combination of unions) to call a strike that brings to a halt all, or the preponderance of the production in a vital industry." [13]

Labor members of the committee were of course incensed, and responded in kind. But what worried Kennedy and Labor Secretary Arthur Goldberg most was that the argument over monopoly power would erupt anew at a National White House Conference on Economic Issues, which 225 prominent business, labor, and academic leaders would attend during the week of May 21. Originally, the White House conference was designed by Goldberg as the capstone to a year's work with the labor-management committee, a goodwill meeting that would seal the bonds of harmony carefully nurtured through the previous 15 months. But in the aftermath of the steel crisis, the pending White House conference took on a new significance: it would be the first opportunity for the President to address as one audience a substantial cross section of the real leadership of the business and financial community—not the Babbittish Chamber of Commerce, nor the exclusive blue bloods of the Business Council, although some of each would be present—together with top labor leaders.

Opening the Economic Issues Conference, the President talked extemporaneously—quietly and feelingly—about the need to put aside slogans and clichés, to distinguish between myth and reality:

> I would like . . . to say a word about the difference between myth and reality. Most of us are conditioned for many years to have a political viewpoint, Republican or Democratic—liberal, conservative, moderate. The fact of the matter is that most of the problems, or at least many of them that we now face, are technical problems. . . . They are very sophisticated judgments which do not lend themselves to the great sort of "passionate movements" which have stirred this country so often in the past. Now they deal with questions which are beyond the comprehension of most men, most government administrators, over which experts may differ, and yet we operate through our traditional political systems. . . .

So how can we look at things as they are, not through party labels, or position labels, but as they are and figure out how we can maintain this economy so that it moves ahead?

. . . What we want to have is confidence that we will be able to invest and produce and consume, which is what . . . [the] successful countries of Europe have had. . . .

The point I am making, is the problems are all extremely difficult, they require the most sophisticated solution . . . and we ought to work [on them] in the closest concert. . . . We cannot solve any of our problems without the wholehearted co-operation of all groups. . . . These are not issues, there is no Presidential election until 1964. These are problems that are going to face each and every one of you, and unless we can work them out together, all of us are going to suffer.

It was one of Kennedy's most successful performances. His characterization of such problems as solving the balance of payments deficit as "sophisticated and technical" was entirely correct. It had as much point, if not more, for labor than business, and Kennedy himself brought out that his single-mindedness about bringing the deficit under control had resulted in criticism from the labor side. "I know," he told the conference, "that the AFL-CIO feel that perhaps I overemphasize [it]."

Thomas J. Watson, Jr., president of the giant International Business Machines Corp., put it this way after Kennedy's address: "He has pointed out that issues facing the United States are really bigger than any of us, whether we be businessmen or members of the public, or members of labor. . . . When the chips are down, we have always been able to put our narrow business and parochial interests in their proper place. But in previous times of national crisis, the crisis has been a little more obvious, because people have been shooting at us. . . . If we go home with a better mutual understanding of what the important national economic issues of the country really are, the conference will have served its goal." [14]

The conference was a significant plus for the Administration. It did not evolve any new startling concepts, nor did it do much to distinguish, as Kennedy had urged, between economic myth and reality. On the other hand, no new fights broke out over the union monopoly question, and the conference did seem to mark a transition in which the sharp edges of the Kennedy-business conflict were blunted. Within a few days, the Committee for Economic Development took on, at the President's request, a special study of European economic planning and high growth rates. The Business Council and the Chamber of Commerce were asked to study the balance of payments problem, and to bring in substitute ideas for the elimination of tax havens abroad, one of the tax reforms contested by certain business interests.

For the first time, many business leaders at the conference understood, as Heller explained Kennedy's growth and wage-price policies, that the Administration was taking a middle, rather than an extreme position. When Leon Keyserling publicly charged that the Administration was more concerned "with fighting inflation . . . than reactivating the economy," Heller responded that "over the long haul, wage increases that exceed the productivity increase in the economy . . . are going to be self-defeating. That is, we have to look at wages not only as purchasing power, which indeed they are, but as costs. And unless there is a social consensus to shift in our distribution of income from profits to wages, this standard implies not only a noninflationary standard, but really the only non-self-defeating standard for real improvement in our standard of living." [15]

This demonstration of the essentially conservative foundation of the Administration posture was an eye-opener to some business participants. Some conceded that they in fact believed Kennedy wanted to share the fruits of productivity among business and the consuming public, as well as labor. Until the conference, many businessmen had interpreted the guideline theory as allocating all of the gains made by greater productivity to labor. And above all, Heller's answer to Keyserling implying that the Kennedy Administration had no radical ideas about increasing labor's share of the national income at the expense of profits was revealing—about himself and the Administration.

At long last, the Administration felt that it had found a transmission belt for the exchange of ideas with private policymakers. As May drew to a close, the channels of communication that Marion Folsom had feared might be frozen were still open. Businessmen were lionized by the White House, filtering in and out for lunch, for cocktails, and a chosen few were invited to receptions and state dinners. Administration officials belted out speech after speech assuring business that top priority items on the White House schedule included more liberal trade opportunities for American exporters, tax credits, inflation control, fiscal integrity, and maybe even a tax cut.

All in all, great strides had been made since mid-April. Not all vexations had been assuaged. Indeed, businessmen and bankers were still hitting hard at the Treasury proposals for a withholding tax on dividends and interest, the stock market was in a terrible slump, and Kennedy himself was still not at ease in dealing with businessmen.

But the President had arrived at some rationalizations. First of all, he began to concede that an uneasy peace, rather than a warm bond, was all that he should expect in his relationships with the business community. Early in the game, President Kennedy thought that logic would win businessmen to the Administration's way of thinking. Seymour Harris had tried to tell him that a Democratic President who followed a liberal tradition would not be accepted without suspicion by the Republican business community. Averell Harriman's astute, private observation is that businessmen have never forgiven Franklin Roosevelt for moving the seat of power from Wall Street to Washington. Governor Harriman believes that no matter how high their own profits, businessmen will always have that result of the Roosevelt Revolution in the back of their minds, and can be expected to transfer their hostility to almost any Democrat who arrives at the White House. Secondly, President Kennedy expected kudos from the business community for favors— such as the investment credit—that he did for them. It just doesn't work that way, he found out.

The President's approach matured later on. In September, 1962, at a conference of business editors and publishers, a questioner tauntingly asked if he considered himself "unduly" sensitive to the "alleged hostility of the business world."

Kennedy, with a laugh, noted the editorial cast to the words "unduly" and "alleged," but went on to offer this summary:

> I recognize that there is a political difference between this Administration and most businessmen. I am not really concerned about that political difference, because it is traditional. . . . What I am concerned about, is, however . . . that we have as close an understanding as is possible. A good many of the

proposals we may make to improve the state of the American economy require Congressional action. We want to try to make sure to the extent that it is possible that we secure the support . . . of the business community.

In my judgment, we had a good deal of misunderstanding with the business community which did not serve our public interest this year on the tax bill. We really did not get the kind of support that the investment credit, in my opinion, would warrant as a stimulus to the economy. The whole fight against the withholding . . . [created] the impression . . . that this was a new tax rather than a method of collecting a tax which had been in effect for many years. . . .

I would like to describe the relation between business and government as one of co-operation . . . that disregards the alternate Novembers . . . and instead work on this common task of moving ahead.

VIII | *Black Monday on Wall Street— The "Kennedy" Market?*

ON MONDAY, May 28, 1962, the stock market in New York was weak at the opening, and within 30 minutes the ticker tape which records all transactions began to run late. Since December, stock prices had been skidding, and in the previous week there had been a sharp sell-off. As measured by the Dow-Jones industrial stock index, stock prices were off 38.83 points, one of the widest weekly declines in market history. Now, a new selling wave was gaining force: in the first hour of trading Monday on the New York Stock Exchange, 1,090,000 shares had changed hands.[1]

By 10:20 A.M., "flash prices"—the latest prices of 30 key stocks, superimposed on the regular sequence of the tape—were the best rough guide to actual market conditions of the moment. But it was not until noon, when the Dow-Jones industrial index was down 10.98 points, that it became clear that something extraordinary was in the making. The nation's press, radio, and television networks began to spread the word that an historic stock market crash was taking place.

The full extent of it couldn't be measured because of the flood of orders to sell, and the delay in the tape. For example, prices appearing on the ticker at 3:30 P.M., which was supposed to be the close of the market, actually represented sales slips which had arrived by pneumatic tube from the floor of the Exchange at 2:21 P.M. The next day, Tuesday, the jam-up was even worse: prices printed on the tape at 3:30 that day reflected sales going back to 1:07 P.M., a lag of 2 hours and 23 minutes.

On a normal stock market day, the tape usually records the last sale within 5 or 10 minutes of the close. But on Monday, May 28, 1962, the last sale didn't appear on the tape until 5:58 P.M., winding up a day in which the Dow-Jones index plummeted 34.95 points, a 5.7 percent decline. The volume was 9,350,000 shares, fifth largest in the history of the Stock Exchange to that date. In terms of points, it was the second largest collapse, topped only by the Great Crash of October 28, 1929, when the Dow-Jones index fell 38 points; it even surpassed the second-day toll of the October 1929 period, when the index was off 30 points.

The percentage decline, however, had been exceeded on 23 other days in market history, including a 6.5 percent drop following President Eisenhower's heart attack in 1955. And, of course, the October 1929 crash was a much deeper one in terms of percentage, the 38-point and 30-point slides representing 12.7 percent and 11.7 percent of the total index at that time.

The collapse in stock prices continued through midday on Tuesday, under the pressure of heavy waves of selling. At 1 P.M. on Tuesday, the Dow-Jones industrial index was reported to be off 13.61 points from the opening, although, as later reconstructed from actual transactions occurring at the time, a turnaround had begun, and the average at 1 P.M. was actually *up* 7.72 points from the opening. Throughout Tuesday, the late tape clouded the rise in prices.

At the end of Tuesday, the Dow-Jones index was up 27.03 points to 603.96 points, a percentage gain of 4.7. The crash, at its widest—from the close of the previous Friday to noon on Tuesday—had topped 48.54 points off the Dow-Jones index. Tuesday volume was 14,750,000 shares, second only to the 16,000,000 shares traded October 29, 1929.

On Thursday, with buy orders accumulated over the Memorial Day holiday, the market closed with a net gain of 9.40 points, or 1.6 percent. At the end of the wild three-day period, 35,000,000 shares—the greatest volume in a generation—had changed hands, and the Dow-Jones index had swung from 611.78 at the Friday close, to a low of 563.24 at midday Tuesday and back to 613.36 at the final bell on Thursday.

This, then, is the bare outline of the three-day market "break" of 1962. The frantic, panicky gyrations of the market, illogical on their face, resulted in big losses for some, big gains for others—and prompted a fear that the very instability of stocks was the signal for a worldwide collapse. The tumult in New York sent a chill around the world, touching off selling waves in the London, Paris, Amsterdam, and other markets. Europeans, even more than Americans, saw ominous harbingers of a deep depression. All too clearly, 1929 came into view again, for despite the Tuesday and Thursday recovery from "Black Monday," the market then drifted steadily lower for the next several weeks. On June 25, the Dow-Jones industrial average sagged to 524.55, the low mark of the year. The next day, the market closed at 535.76, the lowest closing for the year, off 27 percent from December, 1961.

This was the largest decline of any bear market since the end of World War II—and in all cases except one (1946) these traumatic collapses had been the forerunner of recession. But business continued a steady, if unspectacular advance throughout 1962, and the only sector of the economy that was seriously affected was Wall Street itself; public disenchantment with stocks put a pinch on brokerage house profits, and a few over-the-counter houses even went into bankruptcy.[2]

Confidence in Wall Street may have been shaken, but not confidence in the economy—a remarkable thing in light of the tremendous jolt to the market. No one knows what the "paper" loss in over-all values was at the bottom of the cycle, but government data show that at the end of 1962, by which time there had been some recovery, the estimated total value of common and preferred stock had dropped $55 billion from the end of 1961 to a total of $380 billion. Individual savings rose to a record $20 billion, of which an astonishing $15.1 billion—double 1961—was stashed away in regular savings bank accounts, clearly reflecting money moving out of stocks to a safer place.[3]

What caused the stock market crack-up in 1962? The answer, basically, is that prices were too high.

But to those looking for a scapegoat, the Kennedy Administration was a ready-made target, and it didn't take long for another emotional binge, centered on the "anti-business" theme, to get rolling. The rollback of steel prices was assigned, of course, as the major factor for the collapse of businessmen's confidence in Kennedy. But an important additional reason, according to Wall Street, was that the public's faith in the securities business had been shaken with the start of a new investigation of the markets by a special Securities and Exchange Commission Study Group. This was designed to be the most elaborate and thoroughgoing probe since Judge Pecora's in the 1930's, the one that led to the establishment of the SEC itself.

Coming so soon after the steel price rollback, it was natural that the May collapse in the stock market would be linked to it. Edward C. Gudeman, then Undersecretary of Commerce, visited his hometown of Chicago in the week before Black Monday, and found that his old business friends had long since blamed the market slide on Kennedy. "You son of a bitch," he reports one former associate said to him, "you guys down there are to blame for the market collapse." Gudeman said that his "old friends turned on me as if I personally had cost them money. I can imagine what they were saying after Black Monday this week." [5]

Just ten weeks before his death, on September 13, 1963, after the market swept itself back to new highs, President Kennedy observed wryly at a press conference:

"I got . . . I suppose several thousands of letters when the stock market went way down in May and June of 1962 blaming me and talking about the Kennedy market, and I haven't gotten a single letter in the last few days about the Kennedy market now that it has broken through the Dow-Jones [previous high] average."

What businessmen were thinking in the summer of 1962 was painfully clear. In a special report called "The Stock Market Under Stress," the New York Stock Exchange shied away from blaming Kennedy directly, but listed among reasons "which have received widespread" publication and discussion "uncertainty about the national Government's attitudes toward the business community, heightened by the mid-April steel controversy and the Securities and Exchange Commission's investigation of the securities markets." [6]

The other explanations the Exchange report enumerated were diminishing concern over inflation; growing uneasiness over high price-earnings ratios; the squeeze on corporate profits; increased competition from savings banks; the increasing threat of foreign competition; and concern over the balance of payments. Its chronology of events even indulged in the thought that "the degree of attention devoted to the stock market in these [radio and TV] broadcasts may have contributed to the uneasiness among some investors." [7] It's a familiar theme: Don't mention trouble, and it will go away.

One can understand, perhaps, Wall Street's worries about the scheduled SEC investigation. Any salesman is sensitive when someone begins to check the authenticity of his products and the soundness of his sales pitch. But those in the "Street" whose records were clear should have welcomed the sweep of the broom—in their own self-interest.

More than a year later, the SEC study group under lawyer Milton H. Cohen, in one of the windup chapters of its monumental analysis of the securities markets, found no evidence to support the belief that the steel price controversy had touched off the market break. Instead, the Cohen group's conclusions supported the view stated at the time by Treasury Secretary Douglas Dillon and William McChesney Martin, Chairman of the Federal Reserve System—that the market had gotten too high. The big break, Dillon observed, represented "a weakening of confidence [by the public] in the market," rather than a loss of confidence in the Administration. "The stock market always needs an excuse for a big move," Martin told me, "and this time, it latched onto the President's argument with steel."

Martin, of course, is right. Students of stock market swings know that Wall Street generally doesn't react suddenly to a long-developing economic situation; it anticipates the trend. And when the unexpected happens, the market reacts immediately, not weeks after an event. Nevertheless, many businessmen will continue to see a steel-forged link between Kennedy and the May market break. The diagnosis has all of the appeal—and the weakness—of a simple catechism: Who cracked down on Roger Blough? Who forced a rollback in steel prices? Who ordered a probe of the stock markets? Who was anti-business? A year after the market hit bottom and started up again, the president of one of the biggest banks in the nation remarked to me privately: "Last year, Kennedy did everything wrong, and as a result, business was terrible—just terrible. But this year, he's doing everything right, and business is a lot better." My tongue-in-cheek response that Kennedy had apparently found the long-sought-for magic to control the business cycle wasn't considered amusing.

The 1962 "Kennedy market" is on its way to being encrusted as one of the standard legends about the economy, much like other myths that Kennedy attempted to challenge in mid-June, 1962, at Yale University. As he himself told a White House meeting just a few days before Black Monday: "I read that the problem really is that business confidence may be shaken by actions of certain public figures. Now, business had high confidence in the previous administration, yet there was a recession in 1958 and a recession in 1960. And in 1956, there was a very sharp drop in the stock market before a very good year in 1957. So that doesn't give us the answer to the problem at all." [8]

One of the "black marks" the business world scores against Kennedy is that very speech at Yale, although that remarkable effort, in which the President called for an intelligent and unemotional dialogue about the economy, was one of his best—a literate and sophisticated appraisal of the economic problems of the United States in the troubled world of the 1960's.[9]

Many trained hands were involved in the Yale speech: McGeorge Bundy, Arthur Schlesinger, Jr., Walter Heller, and Ambassador to India John Kenneth Galbraith. The final document was a blend of Sorensen's polishing and Kennedy's own penciling aboard the plane to New Haven. The unhappy thing to record is that for all of the brainwork that went into the Yale speech on economic myths, the President did not return to its basic theme until a few days before his death. (See Chapter XIV.) It is sad to record that in his all-out search for a tax cut, and in defense against those who snapped at him for heavy federal spending, he later relied himself on some of the very myths he exposed that June afternoon on the Old Campus.

His main theme that day was that the time had arrived to halt the "current trend toward meeting current problems with old clichés." If we were to look toward the future, Kennedy felt, we had better not rely on the myths of the past. He spelled out three major myths—where "illusion may prevent effective action"—this way:

> *Let us take first the question of the size and shape of Government.* The myth here is that Government is big, and bad—and steadily getting bigger and worse. Obviously, this myth has

some excuse for existence. It is true that in recent history, each new Administration has spent more money than its predecessor. . . . It is even possible something of this trend may continue. But does it follow that big government is growing relatively bigger? It does not—for the fact is that for the last 15 years, the Federal Government—and also the Federal debt—and also the Federal bureaucracy—have grown less rapidly than the economy as a whole. If we leave defense and space expenditures aside, the Federal Government since the Second World War has expanded less than any other sector of our national life—less than industry, less than commerce . . . and very much less than the noise about big government. The truth about big government is the truth about any other great activity—it is complex. . . . Generalities in regard to federal expenditures, therefore, can be misleading—each case . . . must be determined on its merits if we are to profit from our unrivaled ability to combine the strength of public and private purpose.

·　　·　　·

Next, let us turn to the problem of our fiscal policy. Here, the myths are legion and the truth hard to find. But let me take as a prime example the problem of the federal budget. We persist in measuring our federal fiscal integrity today by the conventional or administrative budget—with results which would be considered absurd in any business firm—in any country of Europe—or in any careful assessment of the reality of our national finances. The administrative budget has sound administrative uses. But for wider purposes, it is less helpful. It omits our special trust funds; it neglects changes in assets or inventories. It cannot tell a loan from a straight expenditure—and worst of all, it cannot distinguish between operating expenditures and long-term investments. This budget, in relation to the great problems of federal fiscal policy, is simply not relevant; it can be actively misleading. And yet, there is a mythology that measures all of our national soundness or unsoundness on the single simple basis of this same annual administrative budget. . . . Let me say a word about deficits. The myth persists that federal deficits create inflation and budget surpluses prevent it. Yet, sizable budget surpluses after the war did not prevent inflation, and persistent deficits for the past several years have not upset our basic price stability. Obviously, deficits are sometimes dangerous—and so are surpluses. But honest assessment plainly requires a more sophisticated view than the old and automatic cliché that deficits automatically bring inflation. There are myths also about our public debt. . . . In fact, both the debt per person and the debt as a proportion of our gross national product have declined sharply since the Second World War. . . . Debts, public and private, are neither good nor bad, in and of themselves. Borrowing can lead to over-extension and collapse—but it can also lead to expansion and strength. There is no single, simple slogan in this field we can trust.

.   .   .

Finally, I come to the matter of confidence. Confidence is a matter of myth and also a matter of truth. . . . Let me take the truth of the matter first. It is true—and of high importance —that the prosperity of this country depends on assurance that all major elements in it will live up to their responsibilities. . . . This is the true issue of confidence. But there is also the false issue—and its simplest form is the assertion that any and all unfavorable turns of the speculative wheel—however temporary and however plainly speculative in character—are the result of, and I quote, "lack of confidence in the national ad-ministration." This, I must tell you, while comforting, is not wholly true. Worse, it obscures the reality—which is also sim-ple. The solid ground of mutual confidence is the necessary partnership of Government with all of the sectors of our society in the steady quest for economic progress. Corporate plans are not based on a political confidence in party leaders, but on an economic confidence in the nation's ability to invest and pro-duce and consume.

It was a good, honest, plain-speaking rundown of some of the notable economic fables. But the President's lesson in myth-ology was lost on his Wall Street students. In brokerage offices, it was taken as a sign that Kennedy had returned to his bellig-erent mood of the steel crisis. Indeed, in his prepared text, the President had lashed back at those in the business world "who ignore the realities of our economic life in a neurotic search for unending reassurance." [10] The fact that he inadvertently omitted the line in reading the speech only served to call atten-tion to this expression of his cumulated annoyance with the business community. Even FRB Chairman Martin's character-izing as "childish" those who explained the stock market panic in terms of worries about Kennedy had no impact. The key fact of the day—the only one that businessmen were paying attention to—was that stock prices were still going down, and that tempers on both sides were edgy. Inland Steel's Block said after the Yale speech: "I'm afraid a lot of people will take it as a combative speech. And I think it *was* a little combative when he said these things were 'myths.' When you say, 'Let's re-examine,' that's right. But he's gone beyond that." [11]

The White House noted well the response to the Yale speech on myths. That excellent speech material was put in mothballs.

The coldly factual study made by the Milton Cohen group running the SEC's special study of the securities markets and related institutions showed that for the economy as a whole, the year and a half preceding the market break was a period of hesitation. The pace of recovery from the cyclical low of February, 1961, was disappointing to many economists, and the basic trend of economic growth, while still upward, lagged behind expectations. The stock market itself had hit a peak at the end of 1961, and then began its long slide down.[12]

The professionals evidenced their disenchantment with the market well ahead of the April steel fight and the May market break. Mutual funds began to unload early in the year—a sign of concern that prices were getting out of line with earnings. And the price of a seat on the New York Stock Exchange—always a good, earthy appraisal of the future—having touched a $225,000 peak on August 8, 1961, thereafter dropped sharply to $200,000 on January 17, 1962; to $175,000 on March 27; to $160,000 on April 18, and to $150,000 on May 16. Moreover, since August of 1961, the ratio of daily stock price advances to daily declines was steadily diminishing.

All of these sober portents were there to ponder at the time. Some of the more respectable market letters—and even some cautious financial page stories—laid the prospects before the public. But the economic background of the market slide is conveniently forgotten by those who want to blame the break on Kennedy or, at least, link the break with the Kennedy-business disputes. Long after Cohen's persuasive analysis of the 1962 market break was available, for example, one usually keen commentator on economic affairs wrote: "Business activity . . . has climbed in fits and starts, with a prolonged interval of marking time after the President's dispute with the steel industry and the stock market break that followed." [13]

One factor that had a clear bearing on the turndown in stocks was the new attractiveness in other investments. Beginning in 1962, a sharp rise in savings deposits was stimulated when the Federal Reserve Board authorized commercial banks to pay up to 4 percent interest on savings accounts. This put them about on a par with savings and loan associations, and attracted a steady inflow of funds from the stock market into the banks. A 4 percent interest rate looked mighty good to prudent investors who were earning that or less on highly priced speculative stocks. The floodtide of deposits gave banks a bulge in liquid reserves, and they, in turn, looked increasingly to corporate and municipal bonds, infusing new strength in these markets.

Toward the end of April, Wall Street analysts noted that stocks had plunged a full 10 percent since December. But this was just an average; many of the best-known names on the Big Board were down even more. IBM, for example, was down 22 percent, and someone noted that the 94 points it had lost since the beginning of the year were the equivalent of 31 years of dividends at $3 a year. National Cash Register was down 26 percent; Bell and Howell, 38 percent; and Transitron, 45 percent.[14]

Thus, those acting on professional advice had begun to put a new valuation on stock prospects, well ahead of the steel controversy. The overriding economic fact was that the long period of continuous inflation was at an end, even as the late Per Jacobsson had predicted months before. Americans had for so long been used to inflation, or the threat of it, that it took a while to get accommodated to the idea that it might disappear. But the absence of inflation was increasingly hard to ignore. As a matter of fact, Kennedy's ability to force a rollback was symptomatic of the weakness in steel prices. It might fairly be said that Blough's capitulation to Kennedy on April 12 was a decisive recognition that the inflationary joyride was over for the moment. It is perfectly plain, in retrospect, that as 1962 began, the stock market, luxuriating overlong in the hyperactive inflationary boom of 1961, soon had to come back to reality.

There had been an ugly stampede, in the late fifties, to get rich quick, and some of the so-called "glamour" stocks rose to unconscionable levels. Just a scientific-sounding name was all that was necessary to feed a wild, illiterate stampede to buy.[15] It happened in better-known stocks, too. Polaroid, with a magical print-making device built into its camera, rose from an average of $4 a share in 1953 to $238 a share in 1961, after having touched an all-time high of $261 the year before. The Cohen report notes that Polaroid's earnings were in a declining trend from 1959 through 1961—but the price an anxious public bid it up to was 100 times earnings in that year.

Exactly one week after Black Monday, Dillon told a dinner of the Financial Writers Association in New York that all vestiges of reason had been cast aside by buyers and sellers of securities. The 1961 bull market, he said, was built on expectation of an inflation that was never realized. For three years, he insisted, stock prices were ballooned higher than justified by earnings—and principally on the conviction that a round of unbalanced Kennedy budgets would produce inflation. Businessmen, Dillon was saying somewhat indelicately, had been trapped by a devotion to their own clichés; they howled about the dangers of inflation, but in reality were dismayed by its absence.[16]

George Mitchell, a member of the Federal Reserve Board, also tagged "the high multiples of earnings" as the root cause of the stock debacle. He pointed out that the market had soared while the economy itself was sluggish and lumbering along well under its potential. "It could be," he said, "that the structure of costs and prices which has developed is incompatible with full resource utilization, or that the distribution of income is not conducive to sustained high-level consumption."

Long before the May break, it had become clear that the $570 billion gross national product forecast for calendar 1962 by the Economic Council had been much too optimistic. Corporate profits apparently had hit a peak either in the fourth quarter of 1961 or the first quarter of 1962—and would head down from there, or at best stabilize. Unemployment was high, much plant capacity idle, and the private capital boom that Walter Heller had confidently predicted was not materializing. In the Economic Report for 1963, the Council admitted that business investment had fallen $8 billion short of the level expected for

1962.[17] Thus, the private economy was demonstrating an inability to move ahead, which was enough excuse for the market fallout without searching out artificial reasons relating to Kennedy vs. the business world.

Dillon was widely criticized for pointing the finger to overpriced stocks. At the time of the May break, stocks were selling, on the average, at about 24 times annual earnings. A 24-1 price-earnings ratio means that stocks were earning only about 4 percent on investment. With little or no risk, money could be placed in savings and loan associations, or in banks, and earn that much—and the records suggest that many people made that calculation for themselves. And when it became apparent that no inflationary thrust was likely to carry stock prices any higher, a break was almost foreordained. Most Washington officials worry when the price-earnings ratio of the market gets higher than 19-1 or 20-1. The most conservative stock brokerage houses try to recommend stocks to their customers that are priced no higher than 16 times earnings. "When I consider the elements of risk and all the other factors involved," a prominent Washington broker says, "I prefer to earn about 6 percent [16-1 price-earnings] on my investments."

In retrospect, the most amazing thing about the 1962 market break is that it did not lead the nation into a depression or even recession. At worst, the economy hesitated a bit, a remarkable performance in face of a paper loss measured in billions, which always has a residual effect on spending decisions by individuals as well as business. That new car or trip to Europe comes a cropper in the wake of declining stock values. Heller worried about a recession, and tried to convince the President that a temporary tax cut was in order (see Chapter IX). But Kennedy and the nation rode out the storm without a tax cut. The market stabilized, recovering about half of its losses by the end of 1962, and the gross national product crept up—not enough to bite into unemployment, but at least up, instead of down. The entire experience, however, helped to convince Kennedy and a unique cross section of business and labor that some basic new stimulus was needed for the economy. "We'll rue the day that we didn't get a tax cut in 1962," a Kennedy Administration official said reflectively later. "But even the businessman who accepts the old myth about the virtues of a balanced budget will be ready to take a tax cut now, after the market crash. The basic cause of the crash, remember, was a sudden realization in Wall Street that the economy would not climb forever without something pushing it. So business will be for a tax cut, eventually, deficit or no." It was one of the best "economic" predictions of the year.

It is not, of course, surprising, when one considers the magnitude of the 1962 stock market swings, that many investors and speculators—professional as well as amateurs—were hurt. This is borne out, first, by direct observations by brokers of the impact among their own customers; second, by the more scientific observations of the Cohen study group; and third, by the evidence during the course of the recovery of the market late in 1962 and 1963 that a disenchanted public was staying, mostly, on the sidelines. Many of those who bought high and sold low didn't recoup while the market did. As onlookers, they nursed their wounds, and hesitated to take a new plunge into the market. The public, as another generation before it did in 1929, learned that what goes up in the stock market can also go down —the game is played for keeps.

This is not to say that there was any conspiracy or manipulation in the 1962 market, as some hinted darkly at the time. The Cohen study group gave Wall Street a clean bill of health on that score, although, according to the NYSE study, the public sold heavily on Monday and Tuesday while prices were going down, and professional traders, on a net basis, were buyers.[18] This is almost normal in a deluge; a market break doesn't have to be deliberately precipitated for the lambs to be shorn.

The Cohen study group *did* criticize some of the stock exchange specialists—those who are supposed to maintain orderly markets by stabilizing prices—because they "were passive or actually net sellers at critical junctures." [19] Mutual funds and other institutions also were persistent sellers of certain stocks in the public eye, such as U. S. Steel and General Motors, and the Cohen report suggested that the continued, heavy pressure on such "leaders" may have had a significant over-all influence on the market.

The public got a certain clear message from the 1962 market. According to the University of Michigan's highly respected survey center, only 11 percent of families in fairly low income brackets considered the stock market the "wisest place to invest money," after Black Monday in 1962. Back in November, 1961 —around the peak of the boom—almost twice as many such families couldn't think of a better place for their cash. (Some people have never heard of banks.) Similarly, only 16 percent of high-income families, compared to 26 percent in the pre-crash period, thought stocks were the safest investment.[20]

Unhappily, there is little evidence, if any, to suggest that the public has paid adequate heed to the results of the Milton Cohen investigation, unquestionably the most important development in the securities business since the Great Crash of 1929, and the basic regulatory act which followed. When Kennedy came into office, the Securities and Exchange Commission got a new lease on life. A reinvigorated SEC, headed by William L. Cary, quickly sensed that a major overhaul was necessary, because the markets and their networks of brokers and associations—allowed, for the most part, to police themselves—had gotten dangerously lax.

There had been, first of all, a tremendous expansion of the stock and bond business since the SEC came into being in 1933 —some 17,000,000 Americans are reported to own securities. Many are low- or middle-income families who own only a few shares of stock. In recent years, a great number of speculative issues had sprouted, many of them floated by unseasoned companies and touted by salesmen who knew little or nothing (except how to make a commission) about the securities business. More and more of the public, as per capita incomes rose, began to be enticed by the lure of fortune just round the corner. This combination of pressures clearly called for greater guidance to and protection of the public, and what began to dawn on the SEC—perhaps too slowly—was that the existing "self-regulatory" agencies were not providing such guidance or protection.

A big "sell" was on in the markets, especially of the "hot" issues, featuring high-pressure huckstering more commonly associated with door-to-door vacuum cleaner promotions. "There was unusually high activity in new issues accompanied by an atmosphere of feverish speculation during the early months of 1961," the Milton Cohen report said in its Chapter XIII. "The new 1961 offerings represented in many instances, young, untried, small businesses frequently with scientific sounding names ending in *-namics, -onics,* or *-mation.* Among these were Digitronics, Hedtronics, Pacotronics, Microsonics, Nuceleonics, Techmation, Pneuomodynamics. There is little doubt that some of the many first-time investors who eagerly bid for shares in these companies had little understanding of what these companies manufactured."

Most of the troubles that the SEC staff had uncovered came from new and unscrupulous firms out to make a fast buck at the expense of an unsuspecting public. But the real shock came, SEC Commissioner Manuel F. Cohen revealed, when the Commission learned "that in instances too numerous to ignore, customers of large and respected firms have found themselves the victims of flamboyant and high-pressure sales campaigns." He added: "The persistence of boiler-room operation despite vigorous enforcement efforts, the lack of effective controls over the hot-issue phenomena, and the failure of self-regulation on the American Stock Exchange served to heighten our concern and increase our frustrations." [21]

It is to Kennedy's great credit that he gave his blessing to a full-scale probe into the markets in the face of certain knowledge it would harden the attitude of those who wanted to consider him anti-business. And compliments should also be extended to the Congressional committees that pushed through the enabling legislation—wisely setting up a study group independent of the SEC—in the teeth of bitter opposition from Wall Street, especially from the New York Stock Exchange. In June, 1961, testifying before the House Interstate and Foreign Commerce Subcommittee headed by Representative Peter F. Mack, Jr. (D. Ill.), NYSE President Keith Funston said there was no need to include *his* exchange in any investigation. But Congress nevertheless authorized a full investigation into the securities markets on September 5, 1961, appropriating $750,-000 for the study, and Chicago lawyer Milton H. Cohen was named head of a special team of investigators to carry it out.

It was, of course, a cumulative deterioration in standards that gave the investigation its impetus. But the specific trigger was a scandal involving a father-son operation on the American Stock Exchange (New York), a firm of specialists called Re & Re. Their activities had aroused the suspicion of the SEC as early as 1957. An initial inquiry resulted in suspension of the Res in 1960, their expulsion from the exchange in 1961, and a 6-month jail sentence in September, 1963. Meanwhile, for his involvement in various phases of activity relating to the Res, and for questionable management of the exchange, Edward T. McCormick, then president, resigned and a thoroughgoing reorganization of the exchange was undertaken.[22]

What the investigators found out in the Re & Re case brought into question the whole concept of self-regulation. For six years, Re & Re, specialists on the exchange, had rigged and manipulated markets in at least 20 stocks, bilking the public for their own private profit—right under the eyes of exchange officers. Over this period, the Res peddled $10,000,000 worth of questionable stocks, and pocketed profits of more than $1,000,000. Frank Cormier, able reporter for the Associated Press, says in his *Wall Street's Shady Side:* "Prior to the Re case and its two follow-up investigations, a great many Americans assumed that flagrant criminality was virtually impossible in the major stock exchanges. . . . If there were a few bad apples, they were in no position to contaminate the barrel; such was the belief, at least, until the Res were found at the center of the barrel. For the SEC, this discovery climaxed a decade of growing disillusionment with the moral standards of certain segments of the stock market." [23]

After 20 tireless months, the Cohen study group produced during 1963 a 5,400-page report, with more than 100 specific recommendations to correct unbelievably bad conditions in the markets, and a lassitude in the Commission itself. The picture Cohen drew was not one of "pervasive and fraudulent activity," thanks to the existence of the Securities and Exchange Act. But there were "grave abuses." Space does not permit listing all, but the chief offenses include lack of controls on the over-the-counter market; low standards that permitted salesmen of little character and less competence to enter the securities business; a bland acceptance of market "letters" with deliberate exaggerations or even misrepresentations; high-pressure sales tactics by mutuals; and trading for their own profits by stock exchange "specialists," whose function is supposed to be the stabilization of prices.

And as for the New York Stock Exchange—which didn't

want to be investigated—the Cohen report said that it treated violators of its own rules with "tenderness rather than severity"; that it operated like a "private club," and in its public relations program was excessively concerned "with the image of itself and its members."

But for all of the specifics found by the Cohen report, the most important contribution it made was calling into question the success of self-regulation of the markets. The whole underlying concept of the 1933 securities legislation was the disclosure principle: the Government would force those who offered stock to the public to tell the truth about it. From then on, it was *caveat emptor*. The policing function was left to the exchanges, the brokers, and their associations. It may have been what was needed in the 30's. But it wasn't enough for the 1960's. Over the years, the SEC has not done the same thorough job of regulating the conduct of those in the securities business that it has done in administering disclosure requirements. Now, the SEC is prepared to assume a new role, in response to the Milton Cohen findings, under which it will set up "an effective system of regular surveillance of the exchanges' enforcement and disciplinary activities." The public deserves nothing less—it should have had it a long time ago.

Not only had trading volume on the New York Stock Exchange doubled in the 1950's but there was a mushrooming in other markets with even less protection for the buyer. For example, stocks traded "over the counter"—that is, on no organized exchange—were becoming increasingly popular. Sales leaped from less than $5 billion in 1949 (excluding mutual funds and syndicated distributions) to $39 billion in 1961—yet for these stocks, the same disclosure controls applicable to listed stocks were not required. Cary told Congress in midsummer, 1963, that the Cohen report "demonstrates that irresponsible selling tactics, reckless investment advice, extravagant public relations and erratic markets for new issues of securities thrive best where lack of information is most marked." [24]

The sad history of most Washington probes and studies is that they live briefly in newspaper headlines, then flicker out. Not so with the Milton Cohen investigation. Even before the final group of chapters was issued—the report was parceled into three stages—the Senate had adopted a bill embodying the recommendations in two areas: new and strict qualifications for entering the securities business, and disclosure requirements for actively traded over-the-counter securities.

In April 1964, after weeks of bitter argument with New York Stock Exchange officials, the SEC issued new rules on floor trading, severely limiting floor traders' activity for their own accounts. This, the first major change in stock market regulations to grow out of the Cohen study, was a major victory for the SEC, which had charged bluntly that some traders put their own interests ahead of the public's with "consequences . . . hardly distinguishable from those of a manipulation." But the real importance of the decision on floor trading was even greater: the SEC for the first time threw down a real challenge to the existing power complex of the NYSE—the floor professionals—and promised, in effect, to enforce the kind of continuing reform movement that the Exchange had refused to undertake on its own.

To a considerable extent, the therapeutic value of the Cohen investigation may be countered by the sugary assurances of those with a vested interest that "everything's all right." The mutual funds industry, for example, is ready to fight the Cohen suggestion that so-called "front-end load" plans be ruled out of existence. In a "front-end load" plan, the buyer agrees to a monthly installment purchase plan for securities, usually over a 10-year period. But in contrast to other mutual plans, the 8½ percent sales or commission charge is bunched heavily into the first 13 payments. Usually, half or more of the total commission due for the entire 10-year contract is "loaded," in such plans, into the first 13 months. In many plans examined by the Cohen study group, an "investor" had paid as much in commissions in 13 months as the amount actually invested in the fund—for every $2 installment, in other words, he owned only $1 worth of investments. Thus, the buyer who decides to or is forced to sell his holdings in a "loaded" mutual early in the game takes a terrible beating.

More than 1,000,000 Americans have already been wheedled into such contracts. Many of these are low-income, unsophisticated families, looking for a rainy-day nest egg. The "typical" mutual fund investor, according to the Cohen report, is a high school graduate, head of a family, earning $5,000 to $10,000 a year, in his middle to late forties, with an insurance estate of under $15,000.

There are other than "front-end loaded" mutual investments available, of course, but the industry's salesmen naturally like to push those which yield up such fat commissions in the first 13 payments. There are "level-load" plans, in which the 8½ percent commission is spread evenly over all payments, and also many "no-load" plans, selling directly to the buyer.

The mutual funds industry has grown at a fantastic pace— from $2.5 billion in 1950 to an estimated $25 billion in 1963. Back in 1962, the Wharton School of Finance, acting for the SEC, made the first comprehensive study of the "mutuals" in 20 years; and this showed that investors needed greater protection. There was found to be a direct correlation between the commission that a fund paid to its salesmen and the sales they racked up.[25] Thus, much of the growth of the mutual funds industry, like soap and detergents, is the result of a Madison Avenue huckstering."

The enormous stock holdings by the funds today constitute a powerful market influence. The Wharton study estimated that as of September 30, 1958, common stocks owned by all investment companies amounted to 3.5 percent of those listed on the New York Stock Exchange. This makes funds a tremendous force in the markets, and whether this is a good thing for society is debatable. The funds presumably put some kind of floor under the stock market because, even in the face of wide declines, their business is to acquire stocks. But whether a relatively few men who make the selling and buying decisions for the fund should have this much power is an open question.

However, there is little doubt that the myth underlying the attractiveness of ownership of mutual funds should be revised. Presumably, the man who saves for the "rainy day" by investing in mutuals thinks he is buying not only diversification, but the best professional advice; and he *is* paying for advice—through the nose. The Wharton report indicated that professional advisers to mutual funds charge rates that are higher than the aggregate of fees charged other clients. Such high fees would be worth paying, if ownership in mutuals were something special. But mutual fund performance, says the Wharton study, "did not appreciably differ from what would have been achieved by

an unmanaged portfolio consisting of the same proportions of
. . . [securities] as the composite portfolios of the funds. About
half of the funds performed better, and half worse, than such an
unmanaged portfolio."

The mutual funds naturally resent the sharp criticism by the
SEC and its agents, and blames them for a lessening public interest. The Investment Company Institute, an industry trade
association, reported in September, 1963, that redemptions for
the first eight months of the year were $976,316,000—or 30
percent above the similar period of 1962. As a percentage of
sales, redemptions were running at a rate of 65 percent, the
highest in years.[26]

The SEC is now proceeding to move toward the new and
broader regulatory function that the Cohen group insists is
necessary. This has tremendous implications for the future.
Wall Street may not like it, but the SEC will no longer be the
sleepy cop on the beat, roused to action only in the plain sight
of theft and housebreaking. Through an expanded Division of
Trading and Exchanges, headed by Ralph S. Saul, a member of
the Cohen study group, the SEC will actively review all of the
practices and rules of the exchanges and dealer groups, and
force changes where necessary.

Moreover, the industry is on notice: not only is there a new
SEC Division of Plans and Programs that will stand apart from
routine supervision of the market, and assess new problems as
they arise, but the purgative of new, special investigations is
always in easy reach. In a *Newsweek* interview as he headed
back to his Chicago law practice, Cohen said, "It may still be
desirable . . . occasionally to take a broad look at the markets
through a special study." [27]

Thus, the SEC's new basic guidepost, while giving maximum
scope to self-regulation, is the "crucial function of public over-
sight." This will necessitate a major reorientation of the Commission's work, and the new posture will stand as one of the
major accomplishments of John F. Kennedy. The Administration was acting in the highest tradition of the public service
when it sensed the long-overdue need for an investigation of the
markets, and proceeded to start one and put reforms into effect.
Those who chose to blame Kennedy for the many aberrations
in stock market prices would have found ways to do so, with

or without the Cohen investigation. If new legislation creates a stronger as well as revitalized SEC, the beneficial effects for the public will be an enduring monument to the Kennedy Administration.

Part Two | GROPING FOR FULL
EMPLOYMENT

The Economic Advisers' Pecking Order: Dillon and Heller

ECONOMIC advisers to the President are a relatively new breed in Washington. Until the Employment Act was passed in 1946, Presidents relied mostly on their Secretaries of Treasury for advice on fiscal and economic issues. Under a man named Kennedy, as Economic Council chairman Walter W. Heller found out, this was *still* often true.

The popular impression about the economic forces jousting for attention inside the Kennedy Administration is that they polarized around Heller as the liberal, expansionist-minded innovator—and around Treasury Secretary Douglas Dillon as the conservative, cautious, sound-money man. There is some truth in this oversimplification. But it *is* an oversimplification which misses the full assessment of both men.

Because Heller lost more fights than he won, the over-all coloration of the Kennedy Administration took on much of the Dillon hue. At the same time, it must be noted that Heller had an impact on Dillon's conservatism, successfully pulled both President Kennedy and Dillon along the road of a more aggressive fiscal policy at home, and exacted from them a brand-new willingness to explore new methods to deal with our international money problems.

When one gets right down to it, both Dillon and Heller so much enjoyed their respective roles close to the seat of power at the White House that they were always willing to edge toward John F. Kennedy's notions—one moving from the right, the other from the left—in order to protect and preserve those roles. Long before becoming Council chairman, Heller—during testimony before Congress in 1959—observed that "in determining the level of government activity, the policy-maker cannot live by economics alone." This is the facts-of-life approach, and such economic pragmatism was keyed nicely to the brisk, professional air of the Kennedy White House staff. It is of a piece with Seymour Harris' observation that "*qua* economist I would accept larger deficits, but in view of other considerations, I am not equally enthusiastic about large deficits in the present milieu." [1]

The net result is that Heller moved carefully to see how he could bring his influence to bear within the Government, and although he is a driving, ambitious taskmaster to his staff, the Economic Council doesn't often stray far from the main party line. Some of the bolder notions about the domestic economy, as a matter of fact, have originated in the Department of Labor, and Heller is not at all unhappy to have Secretary W. Willard Wirtz just a little bit to his left.

At the beginning, Heller was a symbol of what the business world—somewhat irrationally—complained about in the Kennedy Administration. Heller was committed to the notion, as are most Democrats, that the basic need of the U. S. economy at the end of the stagnant Eisenhower years was faster growth. Lumbering along at a growth rate of less than 3 percent, much less than half the pace in Western Europe or Russia, the U. S. economy was wastefully sluggish in real and human terms. The losses in potential national wealth had been staggering.

Heller rejected the Galbraithian theory that the affluent United States society is "saturated" with production, and needs only to allocate its wealth more sensibly. Faster growth, Heller argued, would provide a bigger economic "pie," with more resources available for both private and public sectors. He calculated that there was a "gap" of at least $30 billion a year between the economy's performance and potential, and if this were closed by stimulating the nation's production, it would obviate the necessity for the Government to decide—as it would have to under the Galbraith system—how the resources would be split between the public and private sector. But this called for a more aggressive fiscal policy—some combination of higher spending and reduced taxes—and an overthrow of the Eisenhower "tight money" policy—which, designed to eliminate inflation, was one of the major causes for the slow pace of economic growth in the 1950's. We need to keep "an eye cocked, but not glued" on the dangers of inflation and gold outflow, Heller said.[2]

It was a bold concept that Heller, along with his first fellow council members, James L. Tobin of Yale, and Kermit Gordon of Williams College, brought into office, and they knew that there would be vigorous opposition. Heller, who has the happy faculty of sprinkling wit into the often dry subject of economics, himself observed that he had to be judicious in making suggestions about money policy, the private preserve of Federal Reserve Chairman William McChesney Martin: "We have to aproach this the way a porcupine approaches making love—and that's carefully."

Heller has never quite understood—and has spent much time trying to eradicate—the business world's notion that he is a radical. This stereotype appears to have been established by the first flush of newspaper and magazine stories on Heller's appointment by the President. Articulate and personable, Heller was fairly well known in Washington, where he had served in the Treasury and on various government committees in the postwar period. He had also acted as fiscal adviser to Governor Orville Freeman of Minnesota (now Secretary of Agriculture) but was hardly a prominent figure. In the academic world, he had a high rating for intellectual integrity and drive. But there were better-known names among the Democratic liberal economists—Seymour Harris, Paul Samuelson, and John Kenneth Galbraith, to name a few.

When it was reported that Kennedy had offered the CEA post to Heller, some publications, combing over speeches and Congressional testimony, played up his demands for an easier money policy and tax reform. Columnist Arthur Krock furrowed his brow and wrote: "Professor Heller has expressed economic views, which though contradictory at points, have classified him as an 'inflationist' in the opinion of some fiscal moderates and conservatives." [3] His source for this was a series of excerpts from Congressional testimony. Then Krock continued: ". . . The sound-dollar groups continue to be worried over Mr. Kennedy's statement that his CEA chairman will be on his top advisory level."

One suspects that the "sound-dollar groups" consisted largely of Mr. Krock himself. But the barrage continued. The *U. S. News and World Report* strung together a list of Heller quotations, some of them out of context, which gave the impression that the man from Minnesota was wild and woolly-headed, the very prototype of the economist who had "never met a payroll," and who would pump the President's head full of schemes leading to rack and ruin.

Heller is of course a modern man and economist. But some of the extreme characterizations that Krock, David Lawrence and others offered, even though journalistically sloppy or incomplete, have stuck. Heller, like most fellow Frontiersmen, is sensitive to criticism, and this overdrawn picture still bothers him. Heller, as a private citizen, had said that in breaking away from the tight confines of the Eisenhower era, we had to move more confidently into public expenditures, especially those that relate "to our most valuable resource, the human mind." He also had urged Congress in formal testimony to abandon such archaic fiscal concepts as the ceiling on the national debt: "In the name of budgetary integrity, financial prudence, adequately financed national security, and aggressive policies to combat inflation and counter recession—in other words, in the name of everything that is fiscally holy and wholesome—our anachronistic federal debt limit should be abolished."

Such a flip challenge to orthodoxy not unexpectedly sent a chill down the spines of some businessmen to whom, like Senator Harry Byrd, the national debt limit is one of the few remaining bastions of financial virtue and fiscal sanity. It is the one barrier that can be locked against the "spenders," and Heller obviously was a "spender." On a *Meet the Press* television show in September, 1961, Heller was asked if he were not a "spender," and he responded this way:

> I hate labels. And I don't characterize myself as a "spender." You know, I think it is wrong to put the emphasis constantly on the label "spending." After all, if we think of the government's activities in part as investing, investing in human minds, investment in highways, investing in social overhead—if we put our emphasis on the service provided by the government, to the

aged, to the unemployed, and so on, we get a little different concept of it.

No. As an economist, my approach to this general question of government spending is that where government spending represents a better use of the resources than private spending, there, of course, it should be undertaken. Where this line is drawn is different for different people. I would not label the President or myself as a "spender."

Heller was introduced to Kennedy by Senator Hubert Humphrey in October, 1960, when the Senator-candidate was in Minneapolis for a speech. During a swift change of clothes in his hotel room, Kennedy fired one question after another at the tall, eager professor: Could we really get to a 5 percent growth rate? How? What effect would it have on prices? Would a budget deficit trigger inflation? Could small spending programs swing a $500 billion economy out of the doldrums? Heller was entranced, and Kennedy impressed; Heller was an enthusiastic Democrat, articulate, with a sense of the real world mixed in with a certain professorial reserve. Nothing was said then about the Council chairmanship, but when Paul Samuelson of M.I.T., Kennedy's favorite economist, turned the job down, he recommended Heller, among others. Heller also was mentioned by most other experts whose views were polled for the President by Sorensen.[4]

Kennedy grasped as soon as he met Heller what has not come through yet to some of the nation's business leaders: he is a liberal, but far from doctrinaire, and above all, he is flexible. Not only could he learn "the art of the possible," but he could be counted on to be a team player. The Irish Mafia in the White House did not always agree with Heller, but they considered him a "pro," a high compliment from a tough-minded bunch of successful politicians. He became one of the most important Administration salesmen for the 1963-64 tax bill, even though it is far different from the way he would have shaped it himself.

At the Treasury's insistence, he has kept the balance of payments problem to the fore. In sum, as one White House official said, he "acclimated himself to President Kennedy's needs and views." The actions of a public official cannot always be predicted from an examination of earlier articles and speeches. To be an outside critic is one thing, and to have responsibility is another—a simple fact of life in Washington that some academicians do not always appreciate. Arthur Goldberg once told me with a smile after becoming Secretary of Labor: "You must learn to distinguish between what I said before and what I'm saying now—not that I've changed my mind about anything. But the circumstances are different."

To illustrate the point: When John P. Lewis, newest Council member, was still an Indiana University economics professor, he won great praise for a bright and free-swinging speech at the White House Conference on National Economic Issues in May, 1962. He picked holes in the Council's wage-price guidelines policy, and also was gently critical of President Kennedy's role in the struggle with Roger Blough.[5]

But Lewis acknowledged after taking office: "You can't be a white-smocked scientist here. You have to share the objectives of the Administration. But you also have to say your piece—say it inside—and if your point of view seems too far at odds with the Boss', you can quit." [6] Council member Gardner Ackley, a professor from the University of Michigan, feels much the same way. "The role of the economist in public affairs can be extremely frustrating," he says. "Economic policy is as much politics, in the broadest and best sense, as it is economics. . . . In no previous administration have economists had more opportunity to influence policy. . . . That still does not mean that Kennedy's economic policies are straight from the textbook—either of Samuelson or Ackley. It does mean that the President —as he must—considers the 'art of the feasible' as part of the 'science of choice.' " [7]

If the business world had understood this as well as most of Kennedy's appointees, it might have acquired a more rational perspective on Heller. There were strong countervailing influences for him to contend with, not the least of which was President Kennedy's own innate conservatism. There were other strong powers on the side of caution: Dillon, Martin, and the White House staff itself, especially Sorensen.

In three years with Kennedy, Heller had his ups and downs. If there were an Economic Council chart on the Heller impact on the White House, it would be full of peaks and valleys—but the trend line at the end would be slightly up. He has had a free hand in picking his associates, and the first Council—Heller, Tobin, and Gordon—was a superb team. Tobin has since returned to his professorship at Yale, and Gordon, on the point of going back to head the Economics Department at Williamstown, was selected by Kennedy to replace David E. Bell as Director of the Budget at the close of 1962.

Heller decided that Tobin was the man he needed most, in running over possibilities with his old friend, tax expert Joseph A. Pechman, director of the Brookings Institution. Tobin, a brilliant, original thinker, demurred at first when Heller talked to him. He had just written an article for *Challenge,* published by New York University, highly critical of the Federal Reserve, and he thought this would prove embarrassing. When Kennedy himself phoned Tobin, at Heller's request, Tobin said: "Senator, you don't want me in the Council. I'm an ivory tower economist." Kennedy convinced Tobin with the response: "That's the best kind. I'm an ivory tower president." [8] Later, Heller, Tobin, and Pechman plus a Presidential phone call sold Gordon.

All in their forties, economists who had begun their professional careers in the midst of the big depression, Heller, Tobin, and Gordon were attracted by the prospect that a liberal Democratic Administration would stir a lot of action, and modernize economic thinking in Washington. They were enticed by the exciting notion of participating in Kennedy's program to "get the country moving again." Kennedy was delighted with all of them—he once told Sorensen that any one of the three was qualified to be chairman of the Council.

Heller was the "front man," the skillful general who hammered out a program and then set out to sell it to Kennedy and the rest of the Administration. Tobin, an intellectual giant, generated most of the ideas and undertook the tough jobs. For example, it was Tobin who worked with the Federal Reserve to set up a process of modifying the bills-only policy. (See Chapter XI.) "Tobin set a high moral tone," Heller says. "His adherence to principle was undeviating, even when it wasn't expedient." Gordon, with warmth, charm, and practical sense, was a Council workhorse who gained Kennedy's admiration even though Gordon in 1958 rejected a Sorensen request that he become part of an informal brain trust for the then Senator.

When Heller first proposed Gordon, Sorensen objected, but Heller bulled it through.

The common denominator among all the Council members under Kennedy—Heller, Tobin, Gordon, Ackley, and Lewis—and key staff men such as Robert Solow of M.I.T., Arthur Okun of Yale, and Richard Cooper of Yale has been an extraordinary level of talent and inventiveness. If Heller never does anything else, he performed a service in re-establishing among academic economists the fine reputation of the Council, here and abroad.

But mere brilliance of an economics general staff doesn't assure that it will dominate the thinking in a politically sensitive capital. The Council of Economic Advisers, after all, is not an economic Supreme Court; it is just a staff agency of the White House. Where a Dillon or a Martin have major operating roles and large staffs to help them, the Council chairman must survive by his wits, agility, and power of persuasion. Kennedy liked the counterpoint of different advice against which to check the opinions which funneled up to him. He used Galbraith to second-guess both Heller and Dillon, on different occasions. In the summer of 1963, for example, he turned to Galbraith for a hard look at the balance of payments problems, and the solutions the Administration had been devising for it. Heller's policy guidance has sometimes been run through Paul Samuelson, or the White House staff itself, for corroboration.

This caution was part of Kennedy's conservative mold, and it helped to temper the generally liberal philosophy of the CEA. Above all, Kennedy was an expert and practical politician, not a bold adventurer. In the summer of 1962, when Heller (and most academic economists and many businessmen) pushed for a tax cut, the President watched the course of economic indicators like a fever chart. But what really settled the issue was the judgment of seasoned politicians like Wilbur Mills on Capitol Hill, and Lawrence O'Brien of the White House staff that a tax bill couldn't pass.

Professor Otto Eckstein of Harvard University told the Joint Economic Committee that the economic need for a tax cut was so obvious that "it would take someone with a lot more understanding of the political process than I possess to explain the present dim outlook for action. . . ." [9] If Eckstein had been privy to Kennedy's inner-chamber discussions at that time, he

would have found, simply, that the President—as one friend
put it—concluded "he'd be damned if he'd send up a tax bill
only to have Congress knock it down." The lineup was overwhelming: politicians as far apart as Senator Paul Douglas,
Illinois Democrat, and Senator Barry Goldwater, right-wing
Republican, opposed it.

Even on the strictly economic side, there was no unanimity.
Secretary Goldberg felt a cut could wait until 1963. Galbraith
was for larger spending rather than a tax cut. And Dillon, with
some logic, contested Heller's argument, pointing out that if
the Administration wanted tax reform in 1963, it would have
to provide Congress the "sweetener" of a net reduction in taxes.
He warned that if the President allowed the sugar to be consumed by a quickie tax cut in 1962, reforms later on would be
too bitter a pill to swallow. (It turned out that Congress rejected
major reforms even in the setting of an $11 billion tax cut.)

Ted Sorensen confirms, in his *Decision Making in the White
House,* that Kennedy's veto of the 1962 tax cut idea was a political rather than an economic decision. The President leaned
toward the idea that it would be wise to infuse new strength in
a sagging economy, but he waited two months for popular support to develop. When it didn't, he discarded the idea. Thus,
Kennedy eschewed the responsibility of leadership. He could
have tried to mobilize public opinion to support his convic-
tions, but he decided to duck what could have been a losing
fight. If all the economic indicators had pointed down, instead
of being "a mixed bag," Kennedy might have risked the rebuff
from Congress. With some annoyance that things weren't made
simpler for the President, a White House staff man recalls that
"none of those God-damn economists could agree on what the
economy was doing."

One must sympathize with the President's dilemma. Sorensen
believes that "no President is free to go as far or as fast as his
advisers, his politics, and his perspective may direct him." Yet
there is a nagging suspicion, even recognizing President Kennedy's lonely and weighty burden, that he sometimes gave
eloquent lip service to liberal economic theory—and then
backed away from meaningful supporting action.

"The Kennedy performance," as Editor Gilbert Harrison
wrote in the *New Republic,* "is less impressive than the Ken-

nedy style." For example, Heller—with an assist from Nikita Khrushchev, who had boasted that the Russians would out-produce the United States by 1970—persuaded the President to say most of the right things about economic growth rates in June, 1961.

Heller, on short notice, produced a handwritten memo for the President on the morning of June 26, 1961, showing that if the United States could boost its growth rate to 4.5 percent, the Soviet Union wouldn't catch up until the year 2,010. The President, after using the Heller numbers in a private talk with Alexei Adzhubei, visiting son-in-law of Chairman Khrushchev, told a press conference later in the week:

> If our growth rate is increased to even 4.5 percent, which is well within our capability, it is my judgment that the Soviet Union will not outproduce the United States at any time in the 20th century. This faster growth rate is a prime subject of the various measures I have submitted and will submit in the future. . . .[10]

But it takes more than a press conference statement of a goal for growth—which Heller says "is both an end in itself and an instrumentality, both the pot of gold and the rainbow"—to produce it. Its achievement takes a determination, a purposeful willingness to stimulate the economy, public and private. For example, to get to a 4.5 percent rate of growth over a sustained period of time, a very liberal monetary policy would be needed, but there was no evidence that Kennedy would or could wring such a commitment out of Martin. Dynamic actions to accelerate the growth of the economy had to be stacked up against the balance of payments deficit—and caution won out. As was to be seen over the next 18 months, the 4.5 percent growth rate was buried, even for public relations purposes. By the time the January 1963 economic report rolled around, the official White House goal on growth had become "something over 4 percent." And in February, Paul Samuelson, pointing to a "new wave of scholarly revisionism," said that "anything much above 3.5 per-cent will require a great intensification of social and private efforts." [11] (The 5 percent goal of the 1960 Democratic platform had long since been laid away, although it may be resuscitated for a brief appearance on the 1964 campaign trail.)

President Kennedy on other occasions dabbled temporarily in

the theories of his liberal advisers. In January, 1962, he recommended that Congress provide discretionary authority for the President to cut taxes and spend moneys on public works. The bold and perhaps venturesome idea that the President ought to have the power to reduce taxes at least slightly, in certain circumstances, had been current among economists for a decade. It had been one of the proposals made a year earlier by the Samuelson task force on the economy. Now, since it had been given respectability by approval of the Commission on Money and Credit—a group of 25 distinguished business, labor, and public men who had studied the whole range of financial and money problems for three years—Kennedy shipped it to the Hill.[12] (He scrapped Heller's suggestion that the law also include power to raise taxes to clip back inflationary booms.) But this proposal, dutifully made, languished in Congress. There never was any real intention of pushing for it, although, had it been on the books in the summer and fall of 1962, it would have been used if "those God-damn economists" had come up with a consensus that the economy was really going down.

Heller has detractors on the right and the left. The business community, if one takes its complaints seriously, thinks that Heller has too much influence. Invariably, those businessmen who detested John Kennedy had Heller first on their list of complaints. Often, the basis for their rejection of Heller is a compound of misinformation and groundless suspicion. Some of Heller's right-wing critics will be distressed to learn that, unlike Arthur Schlesinger, Jr., he is not a member of the Americans for Democratic Action. Barry Goldwater, of course, suggests that Heller is some sort of evil influence—but where and how is never specified.

Heller himself supplied the critics of the President's tax program with one magnificent piece of ammunition by a classic gaffe before a Congressional committee. Testifying in January, 1963, on the need for a massive tax cut to stimulate the economy, Heller made what was interpreted as a derogatory reference to the "Puritan ethic" of the American people. It happened when Representative Martha W. Griffiths, a Michigan Democrat and member of the Joint Economic Committee, told Heller that not everybody was convinced of the wisdom of a tax cut.

She had polled her constituents, she said, and 62 percent responded: "Don't cut taxes."

Exasperated, Heller answered:

> That does indicate . . . an enormous need for public education in the field of economics, economic policy, tax policy. . . . Major efforts have to be made along this line. . . . It is quite remarkable that the basic Puritan ethic of the American people should be such that they want to deny themselves tax reduction . . . because of their fears of deficits, and the additions to the national debt.[13]

The "basic Puritan ethic" crack, innocent, accurate, but horribly inept, came back to haunt Heller and the Administration for most of 1963. It provided a field day for editorial writers and Republican critics, who not only could pin the spendthrift label on the Administration, but could now show that the radicals in Washington were contemptuous of the prudent and the thrifty.

Heller tried to explain it away, but it was too convenient a tool for tax cut opponents to give up. Heller wasn't helped when a United Press International reporter misheard him, and wrote a news lead as follows: "President Kennedy's chief economic adviser said yesterday that some American taxpayers are conducting a remarkable 'Puritanical effort' to deny themselves a tax cut." An unhappy Heller called the editor of the Washington *Post,* which had carried the UPI story, and snapped that the *Post* ought to cover future Heller appearances with its own staff correspondents.

But "Puritan ethic" was almost as bad, if not worse, than "Puritanical effort." On *Meet the Press* on February 10, 1963, a persistent questioner asked Heller if his reference to "Puritan ethic" meant that the economist felt the American people were not "smart enough" to figure out that big deficits were bad economics. Heller responded:

> . . . as to the Puritan ethic, let me say first of all that I was citing it in an admiring tone, not as a slur, not suggesting for a moment that the American people don't have the capacity for understanding. What I was saying was this, that because essentially of the Puritan ethic they are willing to deny themselves tax cuts until and unless they are convinced that they are in the national interest. And our job . . . is to show that they

definitely are in the national interest, that the stimulus to jobs, to incentives, to profits, to production, will more than make up the lost revenues. . . .

But Republicans, for whom the whole concept of "a tax cut on borrowed money" is morally wrong, will not forget the "Puritan ethic." It likely will be used and misused, ad nauseam, during the 1964 campaign. The Republican minority of the House Ways and Means Committee, in opposing the tax bill reported out on September 13, 1963, gave a hint of what may be expected:

> Tax reduction financed through additions to the public debt is contrary to the Puritan ethic of an overwhelming majority of the American people. They fully realize it is morally wrong to mortgage the future earnings of their children and their grandchildren in order to enjoy presently the questionable luxury of grandiose spending and lower taxes.
>
> In recognition of this "moral" concern, the Kennedy Administration set about to "indoctrinate" the people in the New Frontier code of economic morality. As much was freely acknowledged . . . by . . . Heller in a colloquy with Rep. Martha W. Griffiths. . . .[14]

At the other end of the political spectrum, Leon H. Keyserling, former chief economic adviser to President Truman, thinks that Heller's approach has been excessively timid, and that he has underestimated both the size of the economic "gap" and the economic growth needed to close it. Keyserling has shown, in a series of his own economic reports, the limited nature of many of the Kennedy Administration's proposed programs. In one bitter speech, he told a meeting in St. Louis that he could explain the facts about the economy to his cook, but couldn't get them across to the President's economists. Needless to say, this didn't add to Keyserling's standing at the White House, although Keyserling's outspoken speeches and writings frequently piqued Kennedy's curiosity.[15]

My own view rejects the business-community-Goldwater assessment in toto, and Keyserling's in part. Goldwater doesn't have the credentials to make judgments on these matters; he comes close to being an economic illiterate. Keyserling, a former Economic Council chairman himself, has to be taken more seriously. He is one of the few Democratic liberals who kept up a steady drumbeat of critical comment on Kennedy's policies, and who can be expected to keep a searching spotlight on Lyndon Johnson as well. One doesn't have to agree with all that Leon Keyserling says to admire his keen mind and his nerve.

The facts are that Heller doesn't have either the dangerous inclinations or the influence ascribed to him by some businessmen and Goldwater Republicans. As is indicated above, there are opposing forces to the influence of the Council of Economic Advisers. Moreover, Heller himself, as a team player, waters down some of his own ideas. But over the long run, he has been neither so timid nor impotent as Keyserling implies. No continuous observer of the Washington scene for the past three years can doubt that Heller left his mark on the economic policies of the Kennedy Administration. Heller himself doubtless wishes the imprint had been greater. But given the importance Kennedy placed on the balance of payments crisis, the President's own conservative instincts, and such a capable and ambitious rival as Douglas Dillon, I doubt that Paul Samuelson, Leon Keyserling, or anyone else would have accomplished any more than Walter Heller has.

Heller had successes and failures in the Kennedy era. He had a direct access to the President unmatched by any of his four predecessors as chairman of the Council. Ted Sorensen says that Kennedy made more use of the Council—all members, not just the chairman—than any other President ever did. Heller also had a key and less well-known role as a member of a "Big Four" who regularly met with the Cabinet to assess domestic programs (the others were Sorensen, O'Brien, and Budget Director Gordon). He was also a member of the "Breakfast Group" that met with the President for pre-press conference briefings. Others in this group were Vice-President Johnson, Secretary of State Dean Rusk, presidential advisers Sorensen, McGeorge Bundy, Myer Feldman, Pierre Salinger, and State Department press officer Robert Manning. Heller had made it a habit to brief the Vice-President on important economic matters, and this relationship gave him an entree to LBJ's inner circle immediately after the assassination.

In many ways, Heller has been closer to Johnson than he was to Kennedy. The late President made a sharp line of demarcation between the end of his business day, and his own personal and family life. Few of Kennedy's associates—not Heller, nor even Sorensen, for example—mingled with the President and his family after hours. But Johnson makes few such distinctions, and in his own gregarious style, "integrates" his team into his family life.

This has opened a new vista for Heller, whereas Dillon—one of the few administration men who was a social friend of John Kennedy's—has been more or less on the outside of the Johnson circle. The Texan had fewer ties to the academic community, and found Heller available—and willing—to serve as his No. 1 economic thinker. Whether Heller will be able, over the long run, to establish the same intellectual rapport he had with Kennedy remains to be seen. The pinch of personal finances, in any event, may force Heller and some of the other original New Frontiersmen to leave their posts soon after the election, or early in 1965. This will point up dramatically the need for a substantial boost in salaries for key Government personnel.

Heller has been a prolific and effective speechmaker, selling both himself and the Administration's programs. His theme in 1962, as the year wore on, was a defense of the Administration's exceptionally optimistic economic forecast—one that didn't pan out. Heller had calculated that the gross national product would zoom a spectacular $50 billion to $570 billion in 1962. He missed by about $15 billion, and his critics don't let him forget it. But in all fairness, it should be pointed out that his $570 billion forecast, which held out the hope for a bigger boom than anyone else foresaw, was necessary to provide the budget "balance" that Kennedy had promised at the time of the Berlin crisis. Thus, it was the President's instinct for fiscal conservatism that forced his advisers to "reach" for a rosy estimate of the economy.

In 1963, chastened by this experience, Kennedy settled for more realistic estimates; not only was no surplus forecast, but a whopping deficit of $11.9 billion was planned, assuming the passage of tax cut proposals which would account for $2.7 billion of the red-ink total. Heller devoted all of his time in 1963 to an exhaustive advocacy and defense of the tax cut proposal, which he regarded as his baby. He stoutly defended the program, even when it was accurately criticized by liberals because it was thinly spread over too long a period. For example, less than $3 billion of the cut would have become effective in calendar 1963, under the President's proposal—a concession to Dillon, who didn't want the deficit to move higher. A $3 billion tax cut was a paltry item, less, in fact, than the total amount by which the public's taxes would be *raised* as a result of higher Social Security, and state and local tax boosts which went into effect in 1963. Heller nevertheless toured the country, urging passage of the tax bill and enjoying his place in the limelight. Excessively conscious of his public relations "image," Heller was most pleased with an uncritical *Look* magazine profile which called him "Mr. Tax Cut."

But the projected $11.9 billion deficit—with the prospect that the budget would be out of balance for at least two and possibly three years following—was a landmark in modern economic thinking, and Kennedy deserves enormous credit for accepting a daring concept. Kennedy boldly abandoned the time-honored theory that a balanced budget was the best national posture, whatever the economic situation. Instead, he accepted the Heller thesis that—faced with a $9 billion deficit in fiscal 1964 anyway—the right course was *not* to cut the deficit, but to add to it through a tax cut which would stimulate economic growth, and produce larger Federal revenues in the years ahead.

This was a long way from the Eisenhower years, and a triumph for the Keynesians, even if Kennedy did make a bow to Dillon by spreading the cut over three years, and later mistakenly agreeing to a commitment for controlling expenditures. The choice, Kennedy correctly said as 1963 began, was not between deficit and balance, but "between deficits born of waste . . . and deficits incurred as we build our future strength." [16]

Kennedy's ability to see economic issues in such a framework represented an enormous gain in his own education, a development to which Heller's Council contributed, and which is one of its great accomplishments. He had an uncanny ability to absorb even abstruse and technical matters. In countless memoranda and private huddles, the faculty of Heller U. made of Kennedy, in Kermit Gordon's phrase, "the best economist who's ever been President." He knew, in 1963, that he would be assaulted by the Republicans for "planning" a deficit, but he went ahead anyway.

The Council economists have played a similar role, perhaps more of a selling than an educational job, among their colleagues in Europe. Europeans no longer run for the lifeboats if a big national deficit is posted for the United States. Some of this sophistication can be credited to the sessions of the Organization for Economic Cooperation and Development in Paris, regularly attended by various members of the Council. In the past three years, Europeans have gained an understanding of American economic problems through these transatlantic missions. In June, 1962, the OECD publicly acknowledged that the main problem for the United States was to accelerate growth, in order to strengthen the balance of payments position. This was a reversal of the European view of two years earlier, and an important "convincer" that a tax cut on top of a deficit would not outrage world financial opinion.

The solidity of relationships among Western World financial and economic policy-makers was demonstrated after the stock market break in May, 1962, to the Administration's private satisfaction. This story has never been told before: a prominent New York banker suggested to a European central banker that his country make a substantial "draw" on gold in this country (by turning in dollars) in order "to teach the Kennedys a lesson." This shortsighted New York banker was lectured by the European, who understood how such a malicious move would jar world confidence. He passed word of the proposal on to the Administration through the OECD.

To go along with a list of Council "impacts," as Heller calls them, there is a plentiful score of rebuffs from President Kennedy. One of Heller's worst defeats came early in the Administration, in May, 1961, when against the unanimous advice of the council that the nation needed the stimulus of a substantial public works program, Kennedy said "No." Instead, on May 25 in his "urgent national needs" message, he submitted new expenditure proposals only for army modernization and the moon-shot effort. Heller, supported by Goldberg, had been urging a public works bill, based on a measure introduced by Senator Joseph Clark of Pennsylvania, which would have "triggered" up to $1 billion of public works, parks, forestry and other projects if the unemployment total remained at 6.5 percent.

Kennedy decided against this, resolving the first behind-the-scenes struggle between the Heller-expansionist school and the Dillon conservatives. National security considerations played a role; spending on guerrilla tactical operations had to be boosted in the wake of floundering in Laos and the Bay of Pigs disaster. Besides, Kennedy felt that the nation's prestige needed the boost of a major moon-shot effort, after Soviet cosmonaut Gagarin orbited the earth. Thus, the Heller-Clark public works idea was discarded, and the only gesture toward the civilian economy that survived the May "second look" was a job retraining program.[17]

To soothe ruffled feelings, Kennedy wrote Senator Clark on August 7, pledging to embody "the principle of stand-by authority for capital improvements" in his legislative program for 1962. "I have no intention of 'learning to live with' prolonged and severe unemployment, with all that it means in human misery and economic waste," Kennedy wrote Clark. But budget considerations ruled it out at the moment.[18]

At a press conference a few weeks later, Kennedy defended these decisions in language quite compatible with orthodox business views:

> . . . Some of this [unemployment] is technological and even if we had a complete economic recovery you would still find some men left behind because of the change in skills.
>
> So I do think that [job retraining] legislation would be helpful, and if these programs do not work, then we're going to have to consider what other steps to take.
>
> But we have a large deficit and it's difficult to think that we could usefully increase that in order to affect unemployment without adversely affecting the cost of living. That's our difficulty there."

This was a very significant statement by Kennedy. It demonstrated, first of all, his earlier resistance to the push by Heller to incur a bigger deficit through heavier expenditures. He believed then that bigger deficits would cause inflation, for a certainty—and the prospects were uncertain that such a move would cut into hard-core unemployment. Essentially, this was precisely the viewpoint of Martin and other conservatives, who believed that much of the unemployment problem was due to "structural" causes—that is, unemployment arising because of advances in technology or other shifts (lesser markets for coal, for example, as other fuels became more popular) which would be little if at all changed by expansion of over-all demand in the economy.

Here, we see some of the evidence of Martin's influence. The importance of structural unemployment has been consistently played down by Heller, who relies on the "aggregate demand" theory: concentrate on getting a booming economy, Heller argues, and the stepped-up activity will cut deeply into pockets of joblessness, even in distressed areas and among the "disadvantaged" groups, such as Negroes and untrained labor.

But against his failure to push Kennedy ahead at a faster pace in the spring of 1961, Heller won an important victory against impressive odds in the summer when the President decided, after a long internal debate, that he would not propose to raise taxes to pay for the $3.2 billion in extra defense costs arising out of the Berlin crisis. To cement this victory, Heller enlisted Samuelson's aid, arranging for the M.I.T. professor to fly to Washington with the President on his return from a weekend at Hyannisport.

Ranged against Heller and Samuelson in this argument were Bobby Kennedy, Health, Education and Welfare Secretary (now Senator) Abraham Ribicoff, Arthur Goldberg, and Dillon (whose views shifted during the debate). This was one time when the Kennedy decision was based on economics, and not politics. The lineup for *raising* taxes was composed primarily of the politicians. The Bobby Kennedy-Ribicoff view, for example, was that a tax increase should be adopted to show the need for sacrifice, and to silence the Republicans who were labeling the President a "big spender."

The Council of Economic Advisers, buttressed by Samuelson, persuaded Kennedy that such a tax increase would stall the economic upswing just getting under way, and which would be further accelerated by the bulge in military spending. This spending increase, Heller knew, would provide the economy with as much lift as the public works plan which Kennedy had vetoed back in May. In a sense, Khrushchev succeeded where

Heller, Goldberg, and Clark had failed in providing the excuse for an economic stimulus for the American economy.[20]

The "no tax increase" decision in 1961 was one of the most notable Heller scores; but there was a high price tag attached. Deferring to the notion that the Republicans would make political hay out of a failure to raise taxes, Kennedy agreed that the budget to be submitted in January, 1962 (for fiscal 1963), would be "strictly in balance." Moreover, the President promised, if the budget couldn't be balanced at existing tax rates, higher taxes would then be requested.[21] This reassured Dillon, William McChesney Martin, and the business community, but the advance commitment to a balanced budget, Kennedy's most open gesture to fiscal orthodoxy, shocked many economists.

Samuelson, for example, said it would be "tragic" if a premature budget balance inhibited the recovery, although he defended Kennedy's promise as one way of "quieting irrational opposition to needed fiscal expansion." Professor Alvin Hansen wrote that committing the nation so far in advance to a balanced budget was a "serious step backward" in the formulation of fiscal policy.[22]

Even after Kennedy had made his decision to balance the fiscal 1963 budget, Heller argued stubbornly against the idea. The Budget Bureau's review of the fiscal 1962 budget, issued in October, 1961, estimated that there would be a $6.9 billion deficit, compared with the surplus of $1.5 billion that Eisenhower, in *his* final budget message, had predicted. The difference was due to a recession that Eisenhower had refused to acknowledge, and major new military and space ventures.

Kennedy met with the Cabinet to discuss budget policy the day before the revised budget figures were made public, and emphasized that each agency head must "follow a most careful frugal spending policy." And because defense and related programs would have to rise in the following year, the decision to balance the budget made it necessary "to defer or limit increases in many programs which in more normal times would be thoroughly desirable." [23]

This statement represented Kennedy's conclusion after long sessions with Heller, Dillon, Sorensen, Martin, and Budget Director David Bell, in which Heller argued that the shift from the $6.9 billion deficit position to a balance might cut short the economic recovery then in process. Kennedy acknowledged that this was a risk, but said frankly that political considerations dictated a "hold-down" in spending. The President was also impressed by Dillon's argument that another big deficit on top of the nearly $7 billion in prospect for fiscal 1962 might rekindle a "confidence" run on the dollar. Bell, in these discussions, sided with Dillon. But the Presidential policy decision incorporated a determination to promote a policy of monetary ease, to avoid a repetition of Eisenhower's mistake of 1959-60, when, in the process of moving from a $12 billion deficit to a $1 billion surplus through a combination of a spending curb, and tight money as well, he brought on the 1960-61 recession.

Kennedy's program was well received on Capitol Hill, but it did not succeed in stilling criticism from business. For example, when Budget Director Bell expressed the hope that a vigorously expanding economy would provide additional revenues that would permit some increases in spending—even if the budget were balanced—a widely quoted business response was this:

> The question asked in the business community is whether we would not be on a sounder basis for accelerated economic growth if a closer restraint on spending were applied to easing repressive taxes.[24]

Or, as the *Wall Street Journal* put it, commenting on the budget message in January, 1962:

> The Kennedy budget all too fully reflects the prevalent notion that unlimited government growth is the key to economic well-being. Unfortunately for the nation, that theory prescribes methods which run counter to the achievement of the President's admirable aims [of growth, high employment, and price stability].[25]

The budget balance policy Kennedy felt impelled to follow in fiscal 1963 called for a whole range of orthodox proposals that should have been agreeable to the business community. There was expansion of government spending only in the areas of defense and space exploration. Moreover, the Administration committed itself to policies directed to halting the gold outflow, including wage-price stabilization measures, aids to stimulate exports, and sufficiently high interest rates to stem short- term capital losses.

And the projected "balance," as we have noted, was achieved by an excessively exuberant estimate of economic recovery that Heller produced. As Walter Lippmann wrote, if a deficit resulted, it will be "primarily because the President is overestimating the strength of the present business recovery. If he is doing that, then the decision to balance the budget will have come too soon." [26] This indeed is what happened. The nation wound up with a $6.2 billion deficit in fiscal 1963, instead of the $500 million surplus in the original budget estimate.

From Heller's perspective, in the 60 days from the end of May to the end of July in 1961, he had been batted down in an effort to stimulate Kennedy's interest in a public works bill, had won a fight against a regressive tax increase, then had to remain silent while the President promised a balanced budget for the following January. This is the pattern that Heller learned to accept: when liberals leave the protection of the campus to play a role in a national political administration, they sometimes must substitute compromise for bold academic assertiveness. This poses a dilemma that calls for soul-searching; one must be able to survive the frustrations of the political process, which is biased in favor of the status quo, in the hope that the constant nudging will have an impact, eventually, in the man at the top.

The very decision against a "quickie" tax cut in the summer of 1962 that represented a reaffirmation of Dillon's top place in the pecking order contained the germ of still another turn in Heller's fortunes. This time, the President promised a substantial net tax cut in 1963 because the high level of taxation, basically unchanged since World War II, acts "as a drag on the whole economy." (See Chapter XII.)

This necessitated some shifts in Dillon's position, for, as the record will show, Dillon had been touting tax reform as the projected cornerstone of the Administration's 1963 tax policy. Even when trying to reassure Wall Street after Black Monday, Dillon talked of tax cuts that would be accompanied by offsetting reforms "in whole or in part." [27] Dillon made no reference to a *net* tax cut until after the President had announced the policy in his August 14, 1962, speech rejecting the quickie cut. Dillon's first reference to the Administration's new policy came when he took his cue from the President, during testimony before the Joint Economic Committee three days later, on

August 17. Thus, it may be said that Dillon was a Johnny-come-lately to the massive tax cut idea; originally, what Dillon had in mind was just enough tax reduction to sugarcoat the unpleasantness of tax reform.

Heller, on the other hand, from the start had seen a massive tax cut as the one remaining hope of shooting some life into the economy. The spending route, he concluded, was a difficult if not impossible one—it was just as hard to persuade President Kennedy to take on new programs as it was to sell them to Congress. Heller envisioned a sharp slash in rates, encumbered by only enough reforms to make a package bill salable to the House Ways and Means Committee. And these could always be divorced from the tax cut itself if, for example, there was a renewed threat of recession.

The way it turned out, by the time Dillon finished reshaping Heller's original ideas, things looked quite different. There was still a large over-all tax cut figure—slightly more than $10 billion—but its impact was watered down by the timetable that spread it over three years. But Dillon had moved his position, too. In his August 17 testimony, he accepted the Heller "drag" theory, saying that "the tax system that was appropriate during the inflationary postwar epoch is now too onerous." Moreover, although fear of deficits "is deeply rooted in our thinking," Dillon said, "a temporarily larger deficit . . . is a reasonable price to pay for a program of basic tax reform and tax reduction."

The Dillon shift on tax cuts, and his open-minded position on deficit spending, serves to reinforce the belief in Washington that the Kennedy-Dillon relationship was one in which the President was as much or more of an influence on Dillon as the other way around. "Much of the so-called Dillon influence in the Kennedy Administration," says a well-posted insider, "represented Dillon's willingness to adapt to the President's views. Of course, they were close on most things, anyway."

One of the most astute observers of the national scene, himself in a high post, says: "To some extent, Dillon and Heller made a bureaucratic accommodation to each other's views and the desires of the President. This is often ignored in the conventional Washington appraisal, which likes to rack up a scorecard in terms of 'wins' and 'losses.' To see the Dillon-Heller relationships in blacks and whites is to deal in clichés that don't fit the situation."

Any assessment of the role of Treasury Secretary Dillon that failed to acknowledge his concessions to modern economics would be just a narrow view held only by highly partisan Democrats. One doesn't have to insist that Dillon think like Alvin Hansen or Leon Keyserling, or even Senator Paul Douglas, before giving him proper credit.

One scene that sticks in my mind took place in the Indian Treaty Room of the Executive Office Building, in January, 1962, when Dillon sat side by side with David Bell, a Truman Democrat, to brief reporters on the President's budget message. For 70 minutes, the Dillon-Bell team explained the President's budget and his economic philosophy. They were in complete harmony, and no one present could have identified the answers by political affiliation. Dillon explained the last Eisenhower recession developed because of a "decline in government expenditures . . . [and] there was also one of the sharpest and most restrictive monetary actions that we have seen, I think, in this century." [28] Shortly afterward, I asked Dillon if he still found it "congenial," as he had said a year earlier, working with Heller and his other Democratic colleagues.

"I don't have any problems," he smiled. "As the economy moved ahead this year, it became obvious we were going into higher ground, and that a balanced budget was indicated. I've argued with McNamara and others who have the job of putting in spending programs. But that's just the standard role of a Secretary of the Treasury, supporting the Budget Director."

Dillon was offered his job, originally, on a "national security, nonpolitical basis." It was made clear that there would be no embarrassing requests for appearances by the Democratic National Committee. (As Undersecretary of State under Eisenhower, Dillon also ducked requests for political speeches. He gave in once to the Republican National Committee, then under Thruston Morton, and made such a dull speech in trade, in which Lincoln was the only Republican mentioned, that he was never asked again.)

"In the areas I'm interested in," Dillon once said, "President

Kennedy is a fiscal moderate, fiscally highly responsible. He considers these things important, as I do. Now, that doesn't mean that he can't be a liberal in other respects, but he's not a liberal in the sense of being a free spender." [29] As for Heller's Council, Dillon said: "I look on them as a group that's supposed to be out front, coming up with ideas. We here in the Treasury, we're running an action Department. So we have to stop, look, and listen. But the Council is very useful and helpful."

The most significant "accord" between Dillon and Heller is on the value of deficit spending as a common, acceptable tool with which to stimulate the economy. This had long been accepted doctrine among Keynesian economists, but not tolerated by Secretaries of the Treasury. The classic observation of Eisenhower's Treasury Secretary, George Humphrey, was still within memory: If the nation didn't cut spending, "I will predict you will have a depression that will curl your hair." [30]

Dillon didn't always view deficit spending as a useful countercyclical device. When Kennedy first took office, Dillon voiced a fairly standard business view of budget deficits. For example, in 1961, after a BAC meeting at Hot Springs, when asked for comment on a Heller speech that contrasted a "constructive deficit" —meaning one that comes at a time when the economy isn't moving at full capacity—with a "destructive deficit"—which comes at a time when inflation abounds—Dillon said with a smile that he didn't know that there was a difference. But by May 18, 1962, Dillon had a different pitch. At a bankers' conference in Rome, Dillon observed: ". . . There is no automatic relationship between budgetary deficits and price inflation, or between budget deficits and the balance of payments. . . . We should always bear in mind that moderate budget deficits incurred during periods of inadequate demand, and which do not exert upward pressures on price levels are quite different in their economic effect from deficits incurred when the economy is operating at full capacity." Heller couldn't have put it much better himself.

Of course, Mr. Dillon doesn't go as far as Heller would. This was made clear by the limitations put on the tax cut measure. And the Secretary clings more steadfastly to the conservative wisdom on monetary policy; here he is close to the Martin philosophy, and whenever the Martin-Dillon-Roosa complex decided that a tight, rather than easy money posture was indicated, Kennedy's CEA was overruled.

To the extent that Heller has helped push Dillon into an acceptance of a more liberal fiscal attitude, the suave Secretary of the Treasury has had a reciprocal impact on Heller. The former Minnesota University economics professor extols the virtues and rewards of price stability—and in the Johnson era, of the need for "a dollar's value for a dollar spent"—with a vigor unmatched at an earlier stage of his career. He responds to the strictures of the balance of payments deficit, and has championed the cause of tax stimulants for business investment with an enthusiasm that mystifies some of his former academic colleagues.

What it comes down to, I think, is this: Heller, to many businessmen who rely mostly on *U. S. News,* the *Wall Street Journal,* and what their instincts tell them they should be thinking, is a bogyman. If they read David Lawrence regularly, the case is closed. But in today's real world, these fears are unjustified, as some businessmen who have met and worked with Heller realize. The fact is that the political realities in Washington do not permit a President to take the kind of initiative that many academic liberals properly urge. I hope that there may be a President some day who will shuck all such political constraints, but I am not sanguine about such a prospect. Says one escapee from an Eastern campus to the New Frontier: "The climate along the Potomac just isn't conducive to crusades."

In the summer of 1963, for example, with the tax cut far from an accomplished fact, Heller had to swallow a painful defeat at the hands of Messrs. Dillon and Martin: an increase in the FRB discount rate from 3 to 3½ percent, the first increase in three years. This decision sharply divided the Administration; indeed, it divided the Federal Reserve Board itself. Dillon had made it clear in testimony July 9, 1963, before the Joint Economic Committee that he thought short-term interest rates had to go up in order to stem the outflow of short-term capital, and thus help correct the balance of payments deficit.

Heller feared that a rise in short-term rates would be accompanied, inevitably, by an increase in long-term rates, which would put a damper on expansion at home. But at a White

House conference conducted by the President, and attended by Dillon, Undersecretary Robert Roosa, Chairman Martin, and Heller, the President ruled out Heller's arguments.

Gamely, Heller defended this turn of the tighter-money screw before the Ways and Means Committee of the House on July 25. But he did "categorically reject" the suggestion—made by the conservative Bank for International Settlements at Basle, Switzerland, among others—that the whole range of money rates be allowed to move up. This could do "serious damage" to the economy, Heller feared.

Even the Federal Reserve made plain its concern about the impact of the higher discount rate on the economy. Normally, the FRB announces any changes in the discount rate in a single sentence, with no elaboration. But this time, the FRB issued an unprecedented two-page press release calling attention to the balance of payments reason for the boost in short-term rates. This time, the FRB said, the increase was not intended as a signal to the business and banking communities that the System was embarking on an anti-inflationary program. "These actions," the announcement said, ". . . do not constitute a change in the System's policy of maintaining monetary conditions conducive to fuller utilization of manpower and other resources in this country."

A cynic observed that a quick translation might be: "Mr. Martin doesn't want to be accused, again, of triggering a recession." The Board of Governors had been fairly evenly split for months on the question of raising the discount rate. It is quite possible that the Board might have hesitated further if Dillon himself were not so completely convinced of the need to take some action to control the enormous balance of payments deficit.

For Heller, it was ironic that a rise in short-term rates was deemed a necessary method of attacking the balance of payments deficit. A year before, the Council of Economic Advisers had warned Kennedy that Dillon and Roosa were too optimistic about the prospects for whittling the deficit down. At the time of the International Monetary Fund meeting in Washington in the fall of 1962, Dillon and Roosa confidently predicted the virtual elimination of the U. S. payments deficit by the end of 1963.

Convinced by their own euphoric appraisal, Dillon and Roosa had put the quietus on the initiative of others, notably the British Chancellor of the Exchequer, Reginald Maudling, who demanded changes in the world's monetary system that could bolster the dollar or pound sterling in time of crisis. The Treasury wanted to follow only limited new ventures. Mostly it wanted to stay on traditional paths, subject to the balance of payments "disciplines," and with Kennedy's blessing, it did— only to find, in mid-1963, that the deficit had risen from an annual rate of a little more than $3 billion to a $5 billion-plus rate in the second quarter of 1963.

However, backed by Undersecretary George Ball and White House aide Carl Kaysen (now back at Harvard), Heller worked assiduously behind the scenes to convince President Kennedy of the need for basic reforms to bolster international liquidity. Walter S. Salant's report for the Brookings Institution on the balance of payments, commissioned by the CEA, helped to support this general view. As a result, the President in one of his final, significant economic policy decisions, agreed to "reopen the doors"—as one insider put it—that had been slammed shut a year before by Dillon and Roosa. And without so much as blinking an eye, Dillon and Roosa at the 1963 International Monetary Fund meeting sponsored a study of international liquidity by the "Paris Club"—ten big industrial nations—to be completed in time for the Tokyo meeting in 1964. Thus, there is at last under way an examination of problems whose very existence the Treasury scoffed at for more than a year. Traditionally, the conservative Treasury looks askance at any international mechanism—scheme, it would say—which not only might involve sharing sovereignty but tends to be inflationary.

The orthodox ways of correcting a balance of payments deficit, of course, are devaluation, trade protection, a major deflation at home, and abandoning commitments abroad. President Kennedy had from the start ruled out devaluation of the dollar, and the nation had no intention of suddenly going protectionist, throwing the economy at home into a complete tailspin, or abandoning our many obligations around the world. The single element working to correct the U. S. payments deficit was inflation abroad, which gave American exports an extra edge in world markets. Thus, the Heller-Ball-Kaysen group successfully argued with the President that the U. S. needed some new approach to relieve present and potential pressures on our gold reserves, and eliminate the need to rely so heavily on drastically restrictive measures like higher interest rates.

The Heller group, as did Maudling in Britain, insisted that they key thing was to solve the international payments problem without deflating the economy at home. The fact that Kennedy eventually swung around to this as a proper goal was a major victory for the liberals. It took a long course of persuasion—but stands as evidence that even though he was a cautious man, the progressive elements around President Kennedy were able to stimulate his thinking, when they tried.

To a great extent, Kennedy gave Heller, as chairman of the Council of Economic Advisers, a free hand to take more advanced positions than the Administration was ready to adopt. To be sure, there was a political dividend in this for Kennedy, in that it accorded the Administration a useful liberal façade. But Heller can also be a genuine front-runner, as Dillon suggests, generating new ideas. The CEA's annual reports have contributed greatly to the public's economic education, especially the 1962 report which developed what might be called the "economic conscience" of the New Frontier. This may eventually be regarded as a unique state paper, because it urged the nation "to face the question of public versus private expenditures pragmatically, in terms of intrinsic merits and costs, not in terms of fixed preconceptions."

This was farther than Kennedy and Dillon were prepared to go. It is somewhat farther than Heller himself has gone since. It is far out front of the Johnsonian philosophy, anchored to reduced federal spending, and a full commitment to the virtues of the private sector.

That report didn't attempt to suggest the right mix of public and private investment, but left no conclusion except that there had to be *some* increase in government spending for transportation, housing, education, health, and other social programs that can't be handled exclusively by the private economy. It pointed to the enormous waste from early school dropouts—and it was a year ahead of the Administration in blueprinting the "national disgrace" of racial discrimination.

It was a strong and courageous document, unhappily unequaled since. It undoubtedly helped shape business opinion of Mr. Heller. But the front-runner has a tough job; to be useful, his ideas have to be provocative. And they will be new to many people. A front-runner for politicians has an especially stiff sales resistance to overcome. This means that if the President's chief economic adviser is doing his job, he will have to accept the strain of leading the way, which doubtless is tougher and less enjoyable than just keeping pace with the man in the White House.

| X | *Kennedy, the Public Interest, and the Labor Movement* |

FOR the leaders of organized labor—excluding, of course, James R. Hoffa—the election of John F. Kennedy amounted to a release from the bondage of the Eisenhower years. Labor had fought hard for Kennedy, and could reasonably expect to play an important role in the new Administration.

But any fears that the Kennedy Administration would be excessively pro-labor were unreal; the hard fact of the matter is that a Democratic Administration does not have to deal out undue favors to labor, which is bound to it ideologically and has, literally, no place else to go.

Moreover, a good President should not be *pro-labor* any more than *anti-business*. He must, as Arthur Goldberg says, be *pro* all of the people, and if that sounds a bit trite, it is nevertheless true. Kennedy's record shows that he was sympathetic to labor's goal of full employment, a rising standard of living, and other social objectives. He even moved ahead of the labor movement on the urgent race relations question.

At the same time, Kennedy insisted on holding down wage demands in order to contain inflation, emphasized the public interest—rather than labor's—in collective bargaining disputes, and although he desperately tried to avoid it, followed the compulsory arbitration route in warding off a national railroad strike in August, 1963. It remained for Lyndon Johnson to recoup this situation neatly in 1964, and to avert a crisis in which some Congressmen might have been tempted to write compulsory arbitration permanently into the Railway Labor Act.

To a considerable degree, the labor movement is trapped by its affiliation with the Democratic Party. It is tied so definitively, in economic and political issues, to the Democrats that it has little independence of action left. For example, when Mr. Kennedy abandoned meaningful tax reform, and accepted proposed legislation favoring the high income groups, the American Federation of Labor–Congress of Industrial Organizations (AFL-CIO) could only sputter helplessly. Its rationale was that if it opposed the Democratic proposals, it would only be aligning itself with the Republican alternative, which it considered worse.

"The unions . . . are being rather careful not to prod [the President] too hard," *The Economist* wrote. "A Democratic President requires the support of organised labour, and Mr. Kennedy has enjoyed such support throughout his political career. But the unions also need the protection of a Democratic President against those elements in the State legislatures and in Congress which would like very much to impose curbs of varying severity on organized labour. The unions may criticise Mr. Kennedy, but not to the point of helping his and their opponents." [3]

In a revealing self-analysis published in 1963 by the Center for the Study of Democratic Institutions (University of California at Berkeley), a West Coast auto workers' union executive remarked: "When I came up in the trade union movement, our teachers were trade unionists with class struggle backgrounds of one kind or another. . . . Now . . . when we go to a trade union educational class, we talk about which wing of the Democratic Party we are going to support."

For Kennedy's years in office, labor leaders were frustrated by his stands on domestic issues they felt too timid. And when Kennedy pleaded the exigencies of balance of payments "constraints," labor leaders privately insisted that this was a convenient excuse for failure to take bold action—but in public, they held their tongues.

In early 1962, for example, AFL-CIO President George Meany told a conference on unemployment that "the great lack in the Administration and in the country is a sense of urgency of this problem." But he added: "The President and his Administration are basically sound." The sum of the Meany criticism: "In some areas, we do question their tactics." [2] In 1963, at the Council meeting at Miami Beach, a devastating analysis of the Kennedy tax program was deleted from the published economic policy statement, in order to keep the AFL-CIO's disagreements with Kennedy out of the public prints. Even Walter Reuther, an activist who feels that Meany is a plodding detriment to the union movement, tended to soften his criticism of the Administration. "The problem is not the Administration, nor Mr. Kennedy," Reuther concluded, "it's Congress. John Kennedy is prepared to do what is necessary, but Congress holds back." [2]

Organized labor didn't see the picture in blacks and whites, and with good reason. The Kennedy years had brought a $100 billion bulge in the gross national product from 1960 to 1963, and for those who were working, wages (and overtime) were at a record peak. From the very first days of the Kennedy Administration, much progressive legislation had been bulled through Congress: the first manpower training act in history, a depressed areas bill, improvements in minimum wages, unemployment compensation, and Social Security, to mention a few.

Moreover, labor had a new role of dignity under Kennedy; its counsel was not sought reluctantly or irregularly. It had favorably disposed friends in both Secretary of Labor Arthur Goldberg and his successor, W. Willard Wirtz. It was a full partner with business and Government in the Labor-Management Advisory Council. And even if he was one of the brains, and not one of the politicians who really run the labor movement, Arthur Goldberg's promotion to the Supreme Court was a prideful moment for every workingman.

Beyond all of this, labor leaders were just as acceptable at the White House dinner as conference table, and this is a status symbol as meaningful to the graduate of the picket line as it is to the president of the Pocatello, Idaho, Chamber of Commerce. In the summer of 1963, finding Meany in Europe, Kennedy took him along on his sentimental trip to Ireland. Once, the burly ex-plumber felt enough "at home" at the White House to climb onto a fragile State Dining Room chair, and announce: "I've always wanted to stand on one of Mrs. Kennedy's chairs."

For all the good fellowship, there was, nevertheless, a basic conflict between the Administration and labor. Kennedy had demanded the same measure of moderation from labor in wage policy and in collective bargaining that he sought from business on the price side. For the first time in U. S. peacetime history, a President—a Democrat and liberal at that—had told the unions they had to limit their wage demands, and that in some key areas, strikes could not be tolerated.

Goldberg argued that the nation could no longer afford to let giant unions and giant industry fight things out while the public—not represented at the bargaining tables—got hurt. It was only logical, Goldberg felt, that the Government should identify the public interest, and actively help labor and management settle their differences. Obviously, this not only meant that the Kennedy Administration could not countenance anything like the marathon 1959 steel strike, but it also had to anticipate and head off such power struggles in the private economy before they started.

To provide a top-level forum for the development of this philosophy, Goldberg persuaded Kennedy to appoint a 21-man Labor-Management Advisory Committee, representing the unions, business, and the public. This committee not only kept key labor and industrial people in continuous contact, it gave the Administration a chance to hammer away at the theme that the Federal Government had to exercise more responsibility in collective bargaining matters.

All told, this was a pretty stiff dose of medicine for labor to take, and it didn't go down any easier at the start because it was prescribed and administered by Dr. Goldberg. If anything, that was harder. Goldberg had not been Meany's choice for Secretary of Labor to begin with—Meany had recommended, instead, any one of six AFL-CIO officers.[4] There were some highups in the labor movement who grumbled that "Arthur leans over backward to show that he is not pro-labor." When Goldberg spoke out vigorously against work stoppages at the nation's missile bases, and toured construction sites to tell workers directly that strikes could not be tolerated, some AFL-CIO leaders considered this grandstanding on Goldberg's part, but there was little they could do about it. Had it been Mr. Eisenhower in the White House, labor leaders would have rebelled openly. But this only shows that there is as much blind faith in the "conventional wisdom" in the labor movement as in the business community. Goldberg succeeded, in the missile bases situation, in contriving a formula to handle the disputes—and still head off a tough, anti-union law that Senator John J. McClellan was driving for, and surely would have obtained. Goldberg set up the Missile Sites Labor Commission, obtained a no-strike, no-lockout pledge from the unions and companies involved, and achieved labor peace in an exceptionally touchy area. It was a brilliant and successful solution.

The new posture that the labor movement had to deal with was the concept of the "public interest." [5] As developed by Goldberg and followed, with some variation in emphasis, by Wirtz, the public interest is paramount, not labor's or management's. Where Eisenhower believed in a pure laissez-faire policy, Kennedy boldly and imaginatively interjected his Administration into wage disputes. Goldberg explained it this way:

> The issues in labor-management affairs are far too complex, far too potent, and far too influential on the rest of society to be resolved on the old testing grounds of force and power. Yet many times the parties are unable to find an alternate ground without the aid and assistance of a third party. The mediation and arbitration process today must be used to a greater extent to avert the wasteful referral of disputes to mere clashes of power.
>
> This truth also calls for the greater exercise of government responsibility in the area of collective bargaining.
>
> When I suggest that government should exercise greater responsibility in the collective bargaining area, I do not mean by this that the government should impose or dictate terms of settlement. I do not mean that it is desirable to impose by law the decisions of a third party. I am sure that I share with you the conviction that compulsory arbitration is inimical to our traditions and system of free collective bargaining.
>
> The government rather should improve its historic role of defining the national goal and of utilizing mediation to assist in keeping the peace and in making sure the peace is a sound and beneficial peace. In the past when government officials were called upon to assist in collective bargaining their only aim was to achieve a settlement.
>
> Today, in the light of our nation's commitments both at home and abroad, government and private mediators must increasingly provide guidelines to the parties to insure that the

settlements reached are right settlements that are not only in the interest of the parties themselves but which also take into account the public interest.

The government must give better aid to collective bargaining through improved good office and mediation procedures but also through better and more precise economic data—which is provided before the fact not as a *post-mortem* inquest; so as to assist settlements, not simply analyze them.

And most important of all, the government must have the courage to assert the national interest as President Kennedy is doing so forthrightly. No one wants government intervention, but everyone expects the government to assert and define the national interest.[6]

The logical follow-through—a legislative proposal to provide the nation with new machinery to deal with labor disputes in key industries—never came. During the 1960 campaign, Kennedy had promised a revision of the inadequate Taft-Hartley law, and both Goldberg and Wirtz tried tentative drafts of a new law.

But the White House temporized here, as it had done in many other situations, fearing, as one aide said, it would open "a can of worms." The concern at 1600 Pennsylvania Avenue was that any legislative request to amend Taft-Hartley would provide a field day for the Barry Goldwaters and others bent on restrictive labor legislation. The unions agreed with this diagnosis. Thus, the utterly sensible idea of providing fact-finding boards with the authority to make public recommendations for settlements in key disputes—which would have been the heart of either Goldberg's or Wirtz's legislative proposals—has yet to come to fruition.

Instead, the Administration depended on Goldberg's willingness and ability—and then on Wirtz's—to spend more time putting out fires than running the Labor Department. This proved unsettling to labor and management, which defined these *ad hoc* government efforts as "meddling." Under the time-honored rules, the American institution of free collective bargaining was supposed to be sacrosanct; the Government's role should be limited to an assurance of equality of bargaining power between the parties.

This is clearly the right policy if there are no overriding considerations. But now, there were. A technological revolution on a scale never faced before was under way, and even more dramatic changes were likely in the years ahead. Moreover, international trade and competition were growing factors in many industries, and the over-all problem of the U. S. balance of payments position affected government policy at home. As John T. Dunlop, chairman of the Harvard University Department of Economics, told the White House conference on economic issues: "We have had stringent requirements on collective bargaining before, but never before has that institution tried to walk the narrow lines of price stability and full employment and other qualitative tests that it now faces." [7]

Public attitudes toward unions and strikes were also in a process of evolution. Even though the loss of time from strikes has been negligible in recent years—one-seventh of 1 percent of all time worked—public tolerance had worn thin because of a few well-publicized strikes, such as the longshoremen and newspaper strikes in New York, and the Philadelphia transit tie-up, where the community suffered immediate hardship or inconvenience, while the parties affected were protected by strike benefits, or strike insurance. Moreover, with growing affluence of American society, including unionized and nonunionized workers, the "public" doesn't identify itself with the "workingman" the way it used to.

Union leaders thus have had to deal with a new mix in industrial society, growing pressures to observe the national interest, a cooling public enthusiasm; and at the same time, act within the framework of restraints on wages contained in the now famous wage-price guidelines promulgated in early 1962 by the Kennedy Administration's Council of Economic Advisers. More properly called "Guideposts for Noninflationary Wage and Price Behavior," this yardstick in essence suggested that wage increases be kept within productivity bounds. In the words of the Economic Report, "The general guide for noninflationary wage behavior is that the rate of increase in wage rates (including fringe benefits) in each industry be equal to the trend rate of over-all productivity increase." For the economy as a whole, such a rule would lead to stable labor costs per unit of output. As for price behavior, the yardstick called for "price reductions if the industry's rate of productivity increase exceeds the over-all rate—for this would mean declining unit labor costs; it calls for an appropriate increase in price if the opposite relationship prevails; and it calls for stable prices if the two rates of productivity increase are equal." [8]

There were qualifications and exceptions, but with over-all productivity estimated at between 2.5 percent and 3.5 percent, the public quickly got the picture: wage increases beyond that level would be considered inflationary.

In December, 1961 (while the Council's guideposts were being formulated), Goldberg carried the campaign directly to the AFL-CIO convention at Miami Beach. When he called on labor not only to show restraint in wage demands, but to abandon resistance to automation and "restrictive practices that cut down industrial efficiency," he got a cool reception. Moreover, Goldberg said, the unions had to adopt a more sophisticated view of profits, which provide new enterprises and new jobs. And his final word struck hardest: the right to strike wasn't unlimited. "The freedom to bargain collectively," Goldberg said at Miami Beach, "the freedom to seek higher wages and better working conditions, the freedom to strike, are not unlimited freedoms. They are freedoms that imply responsibility. They must be exercised in good faith and in full recognition of the public interest."

Labor fussed about the guidelines, fearing that the productivity range would become a ceiling on the wage increases they could negotiate. The unions had a vision of Uncle Sam, with Walter Heller's Economic Report in hand, looking over the shoulder of the negotiators at every bargaining table. But the pressure was for the over-all result, not an automatic application of a 3 percent ceiling to every wage dispute. In some cases, to be sure, that was the precise idea; in the forthcoming steel negotiations, for example, the Government very much wanted wages to be held within the 2.5-3.5 percent range as a symbol of what it was trying to accomplish.

For all of labor's worries at the time that the guidelines were imposed, what developed was that unemployment and the slack economy, much more than the guidelines, set the outer limits on wage advances for much of 1962 and 1963. Some clever labor leaders, like Joseph A. Beirne, president of the Communications Workers of America (AFL-CIO), latched onto the guidelines because they helped establish a floor, rather than a ceiling, for wages. When Beirne got a package settlement of 9 cents, or about a 3.5 percent wage increase, in the telephone industry in 1962, he pointed patriotically to the guidelines. It was the best he could have done without them, but Beirne's stroke of genius in welcoming the guidelines helped explain the settlement to his union, and made the Council of Economic Advisers happy.

By the end of 1963, productivity threatened to scoot so far ahead of real wage increases that some economists feared a recession would develop if the labor share of the GNP did not advance. Moreover, price increases throughout industry were beginning to pop up frequently where a strict interpretation of the guidelines would have called for stability, or even reductions. President Johnson's first economic report early in 1964 recognized the potential for a new round of inflation, and put special emphasis on the need for price reductions in industries which had piled up big profits by ignoring the Kennedy guideposts.

President Johnson continually reiterated a demand that both business and labor show restraint in 1964. He carried this word to the UAW convention in Atlantic City, in March—repeating some of Kennedy's own words in the same hall two years before. As the economy moved ahead, Johnson feared that there might be a "cost-push" inflation more serious than anything that developed during Kennedy's Administration. His notion was that this could be avoided, as he told businessmen and labor leaders (invited with their wives) at a brace of White House dinners, "if everyone behaves."

Looking at it quite unemotionally, the Kennedy Administration established a record for price stability through mid-1963 of which it was egregiously proud. This record—which the Administration emphasized needed to be extended for balance of payments reasons—was made because the economy was sluggish. If Kennedy had been able to slash unemployment, prices wouldn't have been so stable. In his first public address after joining the Council of Economic Advisers in 1963, member John P. Lewis said candidly:

". . . The United States has chalked up a relatively excellent record of price stability since 1958—relative, that is, to all other industrialized free economies except Canada. However, many of us feel that a good part of the explanation of this record is the persistent sluggishness and excessive unemployment the United States has suffered since 1957. And this plainly raises the question of whether the price of our recent price stability has been too high." [9]

When labor looks back on the Kennedy Administration, it finds that its philosophic disagreements stemmed not only from wage policy itself, but with the drift of opinion toward curbing labor's key prerogative—the right to strike. Increasingly, as the "third man at the bargaining table" appeared on the national scene, there seeped into the public consciousness the notion that strikes—big or little, in "key" industries or elsewhere— were wasteful, archaic, immoral, or a combination of all three. [10]

Under President Kennedy, the Government had interjected itself into a variety of labor-management disputes with mixed success, and adopted the policy that strikes in basic industries, such as the railroads, airlines, and other public carriers, could not be tolerated. Some officials looked yearningly at Sweden, where highly organized unions and management groups had worked out a system—including labor courts—that had virtually eliminated strikes. As minimal as is the U. S. loss of worktime to strikes, the Swedish loss, *after* making adjustments for the difference in the size of the countries, is only 1/170 of ours.

Those who were convinced that the collective bargaining system had undergone a serious erosion began to speak approvingly of compulsory arbitration. Walter Lippmann, for example, said: "The country has outgrown the existing machinery for dealing with big labor disputes. But the country has not yet grown up to a consensus on the new machinery to replace it. When a new system of industrial relations is established, it is bound to consist of some form of judicial inquiry and judgment. . . . We may say then that the old system of labor relations with strikes and lockouts is obsolete for the key industries, and that eventually, it is going to be replaced by a system of compulsory arbitration." [11]

It seemed very clear, late in 1962 and 1963, that if labor and management didn't find the means to cope with the larger issues dividing them, and continued on a collision course that disaffected the public-at-large, Congress might resort to compulsory arbitration. As a matter of fact, a precedent for general compulsory arbitration was established when Congress passed, in August, 1963—for the first time—a special law which forced the railroad brotherhoods and rail management to arbitrate the two key issues that had been in dispute for four years.

In November 1963, the arbitration award, as expected, finally settled the issue of obsolescent jobs in favor of the railroads. And it was this determination of the toughest problem that led to the most dramatic labor news story of 1964—an eleventh-hour intervention by President Johnson that postponed, and finally washed out, the threat of a nationwide rail strike over the remaining issues. This doesn't detract in the least from the brilliance of Johnson's determined and successful effort to force the brotherhoods and the carriers to reach an agreement through the process of collective bargaining.

Johnson moved the negotiations into the White House—at times, in his own oval office—hovered over them like a mother hen, and used the full force of his drive and his evangelism to get a settlement. When both sides balked, initially, at agreeing to a 15-day moratorium, Johnson said: "Give me a chance— give me a chance to crack it." Later, Roy Davidson, head of the engineers' brotherhood, defended his withdrawal of the strike call by observing that Johnson was "sincere, even humble." Davidson wrote in his union paper: "You don't defy the President of the United States when he makes a request of you." The Johnsonian "request" for a strike delay was overwhelming. When he discovered that Charles Luna, head of the trainmen's brotherhood, was delayed in Winnipeg, Canada, he sent an Air Force plane at a cost of $3,000 to get him. Then, pleading with Luna, a fellow Texan, Johnson said: "Charlie, I haven't had a crack at this—and it's not one of those Damyankees asking you."

To another recalcitrant that eventful night in the Cabinet room on April 9, 1964, Johnson delivered a folksy account of how, as a young Congressman, he was impatient, and "blew up" at one of his contemporaries. "But I learned," the President continued, "that you can tell somebody to go to hell, but you can't make him do it."

The brotherhood and management men got the message. Although they all were certain that Johnson's effort would fail, they agreed to one more delay, and the unique LBJ brand of earnestness, determination, and cajoling paid off. His *tour de force* was not only a tremendous personal coup, but a restorative, at least temporarily, for collective bargaining engineered by a man who had almost no formal experience in labor relations. It proved that his superlative political skills, finely honed in thirty years on Capitol Hill, were transferable to the White House, and completely adaptable to nonlegislative problems.

One of the reasons that the rail dispute drifted on for four years was the Government's repeated insistence that a strike could not be tolerated: both sides operated with near-assurance that the Government would step in, one way or another, to prevent a strike. But in addition to governmental (and public) distaste for strikes, there was another factor minimizing the usefulness of the strike weapon: automation itself. For example, Beirne, president of the ninth largest of the AFL-CIO unions, has seen his strike power dwindle as automated switchboards replace telephone girls. "The strike is not the weapon it was in the past," Beirne says flatly. Much the same is true of the chemicals, petroleum, and other industries. In an abortive oil refinery strike where a handful of supervisors kept the plant running at two-thirds capacity while the entire production force walked off the job, a frustrated labor leader is reported to have said: "We should have pulled a couple of transistors instead of the men."

In an excellent article in the *Monthly Labor Review*, Joseph W. Block of the BLS observed that ". . . the strike has shed much of its emotional overtones. . . . The labor movement . . . is not about to disown its use of the strike in peacetime, even if, at times, it may deny parentage. It not only remains the ultimate, if undesirable weapon . . . it is, to the labor movement, still the ultimate test of a free society." [12]

Yet, as Block went on to point out, it is the threat of a strike, rather than the strike itself, which is indispensable to labor. Today's public considers strikes a crude way to settle issues, and seems to be saying that there must be some other way. Whether unions like it or not, the way will probably have to be discovered, just in terms of self-preservation, for as we have seen, the strike is increasingly less of an answer in an automated world.

Automation, more than any other factor, brings all the new collective bargaining issues into focus. It is doubtless true that advancing technology, over the long run of history, gives rise to new industries and new jobs. The automobile industry, as we are often reminded, created many more job opportunities than were lost when Henry Ford wrote finis to the horse-and-buggy trade. But the fact is that the new jobs generated by the combined genius of the sciences and the arts are of no comfort to the men displaced today. There is, moreover, some responsible opinion—although many disagree—that automation represents a different and more pervasive impact on the labor force than the technological gains in other periods. (See Chapter XIII.)

AFL-CIO President George Meany says: "The job is the important thing. It used to be, if a fellow lost his job, there was some place or some possibility of some other industry expanding. Now, with automation, people with many years of seniority are laid off—and permanently." [13] Or, as Secretary Wirtz puts it neatly: "It is one thing to bargain about the terms of employment—and quite another to bargain about the terms of unemployment."

The "gut" issue in collective bargaining today—as has been demonstrated in the record 116-day steel strike of 1959, the 1961-62 airlines' cases, the newspaper strikes in 1962-63—is not wages or working conditions, but job security. What is up for discussion, in most cases, is not better pay or hours, but the jobs themselves. Today, the unions are fighting a rear-guard action to hang onto what they've got, spread the work around—and where all else fails, force management to pay attention to the human tragedies involved when a new plant or a new process ends a man's usefulness to society. "Featherbedding" mirrors man's instinctive fight for survival. As Secretary Wirtz once said, "featherbedding . . . is a reflection . . . however unjustifiable . . . of people's wanting very much to work and wanting enough to work that they will resort to the indignity of hanging onto a job which perhaps should not be there." [14]

A look at the steel industry helps to clarify the situation. There have been vast changes in steelmaking in the past few years with the introduction of the oxygen furnace, continuous casting of ingots, and other techniques. These are already beginning to be reflected in productivity increases so great that many experts in Pittsburgh say that "it is reminiscent of what happened in coal. . . . In 10 or 12 years, today's employment figures will look high." In the 12-month span between April, 1962, and April, 1963, monthly output of steel rose more than 1,400,000 ingot tons while the production of work force dropped by 30,000 men.[15] Faced with shrinking employment—10 years ago there were 570,000 steel production workers, 150,000 more than in 1963—it is little wonder that David McDonald bargained not for a wage increase, but for 13 weeks of paid holidays for senior workers every five years. This sabbatical is expected to stretch regular work among 32,000 extra men.

Thus, reduced hours—in the absence of an expanding economy—are sought by labor unions as one answer to the human ravages of automation. The steelworkers boasted that their extended vacation plan lopped two hours off the workweek of those covered, or one full hour, on the average, for the total membership of the union. In the aluminum industry, where a similar but slightly more favorable contract was negotiated, the net shrinkage was 1.5 hours. "The 40-hour week in basic steel, aluminum, and can production in effect has passed into history," the union proudly asserted.[16]

Intermittently, almost from the very beginning of the Kennedy Administration, labor has loudly and persistently demanded a 35-hour week, and the Administration just as firmly and consistently turned a deaf ear to the plea. The 35-hour week, as Reuther says, is a "defense mechanism." Labor would rather see an expanding economy with full 40-hour paychecks for all who want to work, rather than fight to reduce the workweek abruptly. Very obviously, 40 hours' pay for a 35-hour week represents a 14 percent increase in hourly rates—a wage boost that lacks backing by any segment in the economy. But labor's attitude is that it has no alternative to demanding shorter hours, in order to make room on payrolls for those without work. "When society isn't dealing with the unemployment problem," Reuther says, "the labor movement has to fight negatively for a shorter workweek." [17]

At hearings conducted by a subcommittee of the Joint Economic Committee at the end of 1961, Paul Samuelson expressed the official Kennedy Administration viewpoint when he said that a shorter workweek would be "defeatist" and "a disaster of the first magnitude." But Meany, at the same hearings, said: ". . . If this accentuated trend toward automation and technological improvement with displacement . . . continues, we have got to shorten the hours. I do not know of any other approach."

As Secretary of Labor, Goldberg routinely brushed the 35-hour workweek demand aside. "An artifically short workweek," he would say, "is sharing unemployment, not jobs." Wirtz, when he took over from Goldberg in mid-1962, had a slightly different attitude. He agreed that an abrupt change to a 35-hour week, with take-home pay maintained, would be bad economics. But Wirtz recognized that the demand for a shorter workweek represented a real frustration on labor's part that merits attention.

"The proposal is honorably put," Wirtz told the National Press Club, ". . . and on that basis, it ought to be considered honestly. . . . There is only one honest answer to the proposal of the 35-hour week. And that is a proposal as to how we come up with the jobs which will supply work opportunities to the additional four million people in this country who want them. And, until we come up with that answer, I take it that one proposition is as much entitled to . . . our consideration as another." [18]

Labor itself did not expect to win a legislative reduction to a 35-hour week in the near future, unless a real economic depression, meaning a 10 to 15 percent unemployment rate, developed. But the national publicity behind the 35-hour week was designed to put some steam behind local unions' efforts to get shorter hours at the bargaining table.

When Harry Van Arsdale, Jr., won a 25-hour week for his New York electrical workers' local in January, 1962, he was publicly scolded by the President at a press conference ("I regret it"), and by Goldberg in private, unprintable words. Van Arsdale, whose highly paid electricians were already on a 30-hour week, was viewed by the top leadership of the AFL-CIO as greedy.[19] His success also made business scoff at Kennedy's assurances that he could exert pressure on the labor movement.

It was, of course, a special situation, made possible by the fact that the booming New York construction industry played ball with Van Arsdale, and simply passed the higher costs on to buyers or renters (including the Government) of apartments, office buildings, and housing projects.

By midsummer of 1962, George Meany felt that he had to take a more positive stand for a shorter workweek, regardless of the Administration's concerns about inflation. As long as there was a prospect for economic recovery, Meany went along—unenthusiastically—with Kennedy's caution that a shorter workweek would bring inflation. Just prior to Van Arsdale's coup, as a matter of fact, the first report of the President's Labor-Management Advisory Committee—on automation problems—said that efforts should be directed to "full employment, rather than a general reduction in the hours of work." [20] Meany and other labor members of the committee joined in a qualifying footnote warning that unless the economy moved ahead, shorter hours would indeed be necessary, but they didn't argue with the majority view that a shorter workweek was *not* the indicated policy for that time.

But as the year wore on, the combination of the economic gap and the rise of automation forced a change. There was no longer a disposition to sneer at Van Arsdale.

On a realistic basis, neither Meany nor other labor leaders expected to do more than harass the Administration with the 35-hour week idea—and they did this effectively. More than once, Mr. Kennedy interpolated warnings in his speeches to conservative groups about "labor unrest . . . and the drive for a 35-hour week." But even if they do not expect to hit pay dirt soon, labor leaders think that the trend toward shorter hours is inevitable.

It most likely will be, without legislation. Secretary Wirtz points out that since the beginning of this century, the workweek has been reduced, on the average, by one-half of 1 percent —or 12 minutes—a year. That's an hour every five years. Prior to 1860, the work rule was dawn to dusk. That meant six days of 12 hours, or a backbreaking 72 hours each week. The workweek which was 51 to 55 hours in 1910, shrank to 48 hours in 1920; to 44 hours in 1929; to 40 hours by 1946. As Meany says, there is little sacrosanct about any given number of hours to be worked in any one week.

"We recognize the fact," says Wirtz, "that in collective bargaining there will be discussions . . . about the workweek, about vacations, about holidays . . . an adjustment to the increasingly productive economy. . . . The shortening of the workweek which has taken place over the years as a concomitant of increasing production . . . has been considered a healthy thing for society and the economy. That development is still going on." [21]

The talk about the shorter workweek won't die down quickly or easily; and there is no reason that it should. As President Kennedy himself said on his last trip to the West Coast, in the fall of 1963, eventually "we're going to find the workweek reduced." In an impromptu speech at Whiskeytown, California, Kennedy said that in 40 years there would be 350,000,000 Americans, where there are now only 190,000,000. "What will they do? What kind of country will they find? . . . This country is changing. We had a 58-hour week, a 48-hour week, and a 40-hour week. As machines take more and more of the jobs of men, we are going to find the workweek reduced, and we are going to find people wondering what they should do." [22] The President made clear at a later press conference that the main thrust of his California remarks was directed to the greater recreational needs that the nation would have to provide in the future. And he hadn't changed his mind about the illogic of a legislated 35-hour week.

But pressed by time and events, a shorter workweek appeared to be one of the few issues on which labor leaders could unite, and fire up an emotional campaign. It would take careful planning, however. Recent statistics published by the Bureau of Labor Statistics indicate that side by side with steady unemployment, workers who *are* on the job have been getting increasing measures of overtime. Despite the impression given the public by such spectacular developments as Van Arsdale's 25-hour week (his electricians earn $235.60 when working 40 hours) there has been no widespread adoption of less-than-40-hour weeks in the production industries. About 18 percent of the labor force works 8 or more hours above the 40-hour mark, compared with 13 percent in 1948.[23] Leaving agriculture aside, full-time employees in industry average about 44 hours a week, a level unchanged over the past 15 years. It is evident from these figures that most nonfarm employees either need or choose extra income over leisure. It will take some doing to get them to give up their best-paid hours of the week, an effort that President Johnson seems willing to try in an effort to create a few hundred thousand new jobs.

The strains of a slack economy, in which jobs are scarce, have put the whole collective bargaining process to new tests. There are some experts, like Paul Jacobs, former union organizer, who think, simply, that collective bargaining as we have known it is dead.[24] There can be little doubt that automation cuts deeply into the areas where the unions are strongest—manufacturing, mining, and transportation—and that the growth of the working force is among the professional and white collar classes, where the unions are weakest. Walter Reuther's Industrial Union Department, which has done the best job of trying to organize white-collar workers, has discovered how difficult it is to whip up enthusiasm for joining a union. Not the least of the reasons is that the image of unionism has become tarnished by the Hoffas and other hoodlum elements.

Solomon Barkin, Textile Workers Union research director, wrote in 1961 that "a certain lassitude has taken over the union movement itself. Little is left of the proselytizing spirit. . . . The image of the unions as the social conscience of the community has been considerably dimmed." [25] In part, the diminished zeal or sense of purpose that Barkin described is a concomitant of success: the level of pay and working conditions in the United States today is so far advanced over the 1930's that it might be said that the unions have bargained themselves out of their role.

Militancy, once the lifeblood of the unions, has been replaced by conformity. Many old-line unionists consider the AFL-CIO's easy acquiescence in the Kennedy Administration's cautious economic program an abdication of labor's real responsibilities. "Labor's drive has been dulled," one knowledgeable figure in the labor movement says privately. "Labor and management have common ground, of course—the success of the business or industry. But labor and management do not have a common ground in the division of the spoils. If so, why do unions exist? Today, labor leaders are too affluent themselves, and they don't want to rock the boat. They want to be 'one' with the makers and shapers of society. Why, Walter Reuther never even owned a formal dinner jacket until the Kennedy Administration came in!"

There is no doubt that the labor movement in the United States is past its peak. Union labor now represents less than one-fourth of the total labor force, and less than one-third of the industrial work force. Excluded from membership are millions of professional people who feel they can get along well without union affiliation, and also millions of unskilled workers, especially Negroes, without whom the labor movement has chosen to get along. The irresistible conclusion is that just in terms of numbers, the political power of the labor unions is slipping.

"The 'powerful' labor movement . . . today . . . [is] declining in numbers as the labor force grows, its good name besmirched, its expansion blocked by worker indifference and legal obstructions," wrote a thoughtful labor man in 1961. "Only the collective bargaining power of long-established unions and the effectiveness of labor support for social legislation remain relatively unimpaired, and they cannot long survive the present trend." [26]

Statistics on union membership show that in the 1930's, and again in the 1940's when the war was a spur, the labor unions added new members at a rate of about 1,000,000 each year. In the early 1950's, the increment trailed off to about 200,000 a year. In the late 1950's and early 1960's, there has been no growth at all, even though the labor force has grown by millions. For example, the AFL-CIO's own data show a 1963 dues-paying membership of 12,400,000 (excluding Canadians), less than in 1957 or 1959 and only 100,000 more than in 1955, when the merger of the AFL and CIO took place. In the six years since 1957, when the AFL-CIO roster hit a peak, the nonfarm labor force grew by 4,500,000 million—and the AFL-CIO lost 344,000 dues-paying members (not counting the loss of the Teamsters).

Government figures show that in 1962, total union membership in the United States was 16,586,000, or 22.2 percent of the total labor force, a drop from 23.3 percent in 1960, and from the high level of 25.1 percent in 1954. As a percentage of the non-agricultural labor force, the union membership touched a high of 35.1 percent in 1954, and has been trailing off ever since. In

1960, it was 32.1 percent; in 1961, 30.1 percent; and in 1962, 29.7 percent.

The Labor Department tallies AFL-CIO membership, including Canadian affiliates, this way:

1955	..	16,062,000 (year of the merger)
1956	..	16,904,000
1957	..	16,954,000
1958	..	14,993,000 (Teamsters expelled)
1959	..	15,124,000
1960	..	15,071,000
1962	..	14,835,000

Does this mean that unions are on the way out, as Jacobs suggests? Not necessarily, but the shrinkage of the AFL-CIO, at a time when automation is growing apace, indicates an urgent need for both a reinvigorated union leadership, and for new approaches to collective bargaining.

Already, there have been important adaptations in the form of collective bargaining, some of which got their impetus from the Kennedy-Goldberg-Wirtz insistence that the Government should protect the public interest. It has not been easy to persuade the labor union movement that its very existence may depend on the degree to which it can bring a revitalized imagination to older forms of labor-management wheeling and dealing. In the Kennedy-Johnson years to date, the fact is that the transitional problems have been met, mostly, on a day-to-day, improvised basis. Secretary Wirtz once calculated that the 1962-63 airlines' dispute involved 24 private arbitrators and 39 public representatives, including the President, the Secretary of Labor, the Undersecretary, the National Mediation Board, a special Presidential commission, nine Presidential emergency boards, and three boards of arbitration. In the longshoremen's dispute in 1962, all these plus a special board directed by Senator Wayne Morse of Oregon were necessary.

Out of the era of brinksmanship, however, there have emerged some specific new common denominators in the collective bargaining process:

1. Management and labor have come to see the virtues of bargaining, continuously, throughout the contract period. A notable example is the Human Relations Committee in the steel

industry, the one happy product of the tortuous 116-day strike in 1959-60. "We have to stretch things out," Wirtz says, "so issues don't come down to those last 30 days for resolution." In the auto industry, Reuther and the companies actually started talks in 1963 more than a year ahead of contract expiration date in 1964.

2. Introduction of "neutral" or "third party" advisers or consultants. Such professional advisers being more widely used, facilitating the bargaining process. In effect, they represent the public in a realistic, unemotional way.

3. An arrangement for getting from the current contract period to the next, which means that a repetition of crisis may be avoided. There is wider reliance on voluntary arbitration as one means of accomplishing this.

Over and above these hopeful signs, especially forward-looking leadership in some companies has eased the worker's fear— in A. H. Raskin's graphic phrase—that "he will be cast onto the slag heap by a robot." The best-known example of this is the "Long Range Sharing Plan" put in effect by the Kaiser Steel Co., which not only is a profit-sharing method, but a plan containing an ironclad guarantee that no worker will be laid off because of technological changes or improvements. "Progress sharing" at American Motors is another successful experiment.

From these small beginnings, collective bargaining may eventually be transformed into a system where the Government is a full, tripartite partner in labor-management negotiations. Clark Kerr, well-known mediation expert, and president of the University of California, says: "I . . . think we have entered a new stage in the relationships among labor, management, and the Government. When this stage has been completed, collective bargaining in America will no longer have participating in it two major protagonists—management and labor—with the Government acting only as referee.

"Instead, the Government will be a third force, consciously exerting its influence upon the two other groups, and consciously attempting to solve problems that are beyond the capabilities of management and labor alone." As he explained it to friends just before moving to the Supreme Court, this is precisely the view, also, of Arthur Goldberg, who believes that within the labor movement, there are some elements who overprotect the institution of collective bargaining, which needs to be revised to incorporate the vague but necessary "public interest" concept.

The leadership of the AFL-CIO is sharply divided by such notions, and along lines with which the public is now familiar —Meany vs. Reuther. Firmly and deliberately, Meany says: "I don't think collective bargaining is in trouble. Except for this idea of 'permanent contacts'—and that's not new—it's pretty hard to improve on this system. And I don't think collective bargaining is 'on trial,' either. Sure we've had some strikes, but at the same time, there are hundreds—thousands—of bargains that were made collectively. In a system like that, there'll always be some disputes that don't get settled peacefully, but that's all right." [27]

Meany cites figures which show that time lost by strikes in 1961, 1962, and 1963—one-seventh of 1 percent of hours worked —was less than in any similar period since the end of World War II. Of approximately 150,000 labor agreements made through collective bargaining in 1962, 98 percent were settled peaceably, only 2 percent involved strikes. The Labor Department confirms the Meany data: in 1962, there were 3,550 work stoppages in the U. S., involving 1,300,000 workers, and causing a loss of 19,000,000 man-days of time. To put that figure in some perspective, twice as much time was lost due to work injuries on the job.

Thus, strikes are becoming rare—but even a few can be critical and try the public's patience. Meany recognizes this. "The first reaction of the general public is to place the blame on the union," he says. But he insists that labor will fight hard against the imposition of compulsory arbitration because: "We have to retain the right to strike."

Meany acknowledges that the question of job obsolescence presents labor leaders with new problems. In the February 1963 issue of the *Federationist*, Meany wrote an editorial which observed that "sweeping changes are now under way—changes that affect workers first, but which will profoundly affect the future of everyone. While unions are still primarily concerned with raising the living standards of their members, they are today confronted with the basic problem of economic survival of their members."

The way Meany sees it, all that the new situation requires is an extension of the continuous cooperation between industry and labor, as is now the practice in steel. "I don't think that management and labor should come to the bargaining table as enemies to do battle every two or three years," Meany says. "I think they should be in constant contact—that's the sort of thing that brings industrial peace."

This is as far as Meany wants to go in changing the collective bargaining process. Meany would not open the door, as Kerr and Goldberg would, to a bigger governmental role. (The Meany philosophy, it might be noted in passing, is not inconsistent with the argument of the collective bargainers on the corporate side who say to the Government—Stay out!)

Jack Conway, chief Reuther assistant for the Industrial Union Department of the AFL-CIO—in effect, the old CIO wing—agrees with Meany that the criticism of collective bargaining has been overdone. But the Reuthers and the Conways see a time coming when bargaining over specific issues or within specific industries will have to be supplemented by a new kind of negotiating among labor, management and Government on broad national issues.

As Conway put it:

> . . . Beyond the bargaining within the plant . . . unions and employers must inevitably, and soon, begin to engage in a three-sided negotiation over the operation of manpower training programs, or tariff problems, and eventually investment and fiscal policy as they relate to jobs and full employment.
>
> Because when full employment is an established and accepted continuing feature of our national economy . . . bargaining will necessarily continue with plants and companies in the customary dialogue, but the crucial decisions will probably be made regionally and nationally as is beginning to be the case in England and France, and less obviously but with far greater effect, in Sweden.
>
> . . . Under full employment conditions in the United States . . . the traditional demands of the union movement will undergo transformation. . . . The union structure, the union processes, the union activities, which already have changed more than is generally acknowledged, will inevitably undergo a further dramatic metamorphosis. . . . Our efforts to solve today's problems with yesterday's answers may be feeble. But we will adjust to the future, painful as it may be.[28]

There may be an element of wishful thinking in Conway's analysis, because he would obviously involve the nation in national economic planning—a dreaded word!—as well as in more comprehensive collective bargaining. But at least his eyes are open, and he's looking forward. Collective bargaining, old style, can be really meaningful only in an expanding economy which is growing fast enough to absorb the inflationary impetus of bargains struck by big labor and big management. It's the public that pays the price for the success of this kind of collective bargaining. As Professor Daniel Bell of Columbia University points out, industry often chalks up "higher prices than were warranted by the union gains." [29]

But when collective bargaining tries to settle the question of job security, it has almost always been a failure. The nation's growth rate has been slow, and jobs have been cut by technological advances. Detroit's mechanized lines can turn out about as many cars as they did 10 years ago with 20 percent fewer workers. (For additional discussion of the impact of automation on jobs, see Chapter XIII.)

What the unions have tried to do, in this fix, is to fight a delaying action: increase unemployment benefits, shorten the workweek, lengthen vacations, devise substantial lump-sum severance benefits. The nation has been treated, at the same time, to the spectacle of a scavenging operation; the unions fight among themselves for what's left, as witness, for example, the grubby little jurisdictional argument between the steelworkers and the building trades over maintenance and repair jobs that are "contracted out" of the plant or mill.

The problem has been handled well in a few cases. The Kaiser plan has protected workers against loss of jobs due to automation, and introduced a genuine, cooperative relationship between management and workers. (The handsome returns under the profit-sharing arrangement haven't hurt.) The Pacific Maritime Association and the West Coast longshoremen have an agreement which frees the industry to put in labor-saving devices, while creating a fund to guarantee a fixed income to every longshoreman who was registered in 1960 when the agreement went into effect. Good will and a high sense of social purpose doubtless motivate other companies and unions whose arrangements, formal or otherwise, are not so well known.

But the human costs of technological change in the future may be too great for many industries to adjust unaided. According to IBM President Tom Watson, his giant computer company will double its production in the next 10 years, but he believes that it will be a struggle to keep the present 28,000-man work force from shrinking. The obsolescence of firemen on the railroads became painfully clear in 1963. What was also evident was the practical inability of the presidents of the Railroad Brotherhoods voluntarily to scrap any jobs. And politicians who have to get elected again must understand the problem.

"Useful as it is in other areas, e.g. grievances," says Bell, "collective bargaining works only fitfully as a way of sharing the burdens of such costs. Given the increasing human factor of technological change and the increasingly linked nature of the economy, it seems unlikely that any of these automation problems can be met by other than comprehensive action at the government level. And the realization of this, which is slow in coming, inevitably must create extraordinary changes not only in manpower policy but in the character of education and training, in patterns of investment, and in the structure of the labor movement."

The Kennedy Administration was slow to come to grips with this overwhelmingly important question. Kennedy—in the heat of the crisis over a threatened rail strike—asked Congress to set up an automation commission in midsummer 1963, and Johnson restated the request in his January 1964 messages. There is some evidence that President Johnson is taking the threat of automation somewhat more seriously; Secretary Wirtz, for one, is pressuring him to do so.

Society's response to the sense of utter uselessness that comes to the man eliminated by the machine has been to say piously that progress, after all, is inevitable. One can't be blamed for thinking, fleetingly, of Al Capp's General Bullmoose's sage remark: "Progress is the root of all evil." In this era of "liberal" Democratic control, attrition through death or dropout (except in the rare cases) has become the basic answer to technological unemployment. The unions, industry and the Government should be able to devise something more humane and workable.

William McChesney Martin and the "Fed"

ON A warm Washington afternoon in June of 1961, President Kennedy stretched out comfortably on the four-poster bed in his White House bedroom, lit a cigar, and listened attentively to the members of his economic brain trust. Scattered around the bedroom were Dillon, Heller, friend and adviser John Kenneth Galbraith, a representative of the budget bureau —and William McChesney Martin, Chairman of the Federal Reserve Board.

The second-floor bedroom setting was, of course, a bit unusual; the President had sprained his back spading dirt at a ground-breaking ceremony, and on Dr. Janet Travell's orders, he was getting a bit of post-luncheon rest. But meetings with the economic and fiscal high command, including Martin, had become a part of regular White House routine, and Kennedy had asked the group up to the family quarters rather than break the sequence.

This was one of a series started within the first days of the Kennedy Administration, primarily to bring Martin into discussions at a top level. They continued on a regular basis—averaging about one every five or six weeks—for the entire course of the Kennedy Administration. The cast of characters would be the "Big Four"—Dillon, Martin, Heller, and the Director of the Budget—with an occasional invitation to a member of the Economic Council, or to Undersecretary Robert V. Roosa. (Galbraith, in the capital on a visit from his post in India, was a special guest at the June meeting.) Toward the end of Eisenhower's second term, Treasury Secretary Robert B. Anderson initiated a similar set of meetings. But Eisenhower's meetings were rather formal, and provided more of a summary for the General than a give-and-take discussion of current and future policy.

Kennedy had more interest in economic subjects than Eisenhower had, and a better grasp of them, as well. Martin had never met Kennedy until his first session at the White House early in February, 1961, and he was amazed by Kennedy's understanding of Federal Reserve problems and money-market techniques. Aided by Heller and Council Member James L. Tobin, the President crammed for that first meeting with Martin, and the homework sessions paid off. Coincidentally, Martin had never met Eisenhower until after *his* Inaugural in 1952, and when he did, he was dismayed at Eisenhower's almost complete lack of understanding of monetary matters.

At first, Martin approached close relations with the Kennedy team with an understandable degree of caution. The campaign was hardly ancient history, and despite the assuring tone and content of the Philadelphia speech, Martin wanted to see Kennedy in action. The President, for his part, knew that he would need cooperation from the "Fed," but expected Martin to be intransigent.

But a broad agreement was reached—broader than either man or outside observers could have foreseen earlier. And this was possible, basically, because Kennedy's own brand of economics was much more orthodox than his campaign speeches had indicated. At his very first Cabinet meeting, the President asked each Department head to designate the key problem in his own area, and Secretary Dillon nominated the balance of payments deficit as the nexus of all economic troubles at home and abroad. Such a pronouncement by Dillon carried great weight with President Kennedy. Often, in Cabinet or less formal meetings, Kennedy pondered a problem, then turned to Dillon to ask: "What do you think, Doug?" And sometimes Dillon's views alone were solicited, even with other Cabinet officers present.

On the weighty balance of payments problem, of course, Dillon was the accepted authority. Kennedy soberly agreed with "Doug's" estimate, and committed the Administration to rely only in a limited way on easy money policies to boost the domestic economy. Meanwhile, in the privacy of his own meetings with the Board of Governors and his top staff advisers, Martin laid down the rule that there would be a high degree of cooperation between the Federal Reserve and the Administration.

On a policy basis, the groundwork for an accord was thus prepared; on the personal level it worked out well, too. Neither Kennedy nor Martin seemed to the other to be the ogre he had been represented. "So far as I can see," former chief economist for the FRB Woodlief Thomas said soon after Kennedy took office, "Chairman Martin has closer relationships with this President than he has had with any other." One reason was that Kennedy worked assiduously to develop further his own understanding of the subtle interrelationships between monetary policy, debt management, and fiscal problems. Once, when the President was looking for a shorthand device to keep the Fed's monetary function distinct in his own mind from the Treasury's fiscal responsibilities, Heller suggested: "Just think of the 'M'— Martin for monetary." That was fine, the President agreed, but what would he do if and when Martin left? "That's easy," assured Heller, "then there'll be Mitchell." The reference was to George W. Mitchell, middle-of-the-road Democrat appointed by Kennedy in 1961 to a vacancy on the board.

To friends, Martin confessed that he was downright enthusiastic about Kennedy's way of doing things. Since he could express his views personally and regularly to the President, he felt he was—for the first time—bringing the conservative influence of the Federal Reserve to bear on the White House. Were it not for the "Big Four" sessions, Martin felt that Kennedy might continue to have misconceptions about the Fed. One FRB policy-maker said privately: "They might have thought we were single-purpose screwballs who didn't give a damn about unemployment. This way they know that Martin is just as worried about such things as Galbraith."

This was a considerable change from the pattern of the Eisenhower years. For example, in the spring of 1956, when the FRB and Treasury Secretary George M. Humphrey disagreed on a discount rate increase, Martin was anxious for a chance that never came to discuss it directly with Eisenhower—although Eisenhower's inaccessibility did not inhibit Martin from proceeding with the boost in the rate, the first of a series which probably precipitated the 1957-58 recession. Martin knew that both Humphrey and Economic Council chairman Arthur F. Burns were bitter about the FRB action, but if Martin's name had shown up on the White House appointment list, the financial community would have assumed that some big financial crisis was brewing—or that Martin was being "pressured."

This almost incredible episode illustrates the absurdity of a rigid concept of the "independence" of the Federal Reserve. Even in a so-called businessman's administration like Eisenhower's, the FRB was trapped by a phony mystique, a protective cocoon of its own manufacture. It can be assumed that Eisenhower because his two principal economic advisers opposed an interest rate increase, also opposed Martin's 1956 decision. But he would not initiate a conversation with Martin, abdicating all responsibility for monetary policy to the Federal Reserve. Historians are thus justified in dividing the blame for the economic stagnation of the Eisenhower years between the President and the Federal Reserve. Eisenhower's failure to exert leadership was as serious as the FRB's rigid actions directed to tight money.

The meetings that Anderson set up toward the end of Eisenhower's terms served mostly to inform the Administration of FRB plans. Martin's dealings, even at these sessions, were with Anderson rather than Eisenhower. The wide-ranging sessions with Kennedy were entirely different. "I wish we had the same entree to his *thinking* that he has to ours," a Heller staff man grumbled good-naturedly.

Out of the initial meetings between Kennedy, Dillon, Martin, and Heller came an historic agreement. Martin announced that the Federal Reserve would cooperate with Administration aims by abandoning its long and controversial "bills usually" policy, and instead would buy some government obligations with longer maturities in an effort to drive down the long-term interest rate. This was a step that the Council of Economic Advisers had convinced Kennedy was necessary. The reasoning was that lower long-term interest costs would help stimulate investment, needed to buck up economic growth. But even though a reduction in short-term rates was the classic response to meeting recession at home, the Government would make an effort to *prevent* short-term rates from falling any further. If short-term rates declined, that might accelerate the flow of money abroad seeking a better return and worsen the balance of payments deficit.[1]

This, then, was the basic understanding of convenience between Kennedy and Martin: Kennedy recognized that he couldn't follow the traditional Democratic, easy-money posture to promote recovery, and Martin acknowledged that he had to do something to prevent long-term rates from climbing too high. First called "Operation Nudge," and then "Operation Twist," this was essentially a water-on-both-shoulders approach. Interest rates are supposed to move in a pattern, and the financial community was amazed that Martin would agree to try anything so unorthodox. As a matter of fact, Martin was privately abused by some in Wall Street who accused him of "selling out" to Kennedy, and he had to buck opposition to the policy right within the confines of the magnificent white Georgia marble edifice on Constitution Avenue that houses the FRB.

Martin himself wasn't sure that the policy would work, but he thought he had an obligation to give the plan a chance, since the Administration wanted to try it. Looking back, the results were limited, but very useful. From January, 1961, to the fall of 1963, while the rate on short-term Treasury bills had increased more than 1 full percentage point, the average yield on long-term government securities moved up only 0.2 percentage points. Yields on local issues, and on corporate issues were below the January 1961 levels, and mortgage rates had dropped about ½ point. Not all of this can be chalked up to "Nudge"; a slack economy played a role, too. But the plan undoubtedly helped—and it represented the FRB and National Administration pulling together, instead of apart.

The Administration later claimed, with some pride, that "the ability of monetary policy to support economic expansion at home without stimulating outflows of short-term funds was simultaneously enhanced by new Federal Reserve open market techniques, and by Treasury debt management policies." [2]

If, as Economic Council member Gardner Ackley has observed, the central bank and Martin had been operating according to traditional mores, the monetary brakes would have been considerably tightened early in the Kennedy era. To be sure, this is a subjective question. For example, Martin and Representative Wright Patman of Texas would not agree on how one defines tight money or easy money. But it can hardly be denied that the Federal Reserve, in cooperation with the Treasury, followed a policy of relative ease, through mid-1963, while promoting a monetary expansion that held down long-term interest rates, curbed bank lending rates, and over-all, promoted the nation's economic expansion and growth. The fact that the Federal Reserve probably should have moved even further in these directions doesn't mean that it didn't move at all. Martin confounded many people by failing to be an obstructionist. Paul Samuelson, for example, says that "many of us were rather pleasantly surprised" by the flexibility of the independent Federal Reserve System in its cooperation with the Kennedy Administration.[3] But Paul Douglas and other Senate liberals argue that the Fed is a hotbed of reaction, and worry especially that a new era of tight money may lie ahead of us.

There is a real limit to the extent that Martin commits himself or the Fed to a more liberal posture. When the Fed buys government securities, it pays for them with its check, which, when deposited in a bank by a bond dealer who sells the securities, expands the bank's ability to make loans to its customers. Since a bank needs to hold only a fraction of its deposits as reserves, each added dollar of deposits represents several dollars' worth of lending potential—in recent years, the ratio has been one to six. Thus, the FRB has the awesome power to create (or extinguish) much of the money supply of the country, and it is little wonder that the managers of the System are impressed with the magnitude of their influence and the scope of their responsibility.

The overriding source of disagreement between so-called "tight money" and "easy money" advocates relates to this power of the Federal Reserve to add to or subtract from bank reserves by open market operation. The Fed can influence the money supply in other ways, also. It can raise or lower the discount rate—the rate at which member banks borrow from the central bank, or it can change the reserve ratio of loans to deposits, so that the multiple expansion effect referred to above can be increased or lessened. All of these tools, used together, are what give the Fed its enormous, pervasive influence over the cost and supply of money.[4]

In 1961, even though Heller kept urging Martin to follow an easier money policy, he had to admit candidly that Martin was more reasonable than might have been predicted some months before. Much effort went into making this possible. Not only were the top-level meetings regularized, and given a genuine policy status, but many other regular points of contact for Martin and his staff were arranged. On Monday mornings the schedule called for Martin to go to the Treasury for a meeting with Dillon and his top aides. On Wednesday, the Treasury would return the visit with a delegation led by Undersecretary Roosa. Both of these weekly meetings were devoted to debt management and related problems.

Every other week, Dillon played host to Martin in his private Treasury dining room (facing the East office wing of the White House) with Undersecretary Henry H. Fowler and Heller usually in attendance. Occasionally, others joined in. Heller and Martin met alone on a less routinized basis, usually in Martin's office next to the Federal Reserve board room, or at lunch in the FRB's executive dining room. And occasionally, Heller, Martin, Dillon and the Director of the Budget gathered in the White House prior to one of the sessions with Kennedy. For all of this "togetherness," nobody—least of all Martin—suggests that there was any loss of the Fed's vaunted independence during the Kennedy Administration. Similar close consultation has continued in the Johnson Administration.

"Independence," as applied to the Federal Reserve, is one of those catch phrases which, as Labor Secretary W. Willard Wirtz once said, "corrupt the conversation and prevent the application of wisdom to the real underlying problem before us." [5] There are some words, like "featherbedding," to which the public automatically assigns a minus value. There are others which have a plus concept; "balanced budget," of course, is one. And "independence of the Federal Reserve" in recent years has acquired a worshipful quality among the faithful. Exaggerated notions about the independence of the Fed have been aided and abetted by the System's eagerness to cloak itself with an aura of secrecy and infallibility. It most often insists that the American people accept its actions on faith. But this is an arrogant posture; no agency is the repository, in a democratic system, of that much wisdom. While preserving all of the proper cautions —for instance, to guard against market speculation based on a foreknowledge of a specific action—the Federal Reserve has a responsibility to explain the rationale behind its various decisions. Above all, it must act in concert with, rather than in opposition to, the elected national government.

No one has a higher regard for the Fed than Roosa, who affirms a "genuine and abiding affection" for the System. Yet, during his confirmation hearings, he told a Senate committee: "I think Mr. [Allan] Sproul [former head of the New York Federal Reserve Bank] might be willing to share with me the invention of the phrase which . . . describes the relation as we have seen it through the years, referring to the Federal Reserve as independent *within,* not independent *from* [the Government]." It has been pointed out by former Economic Council member James Tobin, one of the truly great economic minds of our era, that the question of the independence of the Fed didn't even arise until after World War II, or some 33 years after it was founded in 1913. From 1946 until 1951, the Federal Reserve was concerned that it was becoming, in the phrase of crusty Marriner Eccles, then head of the FRB, "an engine of inflation." Eccles' fear was a real one, because the FRB, to allow the Treasury to borrow at low interest rates, supported, or "pegged," the bond market. The Truman Administration, which was committed to a low-interest-rate, easy-money policy, was able for most of this period to dominate the Fed.

The pegged market was scrapped by the famed Treasury-Federal Reserve "accord" of 1951. And this victory for the FRB, engineered in large part by Martin, who was then an Assistant Treasury Secretary, got much and powerful Congressional support from such men as Senator Douglas. From 1953 through 1960, with the advent of the Eisenhower Administration, there was no real question about "independence" from the Executive branch, because the Republican Administration moved in complete harmony with the Federal Reserve. On the single important occasion when George Humphrey and Economic Adviser Burns differed with Martin, Martin's views prevailed: as we have noted, despite the combined opposition of those two Eisenhower heavyweights, Martin proceeded with the fifth in a series of hikes in the discount rate in the spring of 1956 to slow down an economy he felt was booming ahead too rapidly.

That episode, when brought to public attention, led to a Congressional hearing, and a study by the FRB itself in which the Board suggested that it had resisted political pressure from the Eisenhower Administration. It is one of the documented accounts of Federal Reserve assertiveness and triumph under Martin's management that caused Kennedy to be concerned, when he was a candidate, that the Reserve Board might go off in one direction while his Administration decided another course was proper.[6]

In the Eisenhower years, the Fed had become a power unto itself largely because President Eisenhower failed to pursue his true responsibilities for determining a national economic policy. Eisenhower never attempted to establish a coordinated relationship with the Federal Reserve; there was no integration of Eisenhower Administration policy with that of the Fed. For example, there were, throughout the Eisenhower years, steady increases in credit made available by various federal agencies, and these occurred in periods of monetary restraint as well as monetary ease ordained by the Fed. When the Fed, using broad-scale monetary controls, chose to fight inflation and accept the risks of recession, it, rather than the elected Eisenhower government, was the maker of crucial economic policy.

The Fed's continued emphasis, during the Eisenhower period, on restrictive monetary policies that inhibited growth— yet which failed to curb inflation—stirred Democrats on Capitol Hill, even those who had helped to engineer the Fed's escape from White House domination in 1951. Now, Paul Douglas and others were concerned by the outsize role the Fed was arrogating to itself. This was the beginning of a deeply rooted hostility between the Fed and many influential Congressional Democrats, ranging from the Northern liberals such as Hubert Humphrey of Minnesota to Southerners with a Populist or agrarian background like Wright Patman of Texas.

Thus, "independence" of the Federal Reserve in the late 1950's was again an issue, but this time it was a question not of independence from Presidential or executive pressure, but of independence from Congress which created it. Tobin observed: "Once again, 'independence' of the Federal Reserve became a heated issue, a symbol of irresponsible power to some, and to others, the last citadel protecting the dollar and the country from disaster. . . . Contrary to the impression sometimes conveyed by frantic financial editorialists, the Federal Reserve is not a fourth branch of Government. Even the Supreme Court is said to read the election returns, and the 'Fed' cannot begin to claim the independence of the judiciary." [7]

At one stage in their worrying about handling Martin, the Kennedy team thought of asking Congress to establish a super-coordinating committee for national economic policy, similar to the National Security Council. But this was abandoned when the informal approach worked out well. In the Kennedy Administration, Martin's Federal Reserve did not try to run a course independent of the White House, although it did not move along the always-easy money lines urged by Representative Patman, or even along the more modest expansionary path urged by Walter Heller. But quite simply, Mr. Kennedy never moved along the lines charted by Patman, and sometimes chose the Martin instead of the Heller path. President Kennedy never found the occasion for a brute test of his own strength against Martin's. Nor, so far, has President Johnson, although LBJ issued a fairly blunt warning in the 1964 Economic Report that Martin should not allow tight money to dilute the benefit of the tax cut.

President Kennedy also took pains to assure that Martin's world-wide status as the living American symbol of fiscal soundness not be diminished by any challenge to his authority within the board. On the first occasion that Mr. Kennedy had to appoint a new Governor, he named George Mitchell, a most able liberal Democrat from the Chicago Federal Reserve Bank, passing over Representative Henry Reuss, Wisconsin Democrat who was the preferred candidate of the anti-Martin bloc of Congressional Democrats. And just a few weeks before his death, in the fall of 1963, when the situation on the board was in closer balance, Kennedy named Assistant Treasury Secretary Dewey Daane, a conservative who originally came into government under Eisenhower, passing over economist Stanley H. Ruttenberg, Assistant to Labor Secretary W. Willard Wirtz, whose name was supported with great vigor by both Wirtz and AFL-CIO President George Meany. Kennedy promised Seymour

Harris an appointment to the Board when J. L. Robertson's term expired in January, 1964. But this appointment—which would have balanced the more conservative Daane—never came to pass. Johnson chose to re-appoint Robertson, whose recent views have been quite acceptable to liberals.

Martin's acquiescence in the grand design of Kennedy's economic policy was made possible by the fact that preference and circumstance forced Kennedy to adopt a general posture of "fiscal integrity." He had to rely on money policy as the principal tool with which to manipulate the economy because tax cuts —early in the Administration—had been ruled out, and Congress, as usual, was reluctant to increase spending. In such circumstances—with the promise of a restrained fiscal policy— Martin was quite willing to ease restrictions on the monetary side in order to stimulate the economy. As a matter of history and fact, this was the direction taken by the Federal Reserve even before Kennedy took office. To help counter the last Eisenhower recession in 1960—even while Eisenhower and Candidate Richard Nixon were denying its existence, and while Kennedy was campaigning against "tight money"—the Federal Reserve had begun to supply extra reserves to the banks. When Kennedy came into office on January 20, 1961, the real question was not whether the Fed would adopt an easy-money policy—it already had. The question was, rather, whether it would abandon the policy too quickly, at the first sign of an upturn.

For this queasiness on the Kennedy team's part, there was ample excuse. An authoritative study of Fed operations by Dr. Asher Achinstein of the Library of Congress staff, published in 1958, showed that the Fed historically is slow to appraise turning points in the economy. Thus, at times, it had kept the money faucet running too long, and at other times, nervously tightened the screws before the economy had fully recovered. For example, the Fed followed a tight money policy in the first half of 1957 in an attempt to diminish inflationary pressures. But, says Achinstein, the Board continued its policy too long, due to "miscalculations . . . [which] may be said to have contributed to the sharpest business decline in the postwar period (1957-58)." [8] It is generally agreed by Arthur Burns and others that the 1960 recession was also touched off by tight money in combination with other deflationary influences, especially a sharp contraction in federal spending.[9]

Therefore, while the Federal Reserve couldn't be faulted for the promptness with which it started to move toward an easy-money policy in the spring of 1960, and which it continued into 1961, the wary Kennedy team properly kept a close eye on Martin. If he moved too soon toward a hard money policy, the recovery could be aborted. Tobin, as a matter of fact, publicly urged that the discount rate be lowered from the 3 percent level then prevailing, although Kennedy did not push this idea.

But Martin and the majority of the Board he controls were not ready to take any unnecessary plunges. The predominant philosophy of the Board was—and is—that an excessive dose of easy money leads first to inflation, then to recession, as businessmen expand inventories and consumers go on a buying binge—and an inevitable day of reckoning comes for both groups. The philosophers at the Fed insist vehemently that Dr. Achinstein is wrong in blaming the tight money posture of early 1957 for the recession late in that year; actually, the Fed experts insist, the break in the economic cycle was caused by too soft a money policy in 1955 feeding a boom that couldn't sustain itself.

With such a divergence in the basic approach, the White House looked increasingly nervously in the direction of the FRB in the summer of 1961, as the emergency program occasioned by the Berlin crisis swelled the budget deficit from a promised small one to a fairly sizable one. But Martin took it in stride, and surprisingly observed that the deficit was no cause for alarm unless a wild speculation took hold. "But inflation is in the air," he said, "and if I'm worried about it, it's because my job is to worry. You might say I'm a professional worrier." [10] Martin urged the President at this stage to plan for a balanced budget, and as we have seen in Chapter IX, Kennedy in mid-1961 promised to send a balanced budget to Congress in January, 1962. In doing so, and in overruling a last-minute Heller pitch for a small deficit, Kennedy cemented his relationships with Martin, while alienating some of his liberal supporters.

Kennedy yielded to Martin's argument that if monetary policy were to be maintained in an "easy" posture, it was neces-

sary to resort to a compensatory tight fiscal policy. To do otherwise, Martin argued in the private conferences at the White
House, would assure a new round of wage-price inflation. Treasury Secretary Dillon supported this general proposition, and
Heller alone argued that excess industrial capacity and heavy
unemployment ruled out any real prospect of inflationary pressures. The facts, viewed in retrospect, support Heller. The
federal budget was some $6 billion in the red in each of fiscal
1962 and 1963—more than Martin and Dillon expected—and
about $9 billion out of a balance in fiscal 1964, but wages and
prices were contained in an almost wholly noninflationary framework because of surpluses in the labor market and productive
capacity. But at the time, Martin and Dillon contended that
excess capacity and manpower might quickly be absorbed if
world tensions continued, and they preferred to move cautiously, which they did, with Kennedy's acquiescence.

Meanwhile, the stock market was off in one of its wildly
exuberant bull phases, which eventually resulted in the much-
publicized May 1962 crash. There was considerable discussion
within the Board in the summer of 1961 about the need to raise
margin requirements—that is, to raise the 70 percent cash payment then required. But Martin, although he knew that the
market was moving too high, chose not to hoist a signal that
might be misunderstood by the business community as a shift in
FRB policy toward generally tighter money. The margin requirement was left alone, and wasn't touched until, well after
the May 1962 crash, it was *lowered* to 50 percent to provide a
small tonic for battered Wall Street traders. After the market recovered in 1963, the FRB restored the 70 percent down-payment
requirement.

Congressional liberals were never quite satisfied with Martin's performance during the Kennedy Administration, although, quite obviously, it could have been much worse. Senator Douglas observed at a hearing during the summer of 1962:
"I've heard it said that a new chairman of the Federal Reserve
Board would be worth as much as a $10 billion tax cut." There
was a cutting edge to the half-jest. Douglas was joined by Wisconsin's Senator William Proxmire and Representative Reuss,
who argued that the balance of payments deficit was being used
as an excuse to maintain a more restrictive credit policy than

necessary. Walter Heller, who naturally seeks no public en-
counters with Martin, told the Joint Economic Committee that
a trend toward higher long-term rates was setting in, enough to
undo the gains from Operation Nudge.

Nobody, to be sure, expected Martin to become a New Frontiersman. No central banker believes that easy money is a nos-
trum for the solution of all economic ills. Martin summed it
up for his side in an extemporaneous comment in March, 1963:
"I think the phrase 'easy money' has gotten to be rather ridiculous, because what we are talking about is easy money, less easy
money, and slightly less easy money than that. . . . Now when
money gets to the point [where] you have deterioration in the
quality of credit, then it becomes self-defeating with respect
to enhancing the vigor of the domestic economy. . . ." [11] Martin's argument is that beyond a certain point, easy money assures
inflation without cutting into the level of joblessness, much of
which he believes is structural—that is, unresponsive to general
stimulation of the economy.

Labor Secretary Wirtz and other liberals argue that the order
of priority should be to attack the unemployment problem first,
and worry about inflation second. And although at times early
in the Administration the President said he was unsatisfied "to
have the cost of living remain constant only by having the
economy restrained," Martin's worries about regenerating a
new inflation were an influential force throughout the Kennedy
years.[12]

This conflict in basic objectives was succinctly summarized by
economist John P. Lewis, now a member of the Council of
Economic Advisers, when he was a private citizen in the spring
of 1962:

"Judging from recent experience, we might guess that the
price creep will tend to be neutralized whenever the economy
settles down to a good solid 6 or 7 percent unemployment rate.
. . . We can expect . . . that the creep will become significant
again whenever the unemployment rate is reduced to 5, let alone
to 4, percent." Lewis said that under both Eisenhower and Kennedy, "we have continued to experience an average slack of
some $30 billions in our national output, excusing it partly at
least in the names of budget balancing, fiscal responsibility, and
fighting inflation.

"It looks for all the world as if we have been opting for slack rather than for a little inflation. And this, I think, represents an inversion of priorities that we simply cannot afford as a nation to let persist." [13]

Such a blunt accusation—which implied that fiscal integrity advocates would rather risk unemployment (and provide the necessary unemployment compensation, retraining, etc.) than inflation—is usually met with firm and outraged denials. But an article in the August 1963 *Federal Reserve Bulletin* by staff economist Clayton Gehman reveals general attitudes along these lines at the Board.

Gehman wrote: "Although the rate of expansion has recovered since the beginning of 1959, the economy has been left with larger margins of unutilized plant and labor resources. The larger margin of unutilized resources has helped to forestall general inflationary tendencies and encouraged conditions favorable to sustainable expansion in production." [14]

Gehman alone was responsible for the article. But its publication was objected to, in advance, by other agencies of the Government because its main point challenged the Kennedy-Heller "line" that the economy was suffering from chronic slack. The fact that it was published implies general approval by the Fed of the notion that a margin of unutilized plant capacity and some unemployment can "forestall" inflation and encourage "sustainable" expansion. This is the standard rationale of the conservative central banker that inflation is just as much, or perhaps more of, a threat to the economy than a deflation accompanied by a tolerable level of joblessness. To resort to general monetary ease to soak up more of the hard-core jobless, in other words, would entail the risk of seriously inflated prices. Inasmuch as the Kennedy Administration had set as an interim goal a minimum level of 4 percent unemployment, the inherent conflict between the Martin point of view and the Administration's expansionist line is quite clear.

In an official briefing paper prepared for the White House Conference on Monetary Policy in November, 1962, the Administration said on this point: "In the current economic recovery, the Federal Reserve has, in fact, not tightened up as it did in earlier post-World War II recoveries, but has maintained some degree of ease throughout. Whether this ease has been

vigorous enough to deal with domestic economic slack, or perhaps, too vigorous in light of balance-of-payments situation has
been a major policy issue."

A majority of the Federal Reserve Board felt it was doing
enough, doubted that an easier money policy, even if desirable,
would work. They concede that tight money can have a dramatic
impact on the economy; for example, it can foreshorten an economic boom. But easing the supply is different, they feel, because businessmen won't necessarily borrow money, even at
cheap rates, unless they have confidence that a market exists for
expanded sales. "You can't push on a string" is the familiar
colloquial summary of this view. Reserve Board Governors
J. L. Robertson and George Mitchell disagree. Robertson told
the House Banking Committee in July, 1963: "I do not agree
with those who maintain that we cannot 'push on a string.' If
monetary policy had been used to its full power over the past
two years in stimulating the economy, by providing such an
availability of funds as to cause banks and other lenders to reduce their rates of interest in order to put idle funds to work,
the stimulative impact would have been felt." Mitchell says that
"there are always eager borrowers if the price is right and the
terms are favorable. What is often overlooked is that monetary
action by imposing an investment decision on the most sensitive and versatile financial nerve—the money market bank—is
certain of initiating a succession of investment actions that will
ultimately lead to spending." [15]

Evaluating the pattern for all of 1962, Mitchell said that Federal Reserve policy had been "less stimulative" than it should
have been. During most of this period, the Administration and
Martin struggled politely behind the scenes in one of the most
important and least well-reported battles in Washington: Martin pressed to keep the balance of payments situation to the
fore, while the Kennedy team lobbied with Martin to prevent a
rise in interest rates. After having vetoed the suggestion of a
temporary tax cut in mid-1962 (Martin approved the veto), the
President promised a thoroughgoing tax cut and reform program for 1963, which raised a new problem in relationships:
how to finance the impending large deficit, originally estimated
by Kennedy at $12 billion for fiscal 1964.

Originally, Martin took the position that if the Federal Reserve was expected to provide enough new bank reserves to finance the needs of the Treasury, it would be regenerating a strong inflationary trend. The Fed, he had said, referring to the Eccles' "engine of inflation" description, "will not . . . again become entangled in the vicious role of financing government deficits with bank credit created solely for that purpose." If this meant that extra reserves would not be supplied to the banks, then the Treasury, to cover its deficit, would have to borrow all of its needs from nonbank institutions and other lenders, and the basic result would be substantially higher interest rates.

Dillon insisted that the Government must be able to tap bank as well as other savings. Fretfully, the Administration could see a repetition of a chapter from the Eisenhower era; if money rates were boosted sharply, private investment would be discouraged, thus canceling the prospective stimulus from a tax cut just as effectively as would a reduction in spending. But in February, 1963, during hearings conducted by the Joint Economic Committee, Martin shifted his position perceptibly, and indicated he was willing to meet Kennedy halfway. "I have never said that there should be no monetary expansion in a year in which the Federal Government is incurring a deficit," Martin testified. "What we should do, and will try to do, is to maintain conditions of reserve availability in the banking system, which will help to match the total rate of bank credit and monetary growth to the needs of the total economy." In other words, Martin would not run a printing press to pay for the entire deficit, but he would allow some increase in bank reserves so that the stimulus of the deficit wouldn't be erased, dollar for dollar. This portended some tightening up of money, and a moderately higher interest rate pattern.

Administration acquiescence in this policy was indicated at the March 14, 1963, meeting of the Advertising Council—one businessman's forum to which Kennedy enjoyed going—where Dillon observed that given a tax cut, "we'll have greater freedom for the monetary authorities to act in accordance with reality." [16]

This was a clear-cut signal that the Kennedy Administration would not interfere with a moderately higher interest rate pattern, although the Democratic majority of the Joint Economic Committee had just issued a report which blasted Federal Reserve policy in unusually strong terms—and that is just the way things worked out.

Dillon, concurring with Martin's view that the balance of payments problem "is the principal shadow over the domestic economy today," pinpointed the lower interest rate structure abroad as a key factor. "We—the Federal Reserve, the Treasury, the Administration—have tried as a definite matter of policy," Dillon said, "to hold the short-term rate here at as high a level as we can without disturbing economic progress in this country, and we think we have been successful there . . . [but] there are substantial volumes of funds that are still going out to Canada and to the United Kingdom, averaging at a rate of something like half a billion dollars a year. So the problem is to decide, and I think something will have to be done to stop that either by still lower rates abroad, or somewhat higher rates here. . . . It isn't a very large change that would be involved. . . . We do not want to do it until it is clear that it will not have any harm in our economy."

Dillon thus was suggesting that once a tax cut was passed—which the Administration optimistically assumed might be before the end of the year—Kennedy might abandon his opposition to an increase in short-term interest rates. But by July, with the balance of payments deficit having swelled to record proportions, panic took over both in the Administration and at the Federal Reserve.

On July 16, 1963, after a bitter wrangle within the Board, the discount rate was raised from 3 to 3.5 percent—a very substantial boost in this sensitive determinant of all other interest levels. At that time, the tax bill had not even been reported out of the House Ways and Means Committee. As a coordinate step, the Administration a few days later proposed an excise tax on the sale of foreign securities to American citizens. This "interest equalization tax" was designed to check the long-term borrowing by foreign investors.

The dramatic boost in the discount rate—the first increase since August, 1960—was a risky step, and both the Fed and the Administration knew it. The Board abandoned all precedents to offer an explanation to the public instead of letting the action speak for itself. Aware of real fears that a discount rate increase would put a crimp in business, the Board said it was motivated entirely by balance of payments considerations, and, in a refinement of the original "twist" operation, it would attempt to keep long-term rates down. The boost in rates did not signal, the Board said, "a change in the System's policy of maintaining monetary conditions conducive to fuller utilization of manpower and other resources in this country." Yet, the discount rate hike was the precise weapon used by the FRB during the Eisenhower years to choke off or slow down a boom, and it was against this consistent policy that Mr. Kennedy had campaigned in 1960. Now, Kennedy was willing to risk deflation at home in his desperate need for a weapon to combat the loss of dollars and gold.

In a private conversation with Martin, Kennedy offered to make a speech urging the Fed to raise discount rate. Kennedy's liberal friends on the Hill would have been outraged had they known the full extent of Kennedy's insistence on tighter money at that point. It was all Martin could do to dissuade Kennedy from taking a public stand; the chairman of the Fed, happy with Kennedy's support, nonetheless didn't want to appear to be pressured by the White House.

Only shortly before Kennedy's tragic death, the President invited Martin to a session at the White House. Alone with the Fed Chairman, Kennedy said that he couldn't understand why it was generally assumed their views were wide apart. "Let me put it to you this way, Mr. President," Martin said. "You're an activist, you've always got something going. You and Walter Heller always want to be doing something for the economy. But I believe that the economy, like an individual, occasionally needs a rest—a time when nothing is going on." Kennedy laughed, and said he still didn't think he and Martin were far apart. Earlier, when Martin wanted to retire by the end of 1963, Kennedy told Martin he wouldn't let him go—and Martin accepted re-appointment to a new term as Chairman.

Within the Fed in the summer of 1963, there was a sharp division. Robertson believed that the increase would have but a "trivial" impact on the balance of payments, and at least two other members doubted the wisdom of raising interest rates while 5.7 percent of the labor force was out of work and the economy was chugging along far below its potential. The normally reserved Federal Reserve Board of Governors' meeting, one responsible source revealed, was a "donnybrook."

"I voted against a discount rate increase," Robertson said in his House banking committee testimony, "because I did not think it was worth the cost. . . . My view was that the probable benefit to the U. S. balance of payments resulting from a discount rate increase would be so small as to be considerably outweighed by its potential adverse effects on our domestic economic activity. . . . The real basis of the world's confidence in the soundness of the dollar is not the gold in Fort Knox or the balance of payments statistics, but rather the underlying strength of the American economy. Hence, there is a compelling need for invigorating our economy . . . with a corresponding strengthening of the capacity of the United States to exercise its role of leadership of the free world." [17]

Kennedy's positive approval of the Federal Reserve action was unprecedented. It was not an angry, frustrated acquiescence; it was complete support. On Capitol Hill and in a press conference, the Administration was accused of betraying its 1960 campaign pledges to overthrow the Eisenhower tight-money policy. The Administration defense was that "the policy we took"—note the "we"—was necessary because of the overriding importance of the balance of payments problem. Moreover, Mr. Kennedy insisted, both the Administration and the Federal Reserve were committed to an attempt to keep long-term rates from rising. All agreed that a substantial increase in long-term rates would put a crimp in plant expansion, home building, and other "growth" components of the economy.

The quarterly balance of payments figures indeed looked bad in 1963: for the second quarter, the deficit was at an annual rate of $5.2 billion, up from $3.6 billion in the first quarter. Although there was a prompt correction to an average of about $1 billion in the deficit rate in each of the final quarters of 1963, the total for the year was $2.7 billion, the biggest, since 1960. Prospects for 1964 seemed more favorable, largely because stable prices here contrasted with inflation abroad gave American exports a continued good edge in world markets.

By boosting the discount rates, the Government hoped that the return on American short-term issues would make them as attractive or more attractive than similar investments in foreign countries, and thus reduce the flow of money abroad. Although there was a sharp division of opinion, as Robertson's views indicate, Treasury officials claimed that money outflows might be cut by up to $500,000,000 a year by an increase in short-term rates. If long-term rates were also allowed to rise, that would discourage some foreign borrowing at the expense of choking off investment at home. The "gimmick" of the interest equalization tax, actually a sales tax on the marketing of foreign securities, was a last-minute, desperate substitute concocted in the Treasury.

President Kennedy sensed that the close new bond between his Administration and the Federal Reserve needed some public explanation. In a special message to Congress on July 18, 1963, he said:

> While none of us welcome higher interest rates at a time when our economy is operating at below capacity, an increase in short-term rates—at a time when liquid savings are growing rapidly, and when there are no accompanying restrictions on credit availability nor parallel increases in the interest rates on bank loans, home mortgages, or other long-term obligations—should have little, if any, adverse effect on our economy. The unprecedented flow of liquid savings should largely insulate the longer-term markets from the effect of higher short-term rates.

It is perhaps a tribute to the potency of the Federal Reserve in the Washington complex that there were only scattered anguished cries from liberals protesting the rise in rates. There were a few speeches on the Senate floor, and the AFL-CIO ground out a critical press release. But it hardly seemed patriotic to argue with a President valiantly defending the dollar. Teamplayer Heller dutifully payed a visit to the House Banking and Currency Committee to defend the policy (see Chapter IX) and Samuelson made the rather wistful observation that "if it had not been for the balance of payments problem, it would have been optimum policy in this era of unemployment for the Federal Reserve to have made itself unpopular with the New York banking community by making money much easier than it has been."

All Kennedy could do was to voice the pious hope that higher interest rates wouldn't pinch off economic recovery. It seemed to weigh on his mind, because he told a group of college students who visited the White House in late August, 1963, that one of the difficult judgments he had to make was "what actions the Federal Government should take in this summer to prevent economic downturn in 1964." It is clear that Kennedy felt the tight money maneuver was necessary. It was a telling illustration of the influence of William McChesney Martin: when Martin's policies coincide with the "conventional wisdom" (as they usually do) his views tended to prevail—even in the Administration of John Fitzgerald Kennedy. Orthodox tactics, in the face of a worsening balance of payments problem, called for tighter money, with some offset in the form of lower taxes. This prescription was increasingly pushed upon the United States by European central bankers and others for much of 1962, although tighter money can be made effective overnight by the FRB, while changes in U. S. fiscal policy are a tricky business: the Congress of the United States must be consulted.

Typical of the conventional wisdom was a report in midsummer, 1962, by the conservative Bank of International Settlements at Basle, Switzerland. "The United States," the report said, "is the only country that has not put major emphasis in monetary measures on external requirements, which has been seen to be necessary since the return to convertibility . . . there is ample European experience to show that the possible internal restraint of a tighter monetary policy can be alleviated by fiscal and other policy means."

For much of the latter part of 1962, the Federal Reserve moved quietly in the direction of tighter money by reducing, week by week, the free reserves of its member banks. By the spring of 1963, the Fed had tightened reserves, and thus the banks' lending power, sharply. The boost in the discount rate completed the shift to tighter money. But the "alleviation" of lower taxes was still in limbo as Congress, caught in a struggle over civil rights legislation, debated and delayed.

Before its dramatic move in July, a top policy officer at the Fed remarked that a decision on boosting the discount rate was difficult, "because we don't want to upset any applecarts, yet we don't want to be irresponsible." The way the Fed looks at things, by raising the rate, it has purged itself of the charge of irresponsibly easy money in the face of the balance of payments deficit. It remains to be seen whether the applecart—the U. S. economy—will be spilled. So far, it's upright, but one can't tell what will happen after the initial effects of the tax cut wear out.

It also remains to be seen whether Martin will have the same influence on Lyndon Johnson as he did in the Kennedy era. Johnson brought with him to the White House a reputation for being a sort of "Populist" in money matters, a man who would instinctively oppose high money rates.

But his assurances to the business community seem to be running along Kennedy lines. At a dinner for top business leaders and their wives at the White House on April 28, Johnson, like Kennedy, pledged that he would defend the dollar. Then, in his best folksy manner, he added:

"I know that some of you are worried that I'll try to substitute friendly persuasion for the hard-nosed monetary and fiscal policy we may need if inflation threatens. I won't.

"Of course, I'll do all the persuading I can. . . . And I hope that Doug Dillon and Bill Martin and Bob Roosa will keep these long-term interest rates down so we can keep the economy up.

"But let me assure you: if the balance of payments turns sour, or if inflation starts rolling, I will look to the independent Federal Reserve as our second line of defense.

"I would have said 'first,' but you in this room are the first in line.

"But right behind you is Bill Martin—a man whom I give full faith and credit as an inflation fighter beyond compare." [18]

Stacked against this were the earlier words of Johnson's economic report: "It would be self-defeating to cancel the stimulus of tax reduction by tightening money." Johnson obviously hoped he would not have to resort to a tight credit policy—that was why he hammered so hard at the theme of price and wage restraint. But if he had to, he seemed ready to accede to the Martin line, just as Kennedy had done.

The Tax Reduction Act of 1964: Will It Work?

FOR the third time since he assumed the Presidency, John F. Kennedy faced a decision on cutting taxes. Early in 1961, and again in the summer of 1962, he had considered, then vetoed tax cut suggestions by his advisers. The first time, his decision was made despite the fear that without it, upturn from the last Eisenhower recession would be slow. The second time, the President had allowed the country to teeter on the edge of a "Will he or won't he?" debate, and the President finally said "no" to a broad group of people, management as well as labor, who urged a therapeutic tax cut to head off a downturn.

But in the winter of 1962, the President accepted the diagnosis and prescription of his economic doctors: the economy had a chronic ailment; it was stumbling along with a 5.5 percent unemployment level, while the gross national product, in real terms, was expanding at just a 2.25 percent rate (1957 through 1961) compared with a 3.80 percent rate in the 1947 to 1957 decade. Recession had been avoided in 1962, but the boom originally foreseen didn't materialize either. A tax cut, Kennedy was finally convinced, was the only effective way to rocket the economy off dead center—more acceptable to conservatives than an expansion of Federal spending. Moreover, a tax stimulus might be just the right antidote to a tighter money policy that might have to be adopted to stem the outflow of gold.

The White House politicians didn't care for the Kennedy

decision, which temporarily assured a larger budget deficit. "We've got to go for it because the economists say we need it," said one Kennedy aide candidly. "But consumers don't get much out of it, then they'll read about all the billions that have been cut, and say: 'The fat cats must have got it all.' " In fact, as was to become evident later, there was little grass-roots demand for a tax cut. But Heller supplied Kennedy with a rationale for cutting taxes: a major slash would be no simple juggling to provide a temporary boost, but an attempt to let the private economy cure itself of a sluggish pallor that had enveloped it for the past five years. This was the tax "drag" theory that Heller had been trying to sell as Administration policy for more than a year.[1] But until late in 1962, the more cautious, don't-tinker-with-taxes guidance of Treasury Secretary Douglas Dillon dominated Kennedy's thinking.

On December 14, 1962, the die was cast. Kennedy flew to New York to address an overflow audience of the Economic Club in the Waldorf-Astoria ballroom. The White House itself had asked for the date so that the President could launch the new tax program before a blue-ribbon business audience. It turned out to be one of the most successful appearances he ever made before such a group.

"I am not . . . talking about giving the economy a mere shot in the arm, to ease temporary complaints," Kennedy said. "I am talking about the accumulated evidence of the last five years that our present tax system exerts too heavy a drag on growth—that it siphons out of the economy too large a share of personal and business purchasing power."

Halfway measures, he insisted, would be self-defeating. He conceded that too large a tax cut might result in inflation, but "the greater danger" would be a tax cut "too little or too late to be effective." And to those who would argue that a reduction in taxes would merely assure a continuation of deficit spending, Kennedy's response was that "our practical choice . . . is between two kinds of deficit—a chronic deficit of inertia . . . or a temporary deficit of transition, resulting from a tax cut designed to boost the economy, increase tax revenue and achieve a future budget surplus." All told, it was a brilliant performance.[2]

The concept was truly audacious. The President was prepar-

ing public sentiment to receive a budget well out of balance—
and on top of that, a tax cut that would make the deficit even
bigger. It was, for the first time in the Kennedy Administration,
a leaf out of the Keynesian ledger. At the same time, the sopo-
rific effects of a large tax cut would be utilized to reduce special
tax privileges, especially those provided the wealthiest income
groups in the country. The fact that Kennedy gave a lesser
priority to reforms was initially overlooked by cheering liberals;
they forgot how easily the reform part of the package could be
abandoned.

Back in Washington, Heller glowed. He had labored long to
convince the President that to push the U. S. economy ahead—
to enable it to compete in world markets and to lower unemployment here—the U. S. would have to adopt a more liberal
fiscal policy. Increased spending of the necessary dimensions
had been shunted aside as politically unacceptable. But the tax
pattern established during World War II, Heller argued, had
the economy in a straitjacket, and what would appeal more to
the business community than a loosening of the bind?

It would require a deft touch with Congress, and especially
with Wilbur Mills, the Democratic tax statesman from Kensett,
Oklahoma (population: 905). For years, Mills had built up a
reputation as a tax reform enthusiast; he had earnestly conducted long hearings which brought prominent academicians
(some of them now in office with Kennedy) to his Ways and
Means Committee hearing room with exhaustive testimony on
every tax loophole in existence, complete with impressive and
logical suggestions for plugging them. But Mills had never been
able to accomplish any real tax reform, save for the few crumbs
saved out of the 1962 Administration proposals.

Now, Mills was determined, as one of the White House "Irish
Mafia" put it, to get a tax reform bill as "his second monument." (The first was his successful sponsorship of the Administration's Trade Expansion Act.) The strategy evolved by the
White House was to work up an extensive package of tax reforms, to satisfy both Mills and liberal Democrats who long had
urged elimination of such things as real estate tax shelters, oil
depletion allowances, special tax credits for stock dividends, and
so on. But reform was the bait—what Kennedy wanted was the
tax cut.

The Mills strategy, as the White House saw it, would be much the opposite: he would yield up a certain amount of tax revenue in order to get reforms of the tax structure. "The function of taxation," Mills told the House in a serious speech, "is to raise revenue. . . . I do not go along with economists who think of taxation primarily as an instrument for manipulating the economy."

Kennedy's political advisers assumed that these two views would not prove incompatible, if they could demonstrate a clear national consensus that taxes should be cut heavily. And this they set out to do. The United States Chamber of Commerce volunteered that it favored cutting taxes, and urged Congress to take action "that would stimulate the economy, promote investments, and create jobs. . . . This proposal faces hard sledding in Congress, unless businessmen rally around."

The influential National Planning Association and the Committee for Economic Development, both highly respected nonpartisan research organizations, swung into line. The AFL-CIO favored a very large tax cut in 1963, emphasizing personal income tax reductions, but postponing reforms until 1964. And most important, Dillon got on the bandwagon, impressed by the fact that even though the economy had recovered from the recession low, businessmen in 1962 were spending at a very unsatisfactory level on new plant and equipment—and even existing capacity wasn't being utilized. He came around to the view that tax rates, developed during the pressures and the aftermath of war, were placing "shackles" on the economy.

But in deciding to cut taxes, the Kennedy Administration ran straight into accepted conservative dogma: how could taxes be cut while the budget was already unbalanced? Conservative spokesmen, with General Eisenhower in the vanguard, warned it would be little short of insanity to cut taxes without compensatory reductions in spending.[3]

Patiently, Dillon warned his friends in Wall Street that "there is simply no possibility within the foreseeable future that expenditures can be reduced below current levels." Tax cuts, in other words, couldn't wait for a favorable budget situation—on that basis there was no telling when, if ever, taxes could be cut. And if spending were cut as taxes were reduced, the stimulative effect of the tax cut would of course be lost. In Heller's apt phrase, acceptance of a big 1964 deficit was necessary as "a down payment on future surpluses."

But there was still another limiting factor to be considered: the balance of payments problem. According to traditional economic theory, big deficits cause conservative bankers to worry about the real strength of a government. A government running deep in the red might decide to pay its bills by the simple, but drastic device of monetary devaluation. If the United States ran a big budget deficit, would confidence in the dollar further erode? It could. But the Kennedy team's conviction was that in the long run, confidence in the dollar would rest on more than just the U. S. federal budget deficit. Evidence began to accumulate that Europeans were more worried about the world-wide impact of a stagnating U. S. economy than a red-ink figure on the budget ledger. A recession or depression in the United States—that was the prospect that gave Europeans a chill. Behind the scenes, the late, great Per Jacobsson, director of the International Monetary Fund, was an important influence in convincing European central bankers that the United States was wise to pursue an expansionary fiscal policy. Jacobsson also bucked up the flagging courage of some American statesmen.

Thus, another very important consensus—an international consensus—began to develop in favor of an American tax cut. This point of view was expressed by the 20-nation Organization for Economic Cooperation and Development, based in Paris. A Chamber of Commerce team, after a two-week survey of Western European financial centers, reported that "U. S. tax cut would be applauded in Europe. . . . So welcome would be . . . an expansion that any temporary increase in the budget deficit, resulting from the cut, would not shake confidence in the dollar in international money markets."

Brimming with confidence, and eager to impress, Kennedy sought further support from business, as he did in his address before the New York Economic Club. Specifics were lacking at this stage of planning, but the President's direction, intention, and conviction on the issue were clear. The Economic Club appearance may have been the high-water mark of Kennedy's relationships with the business community. Malcolm S. Forbes, editor of *Forbes Magazine,* said that the President's basic argument was "indisputable," and called on his readership to give Kennedy "visible, voluble support" to get the program through Congress.[4]

But a funny thing happened to the tax proposal on the way to the Congress. Despite the willingness of business and labor to back a massive tax cut, the President's innate conservatism—fed by Dillon's fear of going too far—took over, and the "working" goal of a $10 billion reduction was trimmed back. This was done at a conference at Palm Beach in late December, 1962, where the President decided that the $10 billion figure would be kept—but spread over three years. Thus, assuming early adoption of the Kennedy program, less than $3 billion of the tax reduction would become effective in calendar 1963, a tactic that would limit the deficit to what Dillon considered reasonable proportions. Not at all coincidentally, the Kennedy deficit would be just under Eisenhower's biggest deficit figure. It was a major concession to the conservative point of view.

A reporter's exchange with Heller in January, 1963, when he briefed the press on the economic report illuminates the Administration's thinking:

> *Reporter:* Would it be possible to achieve full employment much more quickly by having the tax program concentrated in one year? If so, why wasn't it recommended?
>
> *Heller:* It is partly a matter of economics in the sense that you want to stage the tax reductions in a sequence that will get you to your goal but not with . . . inflation. . . . And it is partly a matter of reality and recognition of the legislative process and how fast you can move. Third, it is a matter of holding the deficit, as the President said, within manageable limits.[5]

Ironically, Kennedy's watered-down proposal meant that the net effect of federal, state, and local tax changes in 1963 would be to *raise* the tax burden, not lower it—even if his proposals were promptly accepted by Congress. For simple arithmetic showed that against a potential $3 billion reduction in federal tax liabilities, Social Security taxes were being increased by $2 billion, and state and local taxes by nearly the same amount. Thus, compared to a $3 billion reduction, there was nearly a $4 billion increase in the amount of money to be drained out of consumers' pocketbooks in 1963. Moreover, state and local taxes are, in economists' terms, regressive—they hit hardest at the lowest end of the income scale. Heller disputed this analysis, contending that many state taxes were raised in anticipation of a reduction in federal tax burdens, and that in any event, local collections are poured right back into the economy. But the facts are that these regressive taxes were raised nearly $4 billion in 1963, and there was *no* reduction in federal taxes achieved in 1963.

Dillon was candid, at the Palm Beach discussions, about his fears of overdoing the tax cut. Later, talking off the cuff to the annual conference of the Advertising Council in March, 1963, Dillon said: "We have to do this in a fiscally responsible way because of our balance of payments, the pressure that we have there. In particular, to do it all at once and have a tremendous deficit would not inspire confidence in the rest of the world and could be very dangerous for our balance of payments. Therefore, we have adopted the idea of spreading it in a number of bites as far as the fiscal years, the budget years go, although in actual fact it is compressed." And Dillon again emphasized a policy that Kennedy first hinted at before the Economic Club: that expenditure control would be "an integral part of this program." [6]

Dillon made the policy, conservative on both the tax cut and the expenditure side, stick. Heller was stunned and disappointed, but he did the only thing he could do short of resigning; he defended the program with all possible vigor. When asked on *Meet the Press* in February, 1963, whether the Administration hadn't "oversold the extent of the tax cut it is proposing and the possible impact on the economy," Heller blandly responded: "Not at all. After all, it is a $10 billion tax cut." [7]

But the mere number didn't fool people. A *Business Week* editorial on January 26, titled "The Right Remedy But Late and Little," said: "The Administration is on the right track at last. But its program is still too narrow in scope, too slow in timing, and too complex in detail to be what the country needs."

The enormously complicated and long tax message (it covered 35½ legal-sized, double-spaced pages) proposed gross tax cuts totaling $13.3 billion in personal and corporate income tax cuts carefully rationed over a three-year period, and structural tax changes, usually called "reforms," which would increase tax revenue by $3.2 billion. Thus, the net effect of the whole "package" would be to cut taxes about $10 billion over the three-year period, with individual reductions accounting for just short of $8 billion, the rest going to corporations. (Taking into account that personal income tax cuts in the higher brackets tend to flow into investment rather than consumption channels, the proposed division of the spoils was much more balanced between the business and consumer sectors than would appear at first glance. And remembering the stimulation to investment via the 1962 depreciation and special credit, it is abundantly clear that the over-all effect of Kennedy's original tax program, even with the full "reform" package intact, would have been to give equal thrust to investment as to the consumer side). As later changed by Congress, the bill clearly favored the high income brackets and the investment sector of the economy. Heller made no bones about it. In a speech in Paris to the Société d'Économie Politique on November 7, 1963, he said:

> Traditionally, the Democratic Party has placed great stress on tax measures to benefit consumers. But the force of circumstance has raised investment in productive equipment to a higher and higher priority. . . . New emphasis has therefore been placed on tax stimulants to investment. . . . Such measures would have been considered unnecessary, perhaps even "un-Democratic," 10 or 15 years ago. Today—coupled with over $8 billion of tax reductions to boost consumer markets—these direct tax stimulants to investment are . . . a necessary part of a modern economic policy. This is a distinct change in emphasis.

The principal device proposed to lower individual taxes was a thoroughgoing revamping of the 20 to 91 percent schedule rate. This schedule, almost confiscatory (in theory) at the top bracket, has been universally assailed as too deep. Kennedy proposed a three-stage reduction: to a range of 18.5 to 84.5 percent in calendar 1963; to a range of 15.5 to 71.5 percent in calendar 1964; and to a range of 14 to 65 percent in calendar 1965. Such a personal income tax cut—itself a major reform, in a sense—would have amounted to $11.2 billion over the three years. This was trimmed to about $8 billion by a controversial element in the Kennedy "reform" package: a 5 percent "floor" under personal, itemized deductions for charitable contributions, medical expenses, interest payments, and the like, designed to reduce the freedom with which taxpayers take such deductions, and thereby recoup $2.3 billion for the Treasury. In 1962, about 50 percent of all taxpayers itemized their deductions, lopping an amazing $40 billion off the tax base. The Treasury calculated that by forcing taxpayers to subtract the first 5 percent of their income—$1,000 in the case of a man with $20,000 income—from allowable contributions, it would make itemization hardly worthwhile to about 6,500,000 taxpayers.[8]

"The plain fact," wrote noted tax expert Joseph A. Pechman, "is that the personal deductions in our tax law are too generous. An income tax law is designed to tax all persons with the same income and the same family responsibilities alike. Through the deduction system, our law makes allowances for specific *expenditures* as well, and many of these deductions do violence to the principle of tax equality." [9]

The rest of Kennedy's reform package featured repeal of the dividend credit and exclusion, which would close a $460 million annual "loophole," an attack on the stock option device, which permits corporate executives to benefit, at no risk, from stock market gains, while paying taxes at low capital gains rates— along with an assortment of proposals favoring low- and middle-income taxpayers. President Kennedy did not, however, meet squarely the most sacred cow of all, the 27.5 percent oil depletion allowance. But he did recommend elimination of certain abuses in the way the depletion allowance is calculated, a change that the Treasury claimed would be the equivalent of a reduction of 5.5 to 7 points in the allowance, and one that would plug at least $300 million of the natural resources loophole (which costs the Government an estimated $1.5 billion every year).

On the investment side, the President proposed a change in the capital gains structure which would reduce the effective tax on gains held a year to a top of 19.5 percent (instead of 25 percent in existing law) providing that gains accrued on capital assets be taxed at time of gift or death.

These were important, if not well-understood, proposals.

Existing law gave preferential rate treatment to long-term capital gains. Kennedy suggested keeping and liberalizing this principle. But he asked for a change in existing law which permits capital gains to go completely free if transferred as bequests from one generation to the next. In the case of gifts, the gain is not taxed at the time of gift—or ever—unless sold by the recipient. As Pechman points out, "increases in the value of securities and real estate held in wealthy families for generations may never be subject to the income tax." [10] Pechman estimates that the amount of income that goes scot-free of taxes through the gift and estate tax loopholes ranges upwards of $5 billion a year.

On corporate tax reductions, Mr. Kennedy proposed going a bit further than his liberal advisers had suggested: he asked Congress to lower the top 52 percent rate to 50 percent in 1964, then to 47 percent in 1965. At roughly $500 million per tax point, the reduction would be worth $2.5 billion. Many within the Administration thought it would be adequate to drop the top rate to 49 percent, which would be a $1.5 billion boost for business, and make the Federal Government the junior, instead of senior partner, of the nation's big corporate enterprises. The business community, as it turned out later, had already received the equivalent of a $2.2 billion, or 9 percent, tax reduction through changes in the law in 1962: tax liabilities had been reduced $1.0 billion by the special credit, and $1.2 billion by more liberal depreciation schedules. But Kennedy, acting on the combined advice of Dillon and Sorensen (and Sorensen's views on this were a major consideration) decided to propose a reduction down to the 47 percent level. The overriding consideration: the Administration was anxious to be considered "even-handed" in apportioning the cut between business and consumers.

Between the lines of the tax message, Kennedy made it clear he was not insisting on any rigid formula. He anticipated that Congress would have its own ideas, and he was willing to compromise provided he could get some tax bill, and provided that the tight budgetary ceilings he had set for himself weren't punctured. The $10 billion figure over three years, Dillon told the House Ways and Means Committee, "is the maximum we can stand."

When it came down to brass tacks, Kennedy was guided by two self-imposed guidelines: he didn't want the proposed tax cut to create a bigger deficit than the 1960 Eisenhower deficit—$12.4 billion—and he didn't want the regular budget spending figure (even though it is the least useful of all budgetary statistics) to top the $100 billion level. Thus, Dillon scaled and pared the tax cuts so that in fiscal 1964 only $2.7 billion would be added to the $9.2 billion deficit the Administration faced without a tax cut, making the predicted red-ink total $11.9 billion. And spending, controlled by a rigorous expenditure policy, would be held to a total of $98.8 billion. Thus, for one more year, Kennedy would be spared the noxious task, as he saw it, of sponsoring the nation's first $100 billion budget. Shades of the Yale speech on myths!

There isn't much doubt that the Administration, after all of the fanfare about its need and impact, heavily oversold the potential of the particular tax program it designed. Initially, it had set the stage for a massive cut with a carefully planned conference in November, 1962—just before the President talked to the Economic Club in New York—on fiscal and monetary policy. Here, the Administration sought and achieved a consensus among participating businessmen and labor leaders that something spectacular ought to be done.

But having achieved that consensus, the Kennedy Administration backed away from it in a desperate attempt to accommodate all possible views on Capitol Hill, and to ward off charges—that were certain to be made anyway—that it was following a reckless spending policy.

It is quite true that the President did take the historic step of proposing a tax cut on top of a deficit that already existed. The "planned deficit" was a daring concept, and the Kennedy Administration, sometimes criticized for a lack of courage, ought to receive full credit for this policy decision. But the hard fact is that the President, having broken new ground by presenting and defending an unbalanced budget, a posture well-advanced from his hesitations of just a year before, temporized. He didn't follow his own advice at the Economic Club to shy away from "halfway measures."

The curtailment on government spending was restated with even greater vigor by Lyndon Johnson as soon as he became President. Neither Kennedy nor Johnson was paying mere lip service to the philosophy of fiscal integrity and frugality in government. Each thought it absolutely essential to securing passage of the tax cut—and each accepted budget control as part of his own basic approach to government. Budget Director Kermit Gordon confessed that the "expenditure control" policy effectively placed a ceiling on nondefense spending for the ensuing three years. This was clearly set forth in the fiscal 1964 budget document, published in January, 1963, this way:

> As the tax cut becomes fully effective and the economy climbs toward full employment, a substantial part of the revenue increases must go toward eliminating the transitional deficit. Although it will be necessary to increase certain expenditures, we shall continue, and indeed intensify, our effort to include in our fiscal program only those expenditures which meet strict criteria of fulfilling important national needs. Federal outlays must be incurred only where the resulting benefits to the security and well-being of the American people are clearly worth the costs.[11]

Even Eisenhower, who put a ceiling on defense spending, never enforced one on *nondefense* spending. But this theme was emphasized repeatedly by Dillon and Undersecretary Henry Fowler to business audiences all over the country—and needless to say, they approved. The President himself told a forum of the American Bankers Association in February, 1963, that his whole tax program was devised within the "framework of fiscal prudence and economic necessity." And he added: "No budget will be submitted by this Administration which does not continue a persistent and surprisingly unpopular program of cutting costs, increasing efficiency, and weeding out obsolete activities." [12]

As Republican pressure mounted for specific *reductions* in the Federal Budget, and tying a part of the cut to a new limit on the national debt, Kennedy's pledges on expenditure control grew increasingly specific.

On August 19, 1963, Kennedy wrote Representative Mills as follows:

> *First,* our long-range goal remains a balanced budget in a balanced full-employment economy. It is clear that this goal cannot be achieved without a substantial tax reduction and the greater national income it will produce.

Second, tax reduction must also, therefore, be accompanied by the exercise of an even-tighter rein on Federal expenditures, limiting outlays to only those expenditures which meet strict criteria of national need.

Third, consistent with these policies, as the tax cut becomes fully effective and the economy climbs toward full employment, a substantial part of the increased tax revenues will be applied toward a reduction in the transitional deficits which accompany the initial cut in tax rates.

Fourth, assuming enactment of the tax program incorporated in your Committee's bill with a consequent loss of revenue of $5 billion more in fiscal 1965 than in fiscal 1964, I nevertheless expect—in strict accordance with the above policies, and in the absence of any unforeseen slowdown in the economy or any serious international contingency in the next five months—to be able to submit next January a budget for fiscal 1965 involving an estimated deficit of less than the $9.2 billion forecast for fiscal 1964 by the Secretary of the Treasury in your Executive Sessions last week; and

Fifth, and finally, any increase in the Federal debt resulting from these transitional budget deficits will be kept proportionately lower than the increase in our gross national product, and thus the real burden of the Federal debt will be steadily reduced.

Meanwhile, prodded by Dillon and Fowler, big business organized its own campaign to get a tax cut, effective as soon as possible. With Henry Ford II and Stuart T. Saunders, president of the Norfolk & Western Railway Co.* acting as co-chairman, nearly 3,000 businessmen formed the Business Committee for Tax Reduction in 1963. The name told the story—they were for a $10 billion cut, to take effect if possible in 1963, but they were against reforms. The Ford-Saunders committee consisted of the top brass of American business, and it was not surprising that they openly urged the outright junking of the reform package; most of the reforms would jar well-entrenched privilege.

Kennedy welcomed them at the White House, acknowledging that there was a difference of attitude on tax reforms. As Pechman has observed, the reform proposals were among the most

---

* As of October 1, 1963, Chairman of the Pennsylvania Railroad.

progressive recommendations by the Kennedy Administration in any field. Without the reforms, it is hard to challenge the Leon Keyserling accusation that the tax program is a bonanza for upper-income groups.

From the start, it was evident that the President's commitment to tax reform was tactical, rather than visceral. As far back as the Economic Club appearance, when asked by one of the businessmen, "Why not have a moratorium on reform until we get to full employment?" the President responded:

> "Well, the purpose of reform really is directed to the encouraging of growth, of employment. I quite agree that to launch into a full-scale battle on general reform for academic reasons would be unwise. . . . It is going to be a tough fight, because . . . a reform . . . is bound to affect adversely the interests of some, while favoring the interests of others. Therefore, reform may be a longer task, and we are anxious that in the effort to get reform, we do not lose the very important matter of tax reduction for the sake of the economy. . . ."

Then, in February, 1963, before the American Bankers Forum in Washington, the President said even more plainly that the tax cut itself took priority over reforms. Press officers at the Treasury Department, caught off base, at first denied that the President could have said any such thing; later, they read the transcript. Although Dillon subsequently persuaded Kennedy to reinstate a public "plug" for reforms, the public stood confused about the Administration's objectives. During the spring, there was a period of drift and uncertainty. When prospects for the economy appeared somewhat shaky, Kennedy forgot the whole rationale about the long-term "drag" of taxes on the economy, and warned Congress that the tax cut was needed as insurance against a recession.

Talking of recession if Congress didn't approve the tax cut was a shift in the argument; the President had said very precisely that the tax cut was *not* being engineered as a "shot in the arm." But as the possibility of a downturn in 1963 faded away, this scare tactic was dropped, although the Administration noted deftly that by February, 1964, the upturn in the business cycle would be three years old, relatively well-aged, and the tax cut, if passed, might postpone the next recession. "I would like to see us skip a recession," the President told the nation in a televised address on September 19, 1963. "I would like to see us release $11 billion of extra after-tax purchasing power into the private economy before another downturn can begin. That is why this bill is both insurance for prosperity and insurance against recession."

The Administration's arguments for the tax bill shifted unnecessarily. Its goals seemed confused. In its vacillation, it won few converts to tax cutting, and lost some friends. The carefully constructed consensus began to fall apart when the details were made clear. Business was pleased with the corporate tax cut, but didn't like the reforms; labor leaders felt business and upper-bracket taxpayers were getting too much of a break at the expense of the lower brackets; and Congress was assaulted by various special interests affected by specific provisions. But above all, there was public lassitude. Congressmen discovered from their mail that voters were either passive, or they actually opposed a tax cut because they had heard it would add to the deficit. This was the attitude that Heller described as the "Puritan ethic," and though he expressed amazement that this rock-ribbed feeling should exert such a discipline, it appeared to be genuine.

A Washington *Post* poll conducted by Louis Harris on September 1, 1963, showed that 62 percent of a public opinion sample favored a tax cut at that time, but when those polled were asked whether a tax cut or balanced budget should come first, only 41 percent wanted the tax cut, 36 percent suggested a balanced budget first, and 23 percent were not sure. The Harris interpretation was that "a deep ambivalence among the people themselves" about a tax cut was reflected in Congress. But Harris, as he indicated himself, "reminded" the voters "that the budget is not now balanced." Such a reminder raises a question about some of the responses. Put this way, being for a balanced budget is like being for motherhood. The fact remains, though, that the political appeal usually attributed to tax cutting has probably been overemphasized over the years. Even the basic Harris question, unhampered by a reference to balancing the budget, found 38 percent who opposed a cut or who were not sure.

On August 12, after quiet talks with Mills on what the Congressman thought could be shoved through the Ways and Means

Committee, Dillon brought a greatly revised program to the Hill.[13] It abandoned almost all of the reform package, including the 5 percent floor. The new proposal was for a two-year tax reduction program of $10.6 billion, with corporate rates to be reduced eventually to 48 percent, and individual rates to a top of 70 percent. As finally adopted by the committee, and revised in the Senate the net tax reduction proposed was $11.6 billion, spread over two years. The new rates, applied to a growing economy, translate the actual tax cut into something exceeding $12 billion.

Most of the abandoned reforms would have affected upper-bracket taxpayers. Moreover, to make up for the loss of revenue that would have resulted from plugged loopholes, the new low basic tax rate—14 percent—would apply only to the first $500 of income, instead of the first $1,000 as originally proposed.

The net result of it all was that upper-bracket taxpayers, with most of their special privileges intact, would get a slightly better reduction than Kennedy had first proposed, and lower bracket taxpayers would get a slightly less generous break than promised. In fact, except for the retention of the Kennedy proposal to repeal the 4 percent dividend credit, a mild restriction on stock options for executives, and a small tightening of depletion-allowance rules, the final bill as President Johnson signed it at the end of February, 1964, almost exactly fitted the demands of the Ford-Saunders businessmen's committee: a whale of a big tax cut, and a minimum of reforms. The tax cut more little resemblance to the original proposals for a more fair tax structure—one of the early dreams of the liberals who were attracted to President Kennedy.

Undersecretary of the Treasury Henry H. (Joe) Fowler— who devoted most of his energies over three years to getting tax legislation proposals translated into law—said after passage of the Revenue Act of 1964 that it was a landmark in the nation's economic history, a "break-through" in the effort to promote economic growth. Business Week Magazine, in an editorial February 22, 1964, said that the bill "may prove to be the most important and most constructive piece of economic legislation passed in this decade."

It is of course true that President Kennedy, and after him President Johnson, finally blugeoned Congress into a reluctant acceptance of a modernized fiscal policy, in which irrational fear of deficits was at least temporarily put aside. A Democratic Administration—and two Democratic Presidents—had acted to correct the "drag" on the economy caused by high taxes, an effort put aside for 8 years under Eisenhower, and for the first two years of the Kennedy Administration. The tax bill, even if the "mix" of its benefits could be improved, is a tribute to Keynes' basic idea that the capitalistic system can't always generate by itself the demand for goods and services needed to keep the economy operating at the best levels. The logic of Keynes' conclusion calls for the Government to step in, and boost demand. This gives short shrift to the Puritans, who say that the budget must be balanced and debt not incurred. The tax bill was thus a Kennedy-Johnson monument at the Keynesian altar.

But surely the total performance was less than adequate: the Kennedy Administration had a rare opportunity to insist on real tax reforms, and it was allowed to trickle away. The proposed reforms were mild enough, merely a step in the right direction. Paul Douglas, a courageous advocate of tax reforms, rose in the Senate on November 1, 1963 to "state the urgent need for tax reform and to protest its slow and quiet strangulation." He pointed to Treasury Department data which showed that in 1959, there were 20 persons with incomes exceeding $500,000 each who had escaped taxes completely. Five of these had incomes exceeding $5 million each.

Douglas' bitter words expressed the feeling of defeat that came over Democratic liberals when the Kennedy Administration made its key compromises with the House Ways and Means Committee in order to get the necessary votes for the tax slash itself:

> In 1961, President Kennedy told the Congress that his Administration was preparing a "comprehensive tax reform program" which would be "aimed at providing a broader and more uniform tax base" and at establishing "a more equitable tax structure and a simpler tax law." Originally, that program was to be presented to us in 1962. It was delayed until 1963. When it came, it was, in some respects ambitious, and in other respects timid. But it was an effort at tax reform . . .

> But now, Mr. President, the Treasury has given up on any efforts for the reforms rejected by the House. Supposedly in the

interest of quick enactment of a tax cut, it has decided not to "renew" its request for any of the rejected reforms . . .[14]

The Senate version, which largely prevailed in conference, made one basic improvement in the House bill by rejecting a brand-new giveaway in capital gains taxes that had slipped through the Ways and Means Committee. When Congressional leaders defended the final bill as the best that could have been produced, they were probably correct, because there had been little inclination on Kennedy's part to make an all-out fight against entrenched or sheltered tax interests. And Johnson's role, as he saw it, was merely to drive ahead and get a bill passed, as soon as possible. By grinding the budget down, and exhibiting his concern for "fiscal integrity," he got final action quicker than Kennedy would have.

The sad part of the reform story is that once a big tax cut is actually passed, the opportunity to eliminate special privileges slips away also. Yet there are overwhelming arguments in favor of major tax reform. It is essential as a matter of simple justice. One wonders that the great bulk of ordinary people who must pay their full measure of taxes on ordinary income do not rebel. "Reforms come hard," Walter Heller told the Joint Economic Committee in January, 1963, "the dream of a thorough tax reform is just that—a dream."

But there was a chance for something of a reform in January, 1963, and the Kennedy Administration let it go. It is doubtful, judging by the 1963–64 results, when more than $11 billion worth of bait was dangled before Congressional eyes, that real and meaningful tax reform can ever be passed. The tax havens, the loopholes, the depletion favoritism, will probably go on forever.

Whether the tax program, judged in this light, deserves the accolades heaped on it remains to be seen. The tax reductions eagerly accepted by consumers who found more money in their pay envelopes in 1964 are not going to solve unemployment, or get to the roots of the poverty problem. One needs some income to begin with before a tax rebate is meaningful. Mr. Kennedy might have done better to have mixed in some heavier expenditure programs along with the tax cut. Eventually, such programs are going to be necessary, anyway. No one, not even the optimistic Sargent Shriver, believes that the $500 million re-

quested by Johnson for the new anti-poverty office can be anything except the beginning trickle that must widen into a flood
if the effort is to be meaningful. The 1964 report of the Council of Economic Advisers gives one measure of this problem: to
bring 9 million poor families up to the $3,000 income level
would cost $11 billion a year.

It is inconceivable, of course, that the tax cut will fail to
stimulate the economy: it will certainly drive total consumption
and total profits to a new record. In mid-1964, as a matter of
fact, it was the fashion among business economists to fear a tax-
generated inflation. But the forward push from the tax cut
experienced in 1963 (by way of anticipation) and continuing
in 1964, might very well be short-lived. Knowledgeable economists in and out of the Government had already begun to talk
of the next step—a new cut in taxes (income or excises) or
greater spending—in order to sustain the economy and avert a
recession.

Not even the Council of Economic Advisers pretends that
the whopping tax cut will close the "gap" between the nation's
performance and potential. By degrees, the Economic Report
had postponed that hopeful day when unemployment might be
reduced to 4 percent. In January 1962, the Kennedy Administration set its sights on achieving that goal by mid-1963. This,
Heller wrote in the 1962 report, "would represent a very strong
expansion. But a less ambitious rate of recovery . . . would
prolong the waste of unused resources." By January 1963 the
mid-1963 goal had to be scrapped; but the Economic Report
promised that the tax cut "will surely set us on the path toward
our interim employment target [4 percent unemployment] and
. . . it will lay the foundation for more rapid long-run growth."
And by the time January 1964 rolled around—with the tax
cut almost a reality—the best that the Economic Council could
promise was this: "By the end of the year, it [the unemployment rate] is expected to fall to approximately 5 percent . . .
but the attainment of the interim goal of 4 percent lies beyond
1964." In fact, the Administration did not anticipate that more
comfortable level of unemployment until 1966.

Even the longer-range prospect of new strength in the economy seems dubious, unless the tax cut is soon accompanied by
other public and private action. We need other measures to

focus on specific problems—racial discrimination, inadequate education, inadequate health and hospital facilities, and labor immobility. The basic case for touting a tax cut as a cure-all was that the proposal would have both a "multiplier" and an "accelerator" effect. The first relates to individuals: a cut in taxes (evidenced first in lower withholding rates) leaves the job-holder with more money to spend. And historically—in the postwar years, at least—the consumer spends about 93 cents and saves about 7 cents of every dollar left over after taxes. Therefore, reduce the tax burden, the theory goes, and the consumer will spend practically all of his "extra" dollars. And what he spends is spent and respent, as his purchases raise others' incomes, creating a steadily wider cycle of still new demands. This is the "multiplier" effect, which government economists feel can be conservatively estimated at the number two. Thus, a $10 billion cut in taxes would ultimately lead to a $20 billion increase in the nation's total output, or gross national product. There is a lag of time involved, and the Council makes no specific estimate of how long it takes for the full "multiplier" effect.

In addition, an "accelerator" comes into the picture from the investment side. As consumer spending and the demand for goods and services rises, businessmen will be induced to increase production. They will need to add to inventories to take care of heavier sales. Profits, meanwhile, would begin to climb, providing a new incentive to build more plant capacity while there's additional cash on hand.

The Administration itself never put a number on the accelerator impact, but Dr. Roy Moor, an economist now on Senator Proxmire's staff, developed an elaborate study in which he calculated the combined accelerator-multiplier effect of a tax cut at 3.8 after a period of two years. Give or take a fraction, most economists accept Moor's arithmetic as reasonable.

Thus, applying Dr. Moor's accelerator-multiplier of 3.8 to a $10 billion tax cut, the gross national product might be expected to rise some $38 billion after two years, if the tax cut were made effective all at once. A cut spread over two or three years, to be sure, would not force the economy up that quickly.

But taking the $38 billion as the most optimistic yield of a big tax cut, there is considerable doubt that it would, in today's vastly changing economy, yield enough jobs to bring unemployment down to a 4 percent figure. A provocative study that supports this view was made by Nat Goldfinger, chief economist for the AFL-CIO, and his general conclusions have since been supported by other independent analyses, including one made under the direction of Labor Secretary W. Willard Wirtz, and another at the Bureau of the Budget.[15]

What Goldfinger's research showed was that because of the spread of automation, and a vast change in the composition of the gross national product since the early 1950's, it takes many more dollars of national output to create one additional job than it used to. In the immediate post-Korean War business cycle, from 1953 to 1957, the economy generated one additional job each time the GNP went up by $14,250. In the 1957-60 period, it took $22,335 in added GNP to produce one more job. And in the 1960 to 1962 cycle, it required $28,907 of GNP for every added job. (All figures are in 1962 dollars.)

Goldfinger's figures, tallied from the Government's own reports, confirmed what was evident on all sides in the American economy: despite an increase of $100 billion in GNP in the Kennedy years, the problem of hard-core unemployment had not been solved. Moreover, machines were replacing men in large numbers. This meant that more dollars' worth of products were being turned out with fewer men, and a tax-cut-induced rise in GNP, therefore, didn't necessarily guarantee the creation of the number of jobs required for full employment. Part of the problem could be traced to heavy and increasing military budgets concentrated in space and missile projects, where—dollar for dollar—fewer men and materials were used than in conventional weapons or construction.

Officially, Kennedy's economists scoffed at this analysis, although it received President Kennedy's personal attention and concern.[16] Mr. Kennedy, committed beyond recall to the tax cut, could only hope for the best. The Government, as Johnson took it over on November 22, 1963, had settled for exactly the "less ambitious rate of recovery" that would waste resources. With unemployment well above 5 percent in the spring of 1964, the business world's familiar worries about a nonexistent inflation were trotted out again. The fear of expanding the public sector of the economy, which had gripped the Kennedy Administration, seemed to fit in with Johnson's passion for budget cutting. Suggestions—like one from Senator Clark's manpower committee—that 3 percent unemployment should be taken as a goal, were dismissed as wild and impractical.

Just after Kennedy's death, Arthur Schlesinger, Jr., told the Women's National Democratic Club that in his second term, the President would have swung into a broad program against poverty. Others of his close friends who cringed at the expenditure control policy accepted it as a necessary expedient to get the tax cut—and insisted that Mr. Kennedy would soon have moved again toward heavier spending and a broader governmental role.

The question is moot. But it wouldn't have been easy for Mr. Kennedy to abandon his pledge during the campaign year, and President Johnson has taken up the cudgels for fiscal integrity with such speed and emphasis that he may be locked into a tight spending policy for some time to come. Even with the tax cut now a fact, it is likely that a much bigger Federal budget will be necessary for fiscal 1966 in order to reduce unemployment. If Lyndon Johnson sticks to his initial budgetary tactics, then it can be fairly said that the Kennedy-Johnson-Heller tax strategy set the outer limits of national government policy—more than its originators realized when they started.

Unemployment in America— The Ugly Side of the Affluent Society

SECRETARY OF LABOR W. Willard Wirtz hid his impatience by stuffing yet another bowlful of tobacco into his pipe. "Maybe I *do* get emotional about the unemployment problem," he said. "Maybe I am overconcerned by the fact that there are 4,000,000 people unemployed in this country, people who are denied the essential right to work—using that term in the only true sense it should be. But I think the situation is so deplorable in human terms that it warrants an indignant intolerance of any explanation for it in terms of any kind of economic analysis." [1]

From mid-1957 to the end of 1963, unemployment in America averaged about 6 percent. In this six-and-one-half-year stretch, the percentage never fell below 5 percent, and on some occasions was close to 7 percent. In the midst of plenty, the world's most affluent society quietly tolerated an island of poverty—an underdeveloped nation within a nation as real to those in it as the desiccated South of Italy or the back bush of Africa.

And even the 5 to 6 percent range is not a true measure of unemployment; there are those who must take part-time jobs because full-time work is not available. When allowance is made for this factor, it adds about one additional percentage point to the basic figure. In addition, there are those not counted as unemployed because they had quit looking for work, discouraged and hopeless. Thus, when the "official" unemployment rate is said to be 6 percent, the real count may well be closer to 8 percent.

Yet, among ordinary people, in Congress and in the Executive branch of the Government, there has been little sense of urgency about meeting the unemployment problem. When a general feeling of prosperity prevails, as in the Kennedy years, the anguish of the unemployed is submerged. One has to go, himself, to the half-dead and still dying coal towns in West Virginia or Kentucky, or into the ugly steel slums around Pittsburgh to sense the numbing degradation of unemployment. When one talks to Negro families in Chicago, now in the third generation of relief, or to former steel-mill hands who may never work again—and know it—then unemployment becomes something more than a mere number.

"One of the things that whips us," says Wirtz, "is the 'I'm alright, Jack,' attitude of those who have jobs. Those hardest hit are least able to do anything about their situation. What can a 16-year-old kid do when he's out of a job—pick up a phone and call his Congressman?"

For all of its intellectual concern with unemployment, the Kennedy Administration was never able to grapple successfully with the problem. It is bequeathed, unsolved, to President Johnson. Mr. Kennedy himself, in the privacy of discussions with his advisers, wondered how to get the story across. Even a 6 percent unemployment rate, he sometimes observed, means that 94 percent of the people are working. Moreover, the President also felt there was much merit in the argument made by FRB Chairman William McChesney Martin and others that a big part of the jobs problem was due to technological change, lack of proper training, labor immobility and other so-called "structural" difficulties which are not solved by a general upturn in the economy. His experiences as a Massachusetts Congressman and Senator revolved largely about structural job problems.

President Kennedy's economic advisers played down the significance of structural unemployment, their theory being that the high jobless rate stems instead from inadequate demand. Implicit in the advisers' theory is that automation isn't much different in scope from technological changes in other periods of history.

Professor Paul Samuelson, whose rejection of an official role in shaping economic policy neither inhibited Kennedy's willingness to call on him, nor his prolific public expressions, argues that "not even one-third" of the increase in unemployment since 1957 can be considered structural.[2] Samuelson used no numbers, but his rough rule of thumb seems to be that of an increase of 1,000,000 in the absolute number of unemployment since then, perhaps 300,000 at the very most can be chalked up to structural causes, and the rest is the fault of the sluggish economy.

Other experts hold that automation is no mere extension of the industrial revolution. The key technical advance of the prewar decades was the assembly-line, mass-production technique, which expanded job opportunities for semiskilled workers, many with only limited education. Whatever skills were necessary could be acquired on the job. But today's technology increasingly transfers the materials-handling function to the machines or computers, curtailing the need for workers with little skill. Programmers, not men with wrenches, are in demand today.[3]

The Council of Economic Advisers, under Walter Heller, brushed off the structural theory because of a single-minded concentration on getting the tax cut through Congress. Mr. Heller was determined to "demolish" all arguments on the structural side, and he devoted much energy—probably too much—to the "proof" that structural unemployment was no worse than it was 10 or 15 years ago. This is quite beside the point. Whether or not structural unemployment was worsening in the early 60's because of automation, and whether or not today's technology is a more dire threat than earlier mechanization, *the fact is that there is sufficient technological unemployment to be concerned about.*

To be sure, the basic need is for expanded job opportunities in a more ebullient economy, as Heller has insisted. But the fear of the machine is a pervasive force in labor circles, and understandingly so, because after each postwar recovery with its attendant rise in aggregate demand, the unemployment plateau moved steadily higher.

When Heller came into office in 1961, he predicted that a broad increase in aggregate demand would soak up unemployment. But the record shows that he underestimated the severity of the problem. The recovery from 1961 to 1962 added $28 billion to the economy, and cut unemployment by one point—

from an average of 6.7 to 5.6 percent. And from the end of
1962 through the end of 1963, while the GNP grew yet another
$35 billion, the unemployment rate didn't budge downward
one iota from that 5.6 percent mark.

Heller's response was, correctly, that the economy has to be
stimulated even more. But whether the necessary stimulus can
be produced from a tax cut alone is the real question. Heller for
the first time paid more than lip service to the structural problem in a careful statement on October 28, 1963, to the Senate
Labor Committee, when he said:

> The primary attack on high unemployment must be through
> fiscal measures to speed the growth of total demand and thereby
> to create new job opportunities. But this need not—indeed,
> must not—impede a simultaneous attack on our stubborn struc-
> tural problems. The two approaches are not merely comple-
> mentary; they are mutually reinforcing.
>
> On the one hand, training and other programs to facilitate
> labor mobility can ease and speed the process by which demand-
> stimulated increases are translated into increases in employment.
> On the other, since structural maladjustments tend to flourish
> in slack markets, a vigorous expansion in demand helps cut
> structural problems down to size.

Heller went on to say that high regional rates of unemployment, and high rates among Negroes, the unskilled, and the
undereducated workers "require a more direct attack." But the
trouble is that a more direct attack would involve heavy expenditures for retraining, relocation, and basic education—expenditures that did *not* have backing in the Kennedy Administration and do not have backing in the Johnson Administration
because of the parallel commitments to hold down spending
in order to get a tax bill passed.

This focus on the tax bill explained the frustrations of many.
For example, Ben B. Seligman, research director of the AFL-
CIO Retail Clerks Association, insists that "no amount of Federal fiscal tinkering will meet the immediate needs of those
attached to a dying industry." [4] Seligman, not surprisingly, sees
the shorter workweek as the only practical step for mitigating
the problems created by automation.

The opposing argument was put this way by Economic Council member John Lewis in a speech at Notre Dame University

in September, 1963. "The slack problem," Lewis said, "is essentially an aggregate-demand problem. We are thoroughly convinced that the cause of persisting underproduction and underemployment is insufficient outlays in the economy as a whole.

"To put the point differently, the primary cause is not that our labor force—fairly suddenly, over the space of the last 5 or 6 years—has become too young or too old, or too badly trained, or outmoded by automation, or newly discriminated against on racial or other grounds."

Lewis didn't argue that structural problems were nonexistent. But he insisted: "Employers who discriminate against Negroes, who hesitate to train the unskilled, and who pass over the youngsters . . . do so far less when orders are rolling in, business is booming, and most other job candidates already employed. Greater total demand . . . is the quickest medicine for moderating [special problems] radically while other specific programs are being brought to bear."

Within the Kennedy Administration, there was a sharp split of opinion on this question. Manpower experts at the Labor Department were convinced that the Administration "line," established by Heller, underestimated the impact of automation. Some of these knowledgeable technicians believe—although they admit they can't prove it—that roughly 50 percent of the recent additions to the ranks of the jobless are casualties of automation. In a widely publicized appearance, John Snyder, a manufacturer, told a Senate committee that 2,000,000 jobs each year were being lost to automation.[5] He scoffed at the contention that automation would actually increase the number of jobs and labeled it "the most seductive" of the myths about the new technology. Snyder's may be a high figure; certainly it is a gross figure, unreduced by new and additional jobs created in many sectors of the economy. But it cannot be doubted that there is a noticeable effect on jobs as a result of technological change, as most of us can see as we go about our routine, daily tasks. The most serious impact has been in unskilled and semiskilled jobs in agriculture, manufacturing, mining, and railroading. Craftsmen such as plumbers and electricians have had to take new training in order to keep up with new materials and techniques. In the newspaper industry, linotypists and other highly skilled men in allied trades are being displaced by computer-directed operations. In recent years, employment gains in offices, warehouses and stores have slowed down because machines have replaced clerical workers.

Employment has grown in service establishments such as hotels, beauty parlors, government, and hospitals. But a high percentage of these jobs is unattractive to skilled or semiskilled men pushed out of industry because they involve manual labor at low pay—for example, parking lot attendants, counter workers, charwomen, janitors, busboys.

The other areas of expanding employment are the professions and highly skilled jobs associated with computers and programming. But these occupations are also, for the most part, out of the reach of the blue-collar worker who yields his place on the assembly line to an IBM computer. And untrained youngsters with a minimum of education—there are too many of them—who used to find their first work experience in the factories or the mines, today face the choice of accepting an unattractive service job or nothing at all.

But if Heller and Samuelson are right, the first order of business is to push the unemployment ratio down to 4 percent by a tax-cut hypo. They maintain that there will then be plenty of time to come to grips with the hard-core structural problem that remains. If, in the process, the rich get richer, or if one can't really answer the accusation that this is a trickle-down-of-prosperity program—well, one has to be practical!

President Kennedy, under Heller's tutelage, took 4 percent unemployment as the "reasonable interim target" for full employment, certainly a less challenging concept than 3 percent, the fashionable target among the liberals in the 1950's. The essence of the argument is that about 1½ percent of today's unemployed would be drawn into productive jobs by an expanding economy, and then emphasis should be shifted to a special attack on structural problems.

Among Administration policy-makers, only Labor Secretary Wirtz ever publicly challenged the wisdom of setting the "goal" as high as 4 percent. "I don't think there is any excuse for the figure," Wirtz says. "In some people's thinking, unemployment is accepted—without ever really saying it—as a welcome hedge against inflation, or in other areas even as an excuse to avoid any increase in costs. . . . Inflation, fiscal irresponsibility and international bankruptcy are obvious vices which this economy simply cannot afford. . . . I deny that . . . a choice must be made between these evils." [6]

In defining full employment to mean a 4 percent unemployment level, the Council and President Kennedy put a premium on price stability. It was a basic decision that affected the course of economic policy for all the Kennedy years. It was practical, realistic, hardheaded—but limiting. Heller says that the 4 percent figure was settled on "because, by our best . . . calculations, it is around 4 percent unemployment that you begin to find the bottlenecks developing the inflationary pressures . . . and if you develop a relationship between unemployment and price stability goals, this seems to be the point where you have your standoff." [7]

This isn't terribly convincing. The Council argument rests largely on the fact that there was relative price stability in mid-1955 with unemployment just over 4 percent. If price stability is the sine qua non of Administration policy, would 5 percent become "a reasonable interim target" for full employment if prices start to move up before we get to 4 percent? As a matter of fact, the 4 percent figure already looks so remote that more and more is heard of returning to a 5 percent level as some sort of achievement. In 1961 and 1962, official Administration policy called for reducing unemployment to the 4 percent level by mid-1963. But by the time mid-1963 rolled around, unemployment was 5.5 percent of the labor force, and the 4 percent goal had been put back to mid-1966. In his Labor Day message in 1963, President Kennedy noted that even if the tax bill passed the Congress, it would take another two years or more to get unemployment "under 5 percent."

In his 34-month stewardship, President Kennedy went along with the Heller theory that stimulation and expansion of the economy itself had to be the nation's basic answer to unemployment. "If the performance of the economy is high," Kennedy said in his 1963 Economic Message to Congress, "the aspirations of the American people are higher still—and rightly so. For all of its advances, the nation is still falling substantially short of its economic potential. . . ."

But having gone this far, President Kennedy refused to follow the bold policies needed to provide the necessary stimulation. He felt "constrained" by the balance of payments from moving toward a vigorous, expansionary monetary policy; he delayed and temporized for two years on tax cuts as a device to give the economy a thrust. Although the business community obviously feels more secure in Lyndon Johnson's allegiance to reduced budgets and government economy drives, Kennedy actually tried to follow a "hold-down" policy for most of his Presidency. Thus, even as he supported (in his Economic Messages and in many sparkling press conference exchanges) the validity of the expansionists' prescription for curing unemployment, the President's moves—or lack of them—fitted more closely into a pattern of mild fiscal push and nibbling at the edges of the structural problem through a limited retraining effort and a salvage operation in the depressed areas.

By the spring and summer of 1963, the proposed tax cut had become a panacea: it was the magic cure-all for every problem from unemployment to the balance of payments deficit. And even this was tied to a painful expenditure control policy that became increasingly specific as the Administration tried to push the bill through Congress. The President's home-stretch commitments to "fiscal integrity" as his lieutenants fought for votes on the Hill made it clear that no new programs for badly needed social services would be incorporated in the 1965 budget.

To be sure, Kennedy in his final months was trying to blunt the Republicans' move to tie the proposed tax cut to some sort of budget or debt ceiling. But it was sad to hear the President, in the space of a single paragraph of a speech to the Business Committee for Tax Reduction in 1963, warn knowledgeably that federal expenditures were already a declining percentage of the gross national product—and then promise that in the future, the Government would follow an "even stricter" spending control policy.[9]

The steady growth of unemployment in recent years has evoked two kinds of response among those who wish to brush the problem under the rug. The first is an attack on the validity of the figures themselves. There are variations of this approach, but the common thread is the accusation that the Bureau of Labor Statistics figures overstate the "real" level of unemployment. A particularly shoddy attack in the *Reader's Digest* by a writer named James Daniel prompted the creation of a Presidential Commission, headed by Professor Aaron Gordon of the University of California, which investigated and gave a clean bill of health to the data.[10]

The other approach is more serious. Not only does it represent the privately held view of a large segment of American society, but it is unbelievably crass and wholly indifferent to the human misery of unemployment. The attitude of this group is that the nation "must learn to live" with 6 or 7 percent unemployment. Whispered, not shouted, this notion has wide currency among many important businessmen. And while some regard high unemployment as regrettable, others frankly feel that a pool of 4 to 5 million unemployed men and women is a kind of safety valve against inflation. This is an immoral position that few will defend openly, and many will deny exists.

It is to the credit of the United States Chamber of Commerce that in July, 1963, it flatly branded the current 5.7 percent rate as "too high for economic comfort. . . . Humanitarianism and self-interest considerations dictate that the business community try to remedy the situation." The Chamber developed no policies to cope with the problem, but at least it didn't challenge the existence of persistently high joblessness, or the assertion that it was a drag on the economy.

The fact that a large part of unemployment is concentrated among Negroes has only lately begun to seep into the American consciousness—although the figures have been there to show it all the time. The London *Economist* observed that the racial outburst of 1963 came just 100 years after the Emancipation Proclamation and 30 years after the New Deal, reviving the battle of both. "The answer to it," said the *Economist,* "can only be a synthesis of both . . . the economic and cultural legacies of slavery have to be thrown off. . . ."[11]

Until recently, to the shame and disgrace of organized labor, it openly and deliberately followed and countenanced policies of racial discrimination of the most vicious kind. The AFL-CIO made only token efforts to rid itself of bias against Negroes, especially in the archaic craft unions, until the civil rights' revolution overtook it in 1963. The National Association for the Advancement of Colored People began a fight against discrimination within the AFL-CIO in 1955, almost as soon as the merged union took form. But for years, although the AFL-CIO had a civil rights division, the George Meany leadership took refuge behind the unquestioned difficulty of translating pious national directives into effective action at the local level.

For example, months after a new and more enlightened national policy was established, 35 white plumbers of Meany's own New York local walked off a construction job in the Bronx because the contractor hired three Puerto Ricans and one Negro. To be sure, these four were nonunion—but only because the plumbers had set up racial barriers to union membership.

The AFL-CIO, it is true, was probably in step with local sentiment—the nation itself showed little courage on the discrimination issue in the 1950's. But the AFL-CIO, as an organization representing people, should have taken the lead. It had no courage and muffed an opportunity in the most crucial civil rights' area of all—jobs. Herbert Hill, militant NAACP secretary, is generally disliked in AFL-CIO councils. But his indictment of the AFL-CIO as "negligent and lazy, an active party to discriminatory practices" is hard to challenge. The labor union movement followed four key discriminatory practices: systematic exclusion of Negroes from unions themselves; segregated Jim Crow locals; separate racial seniority lines; and exclusion from apprenticeship training programs. Among the old-line craft unions originally in the American Federation of Labor, there long has been a caste attitude reminiscent of the medieval guilds. The carpenters, electricians, and others successfully perpetuated a "white man's job" aura, which will take time to destroy.

Belatedly, the AFL-CIO moved in 1963 to right some wrongs. Union leaders pledged the President, after he demanded it, that they would end discrimination and would open up apprenticeship training programs. To long-time Negro leaders like A. Philip Randolph, president of the Brotherhood of Sleeping Car Porters, who led the emotion-packed march on Washington in August, 1963, the apprenticeship problem is at the core of the issue. "According to population projections," Randolph said, "there is going to be a great need for skilled workers in the next few years. This will help us if we can only get a foothold. Right now, the young Negro feels bottled up in an economic pocket from which he can't escape."

A nation heeding the demand for job equality and opportunity can ill-afford to tolerate high unemployment—and the enormous technological changes of the next few years will intensify the problem. The kind of skills that even now are in demand are enormously different from the skills available among the pool of unemployed and many young people who enter the labor market. Professor John Dunlop says that "this disparity between the character of our demands for labor, and the characteristics of our labor force is to me one of the most difficult aspects of our whole present situation." [12]

Then, there is the question as to the exact extent to which technological change cuts into jobs. Ewan Clague and Leon Greenberg of the Bureau of Labor Statistics estimated that about 200,000 factory workers lose their jobs each year because of automation. Their study did not cover job losses due to automation in the service industries. But even so, the figure sounds low to some experts. Greenberg, who is assistant BLS Commissioner for Productivity and Technological Developments, himself told a Senate committee that "some significant trends appear to be occurring in the manufacturing sector of the economy." [13] What Greenberg found was that productivity—that is, output per man-hour—had risen 4 percent among manufacturing industries as a whole in 1961 and 1962. Two such successive years of large increase are unusual, and a third—for 1963—would be unprecedented, far above the long-run (1909-1947) average of 2 percent, and the postwar rate of 2.7 percent.

Yet economists like to consider longer trends than two or three years when considering productivity, and a five-year average is thought to be more revealing. And here Greenberg's figures begin to tell a story. For the five-year period 1957 through 1962, the productivity increase in manufacturing was 3.4 percent —well above the long-run or postwar average. And while productivity was going up 3.4 percent, the average increase in *production* itself was only barely higher, 3.6 percent. Thus, the lush output of American factories could be turned out with only a marginal increase in jobs.

Compare this with the first 10 years of the postwar period, 1947-1957. Then, output went up substantially more than productivity—4.3 percent for output, 2.8 percent for productivity —which meant that increasing production was associated with a substantial increase in jobs.

The problem comes into even sharper focus when productivity for production workers alone is set against output. In the past five years, the productivity rate increase for production workers averaged an astonishing 4.1 percent. But output increased only 3.6 percent. Hence, jobs among production workers declined. A study of 200 industries for the four-year period ending 1961 (data for 1962 aren't completed) showed a decline of 747,000 in employment of production workers due to increased productivity, and an additional 576,000 decline because of reduced output in particular industries.

The high rates of productivity increases in manufacturing in the face of declining output, Greenberg testified, "implies a relatively higher impact of technological change or of other labor-saving factors in the manufacturing process. It also points up the problem of job opportunities for blue-collar workers." Unconvinced, the Heller school acknowledges that the rate of industrial productivity was higher in 1961 and 1962—but argues that this gain is no more noticeable than in any other two recovery years. Unless the pattern continues longer, Heller argues, nothing has been proved. More recently, Heller has been hedging his bets. He said on October 28, 1963: "Yet, the trend productivity rate *may* be in the process of accelerating. Technological change may indeed have speeded up, but its impact upon productivity may be only gradually becoming visible. . . ." [14] This thought is elaborated in the 1964 Economic Report.

The Kennedy Administration never developed an official estimate of the number of jobs that will be "lost" to automation throughout the whole economy in the next several years. But Seymour L. Wolfbein, director of the Labor Department Manpower office, calculates that between 1960 and 1970, 22,-000,000 jobs would be "affected" by automation and technological change.[15]

"By 1970," Wolfbein said, "advances in productivity will enable us to produce the 1960 national output with 22,000,000 fewer workers. . . . This does not mean that persons in these jobs will necessarily become unemployed. But it does mean that there has to be a big enough economic growth and demand for goods and services which, in turn, will generate enough demand for workers to account for all of these jobs affected by our advancing technology." In addition, Wolfbein said, there will be a need for another 13,000,000 jobs to take care of the expansion of the labor force during this period.

Wolfbein calls the technological revolution now under way a "literal upending of our occupational and industrial structure. . . . We are now witnessing a head-on collision between advancing automation and technology on the one hand and a tidal wave of manpower, for whom job opportunities must be available on the other." As recently as 1955, in all of the U. S., to cite just one example, there were only 450 digital computers, valued at $250 million. But by the end of 1963, the number had soared to 15,000, valued at nearly $7 billion. Many of these are small units, so other than the giant firms can afford computers today. "We'll begin to see the effects of this later on," says Wolfbein.

In a number of major industries, new machines and methods have already displaced large numbers of men. The bland assurances of some that automation—in the end—will produce more jobs can't obscure the simple fact that the reason for putting new machines or methods in, in the first place, is to *lower* the manpower requirements per unit of production. So the initial impact *must* be a loss of jobs.

The impact can be seen by examining some specific industries:

• The enormous spread of automation into America's farms has chopped employment by an average of about 200,000 a year since the end of World War II. Total agricultural employment has thus been reduced more than one-third (and actual manhours worked cut nearly in half), while farm output has increased one-third.

• In coal mining, 46 miners can now turn out the same amount of coal dug by 100 workers in 1947.

• The railroad industry handles about the same volume of

traffic it did a decade ago, with 40 percent fewer workers—and even the present rail labor force, as is clear from the 1963 work rules fight, can be substantially reduced.

• In the banner years of 1955 and 1963, Detroit produced about 7,000,000 cars of each model. But in 1963, the industry handled its production with 21 percent fewer workers.

• In the electrical industry, output increased 21 percent between 1953 and 1961, while the job total went down 10 percent.

• In the decade of the 1950's, there was a loss of 80,000 production jobs in steel—and the fantastic development of the oxygen furnace and other new methods spell even worse trouble in the 60's.[16]

To look at it in the grand dimension, the nation's total economic output of goods and services from the first quarter of 1962 to the first quarter of 1963 went up $24 billion—while the percentage of unemployment edged up from 5.7 to 5.8 percent.

A steady deterioration in the jobs picture began after the Korean War. From 1951 to late 1953, under the impetus of the war-stimulated economy, unemployment averaged only about 3.1 percent. There was a recession and recovery cycle in 1953 and 1954, and then another stable level of unemployment from mid-1955 to late 1957. But this time the plateau moved up to an average of 4.2 percent. Again, after recession and recovery from 1957 to 1959, the unemployment rate was stable in the first half of 1960—but at a level of 5.3 percent. And then, after the recession and recovery of 1960-61 (when a peak of 7 percent was touched), the unemployment level stabilized around the 5.6 percent mark. Note the pattern—3.1 percent, 4.2 percent, 5.3 percent, 5.6 percent.[17]

Thus, in the 10 years following the end of the Korean War, a period of growing affluence of U. S. society, unemployment settled at a higher level after each recovery from a recessionary dip. Although the recessions were relatively mild, some jobs appeared to be lost permanently after each bout with recession, and the unemployment rate in 1962 and 1963 was almost double that of the Korean War period. If the comparison is unfair because that was a period of forced draft operation (although it raises the question as to why the U. S. economy operates best in wartime) one need only compare the 1962-63 rate with 1955-57. Over that period, the unemployment rate jumped nearly 50 percent.

Defenders of the free enterprise economy might be expected to show more concern over the slowdown in the growth of the private sector. For it is a fact in the years 1957 through 1962, there was a net loss of 425,000 manufacturing jobs, compared with a gain of 1.6 million jobs in the decade prior to 1957. The startling fact that emerges from a cold look at the figures is that only in the public sector of the economy—in government jobs —has there been an increase in the past five years. Most of this increase has been in state and local government jobs, largely in the school systems.[18]

One of the great difficulties in getting across the unemployment story, as we have seen, is the popular impression that the problem is in the rough dimensions of 5 to 6 percent of the labor force. This is the "seasonally adjusted" unemployment percentage which has prevailed for the past many months, the one which is used by newspaper headline and television script writers. But like many averages, it doesn't tell the meaningful story. There is a great variation, according to the separately identifiable problems of age, sex, skill, geographical area, and racial discrimination.

For example, during 1962, when the average annual unemployment rate was 5.6 percent for the labor force as a whole, it was only 4.9 percent for whites, and 11.0 percent for Negroes. Among whites, the percentage of unemployed males was 4.9; of unemployed females, 4.7; and of unemployed teen-agers, 12. Among Negroes, the percentage of unemployed males was 10; of unemployed females, 9.6; and of teen-agers, a shocking 23.6 percent.

For unskilled labor, white and Negro together, the percentage was 12.4 percent in industry. Contrast this with the rate for professional personnel: less than 2 percent. And in the nation's depressed areas—where, by definition, the unemployment percentage was chronically higher than in the rest of the country —the toll was much worse. For example, in Beckley, West Virginia (where once it had ranged as high as 26 percent), 12 percent of the labor was out of work in 1962.

In other words, one had to look behind the bare statistics to catch the tone of tragedy. For the Negro, unemployment was the price of others' prejudices; they have been working, mostly, at the unskilled jobs which are giving way to automation. The market for whatever talents they had is vanishing, and retraining could be meaningful only if there were an answer to the basic question: Retraining for what job?

For the youngsters—and the 23.6 percent of Negro youngsters unemployed is an index to juvenile delinquency statistics, nationwide—only continued years in regular high schools, or special training in vocational schools offers any hope. By the end of 1963, at least 750,000 boys and girls under twenty-one were roaming the streets—out of school, and out of a job. And for the blight in the depressed areas, concealed by national averages, only a bold attack on the immobility of labor would help at all until such time as some future boom picked the most distressed counties up by the bootstraps.

There is yet another area of statistical confusion. The 5.6 percent unemployment rate, in a labor force of some 72 million, represents some 4 million individuals out of work. But that is a very static measure, because it represents the number estimated to be out of work at a given time of the month when the Census Bureau takes a sample. It is not a continuous measure of unemployment.

The problem is more pervasive. There are different groups of persons employed and unemployed at different times—and some of the jobless have two or three periods of unemployment during the year. According to the Department of Labor, in recent years nearly one in every five persons in the labor force has been out of work for some significant period of time during the calendar year. The actual figure for 1962, for example, was 15,256,000 persons, or 18.2 percent of the labor force.[19]

The breakdown for 1962 was as follows:

Total working or looking for work	83,944,000
Total with unemployment	15,256,000
Did not work, but looked for work	1,887,000
Year-round workers with 1 to 2 weeks' unemployment	1,129,000

Part-time workers with some unem- ployment	12,240,000
—1 to 4 weeks	2,993,000
—5 to 10 weeks	2,759,000
—11 to 14 weeks	1,700,000
—15 to 26 weeks	2,768,000
—27 weeks or more	2,020,000
Total with two spells or more of un- employment	5,219,000
—2 spells	2,524,000
—3 spells or more	2,695,000

What becomes clear from this table is that the well-publicized monthly reports on unemployment represent *different* groups of people who are out of work. Thus, in contrast to the 1 to 1.5 million generally listed by the Labor Department as the "long-term unemployed"—those who have been idle for 15 weeks or longer—the true hard core is much bigger. In 1962, the table above shows, there were 4,788,000 unfortunate Americans who at one time or another during the year were out of work a minimum of 15 weeks; and a very substantial percentage of them—46.1—were Negroes. The depressing fact is that the large number of persons unemployed at one time or another in 1962 showed virtually no improvement over 1961 despite new records in sales, production, national income—and even in *employment.*

What does the future hold? One can begin to make an appraisal by noting that there has been a dramatic change already in the character of U. S. employment. We have become the only major nation in the world which has more men and women working in the service industries than in the goods-producing industries—and more in white-collar than blue-collar occupations.[20]

In 1962, the goods industries employed 41.8 percent, compared with 58.2 percent in the services. As recently as 1947, the figures were goods, 51.3 percent, services, 48.7 percent. And among both white- and blue-collar jobs, the trend is, of course, to the skilled occupation. Automation and related processes are raising the skill requirements of the whole labor force. Even in coal mines, where a man used to need "a strong back and a weak mind," most of those who still have jobs in the pits operate a machine instead of a pick and shovel.

As a matter of fact, unskilled jobs now account for only 5 percent of all employment in the entire economy. In the 1930's, 20 percent of all jobs went to unskilled labor. It is easy to see how the rising tempo of requirements necessitates greater training and education. A school dropout years ago, spurred by hunger and equipped with muscles, might find a laborer's job. Today, such jobs are scarce.

Between 1957 and 1962, the total labor force rose by 3,800,-000 persons. And over the same five-year period, output per man-hour rose 12.5 percent. This rise in productivity meant a displacement of about 7,500,000 jobs. With these two key figures at hand, it is easy to see what happened: against a need for 11,300,000 jobs to handle the twin problems of a growing population and technological gains, the economy actually generated 10,200,000 new jobs. Thus, the economy fell short by 1,100,000 —which resulted in a rise in unemployment, as we have seen, from 4.3 percent in 1957 to 5.8 percent in 1962.

What clues does this give us for the years ahead? We know that between 1962 and 1967, the labor force is likely to grow more rapidly, thanks to a bumper crop of war and postwar babies. It is estimated that the labor force will grow by about 1,250,000 a year, or by about 6,250,000 over the five-year period.[21] If productivity should gain even a little more than in the prior five-year period, the displacement due to automation and related causes would be 9,600,000 jobs. On this basis, it would be necessary for the economy to generate 15,850,000 jobs— nearly 6,000,000 more than it did from 1957 to 1962—to keep the unemployment ratio from moving over 5.8 percent.

But if the economy continues to be sluggish over the next few years, there would be more slippage. Experts in the Department of Labor think it quite possible that the jobless percentage could rise to 7 percent by 1967.

And that's the conservative picture. What if productivity is on an upward binge, and the 3.9 percent increase for the private economy Leon Greenberg found for 1962 is equaled or exceeded in future years? It is quite conceivable in such a situation that by 1970, there could be 8,000,000 to 10,000,000 people out of work—with an unemployment rate of 10 to 12 percent of the labor force. Any such trend, even in an incipient stage, would call for heroic efforts, and a casting aside by the Government and business world of (in Gunnar Myrdal's phrase) "a serious and irrational bias" against spending in the public sector.

It is difficult to be optimistic about the future. Both the Kennedy and Johnson Administrations all but shut the door against the kind of public spending needed to accelerate growth and close the jobs "gap." This nation still has too many fixations about the virtues of budget control and "economy," as well as antiquated notions about the limitations on the proper role of government. President Johnson, soon after taking office, declared that the goal of his Administration was 75,000,000 jobs —but he put no date on that desirable achievement. Thus, without programs to achieve that level, it was a rather empty public relations gesture. President Johnson will have to be bolder than Kennedy, and bolder than he himself has indicated he wants to be.

A dramatic attack on unemployment is necessary, as President Kennedy well knew. Just a few days before he died, in a brief talk to a steelworkers' local in Florida, he said: "We have to move tremendously fast just to stand still. I have said before that in the next two and a half years in the United States we have to find 10 million jobs to take care of those who are out of work now, those who will be thrown out of work because of machines, and those who are pouring into the labor market because of the baby boom right after the end of the second World War.

"Ten million jobs in two and a half years!

"We have an extraordinary economic record in the last three years, and yet we still have an unemployment rate of five and a half percent." [22]

In September, 1963, when he addressed Henry Ford's Businessmen's Committee for Tax Reduction, President Kennedy bluntly warned that "this nation must create new jobs by one means or another." The phrase "by one means or another," interpolated in his prepared speech, was taken as a vague warning that if the tax bill didn't pass, increased federal spending was indicated. But what is clearly needed is a *combination* of increased government outlays with a well-designed tax bill, and this is where President Kennedy balked, and where President Johnson—at least in the initial phase of his Administration— drew the line as well. President Johnson told aides soon after taking office that it was worthwhile cutting back $1 billion or $2 billion in federal spending in order to get the tax bill through.

There are some possible solutions to the unemployment problem that should be carefully considered by the Johnson Administration. The first step is to gear American education to current industrial needs—and to wipe out discrimination in the schools, in unions, and in offices. Then, the Government should study the needs of the economy, industry by industry. The failure to do this earlier is hard to justify. If the Council of Economic Advisers is too short-staffed to do this job, it could draw on the personnel of the Commerce Department and other agencies.

To lay the basis for a prosperous future, new areas of public and private investment must be found, since the trend of automation in the auto and other mass industries promises little increase in employment in the next ten years, even if economic growth accelerates. What holds more promise—in the search for something to ignite the whole economy as autos did in the 20's —than a real expansion in housing, schools, urban renewal, and mass transportation? And a heavily expanded, compassionate attack on poverty would doubtless help the economy as well as the poor themselves.

To do all this would require a bold increase in federal spending, as well as a redesign of the Administration's manpower retraining program to meet developing needs (as now constituted, it has been unable to reclaim the most underprivileged of the unemployed), and a willingness to use the federal budget as a tool for expansion. It won't be easy; there are many built-in prejudices against spending money, and many of today's most imaginative thinkers have been shunted aside by Democratic policy-makers because their ideas have been too easy to caricature. But they do have ideas.

Full employment was a goal that eluded Kennedy, and may escape Lyndon Johnson as well. But if Johnson is determined to see the nation move ahead, he must back more than token programs to bolster opportunities for education, and eradication of prejudice and poverty. Budget-balancing as an end in itself will certainly have to be put aside. The tax cut may, as President Johnson hopes, cut the unemployment rate to 5 percent by the end of 1964. But if timidity is to be the guide on federal spending, unemployment could rise again in 1965 and 1966. If a steady decline in federal spending in relation to the rest of the economy becomes the basic theme of the Johnson Administration, the country is in for trouble.

The time to strike out boldly is never better than now—a fact that is so sadly underscored by the cruel fate that befell President Kennedy in Dallas. Almost prophetically, when Kennedy addressed the Business Committee for Tax Reduction in October, he pressed for the tax bill because, as he said, "We may never get another opportunity." It applies to all goals for the people and the economy. Now is the time, not later.

From Kennedy to LBJ:
The Unfinished Business

Four days before he was cut down by a mad assassin in Dallas, Texas, John F. Kennedy—who never won the measure of business approval he so earnestly sought—made a last effort to purge his Administration of the anti-business label in a speech to the Florida Chamber of Commerce at Tampa. President Kennedy never hoped to generate a warm feeling of support for himself or his party among businessmen, but he was dismayed to the end by the suspicious and even hostile attitude displayed by many of them.

At Tampa, President Kennedy catalogued the long list of specific actions helpful to business that he had undertaken: the investment tax credit; liberalized depreciation guidelines; reduction in farm surpluses; reduction in transportation taxes; a private corporation to operate the communications satellites; his proposals to cut personal and corporate taxes; and his plan to reduce regulations on transportation. He could have mentioned, also, the Trade Expansion Act, which was intended to open wider markets to American industry, as well as the conservative fiscal and monetary policy he had followed in order to minimize the balance of payments situation.

These plans or programs, Mr. Kennedy correctly pointed out, were not designed "for the benefit of business alone—they were taken to benefit the country." Nonetheless, even a casual look at the Kennedy Administration record suggests, as Commerce Secretary Hodges recently observed, that "President Kennedy was

274

far more conservative and far more pro-business—as the man in the street thinks of it—than they gave him credit for. . . . Basically, he was conservative in business matters."

Nonetheless, as an exasperated Kennedy told the Florida Chamber, "Many businessmen who are prospering as never before under the policies of this Administration, are convinced . . . that we must be anti-business. . . . Many are still convinced that a Democratic Administration is out to soak the rich, increase controls for the sake of controls, and extend at all costs the scope of federal bureaucracy. The hard facts contradict these doubts. This Administration is interested in the healthy expansion of the entire economy. . . . And it is this kind of program in my opinion, in which American business has the largest stake." [1]

Kennedy then listed four questions he said were asked most frequently by the business community, and, not surprisingly, all four areas of business concern related to the size of the Federal Government, or to government spending and deficits:

"Is the Federal Government growing so large that our private economy is endangered?"

"Are not continuing deficits and the mounting national debt certain to drive us into bankruptcy?"

"Why can't this Administration cut federal expenditures?"

"Will the fiscal policies of this Administration lead the nation to inflation?"

Kennedy drew on the logic of his Yale speech on myths to deny that there was danger in the size of the Government, or in its spending and fiscal policies. And as for a curb on federal spending, he stoutly insisted that he had taken a knife to government spending, and warned that "those who call for larger expenditure cuts are forgetting the growth of our population and the complexity of our problems. . . . The secret of true economy is not blind rejection but prudent selection."

He continued: "I am asked, 'Are not continuing deficits and the mounting national debt certain to drive us into bankruptcy?' And my answer to that is 'no.' Once again, we must look at these facts in perspective. . . . In 1945, our national debt was 120 percent of our gross national product. Today it is 53 percent." Like the debt itself, the role of the Federal Government was shrinking, rather than expanding, in relation to the whole economy. Measured as a percentage of the national economy, federal civilian expenditures are no higher than they were at the end of World War II. Mr. Kennedy cited this fact as proof of the fact that Washington was no octopus about to swallow up free private enterprise. "The Federal Government has no desire to expand the size and scope of its activities merely for the sake of expansion," the President said. He boasted that domestic *civilian* expenditures had been cut below the level of the preceding year for the first time in 15 years, and that "there are no more people today working for the Federal Government than there were 10 years ago . . . [and] less people working for the Federal Government today than there were a year ago." Yet the budgets and expenditures of the states have been growing apace. Mr. Kennedy cited figures showing that while the federal debt from 1948 to 1962 (despite the Korean War and huge obligations abroad) had risen less than 20 percent, the average debt of the states had risen 500 percent.

The picture Mr. Kennedy offered to the Tampa businessmen as proof of the conservative pattern of his Administration should have been impressive. The tax proposal, which forced all forward-looking social legislation onto the bottom shelf, was, moreover, so business-oriented that it guaranteed higher corporate profits for 1964 and 1965, even if it didn't assure higher employment totals. The fact of the matter is that the Kennedy Administration—especially its New Frontier economists—ought to have been pained by the declining relationship of federal spending to the total economy. It was absurd, at a time when the President and Walter Heller daily pointed to a $30 billion annual wastage in unemployment and unused capacity, to find them following a policy of economic restraint. The Administration could prove it held the line on domestic spending, federal job totals, and on wage increases—but could not boast of enough activity, reduced unemployment, or of getting the country moving again. The test of virtue was a preposterous exercise in meaningless and outdated economics. As Professor Francis M. Bator of M.I.T. once asked: "The ideological commitment to budget balance is a powerful force in the land. Does it make sense?" [2]

Some of Mr. Kennedy's liberal friends had tried with no success to convince him in the summer of 1963 that a commitment to frugality would put unnecessary strictures on the economy. He allowed his Treasury Secretary, Douglas Dillon, to praise Congress for cutting the Administration's own appropriations requests, a parallel to an almost unbelievable episode in 1957 when George Humphrey called a press conference to invite Congress to cut Eisenhower's budget. Ten days before his death, Kennedy was importuned by George Meany in a private session at the White House to reconsider his refusal to ask for new public works monies. He listened intently while Meany blistered Dillon, and Meany came away with the impression that Kennedy would take another look at the works proposal after the tax bill got through Congress. But what was uppermost in Kennedy's mind was the need to reduce spending as the "convincer" in his desperate attempt to show the business community that he was a friend, not a foe.

As one result of that effort, the Kennedy Administration itself helped to shape the national preoccupation with spending totals and balanced budgets, which was fed for eight long years by Eisenhower, and is being nurtured again under President Johnson. Back in April, 1962, Kennedy defended modern fiscal theory in the Yale speech. But when the howls arose, as we have seen, Mr. Kennedy quietly laid away most of the principles enunciated at that time. He did move to cut taxes at the beginning of 1963 despite the imminence of a budget deficit, but to make the tax cut palatable, he had to direct much of its emphasis toward business, and promise "an even tighter rein" on total federal expenditures. John Kennedy had many and broader goals than being an Eisenhower budget balancer; the real tragedy of his death is that it cut short his Presidency before he could bring his loftier goals to fruition. An assassin robbed him of the chance to be a great President.

Ironically, Kennedy's abortive campaign to sell himself as a prudent man, or a friend of business (both of which he was) was followed by President Johnson's instant and ringing success in both areas. Despite his roots in Populism, and his schooling in Franklin Roosevelt's New Deal, Johnson seized on the economy issue with such convincing rhetoric and action that he knit a tighter bond with the business community in three weeks than Kennedy did in three years. "We will try our dead-level best to get a dollar's worth of value for every dollar we spend,"

Johnson told a meeting of the Business Council in the Fish Room of the White House.[3] He even imprinted such a quotation on the front cover of the *Budget in Brief*. By carefully training the publicity spotlight on the twin themes of continuity of government and economy, Mr. Johnson won the unrestrained admiration of the business community, the conservative press —and doubtless the ordinary citizen. "Men in the Government are going to be recognized in this Administration by not how much they spend, but by how much they save." Johnson said soberly. Blow-by-blow accounts of each day's "savings" helped forge the image of a new, firm, economy-minded man of action at the helm.

He closed unneeded military bases, cut federal jobs, vetoed many a bureaucrat's time-honored right to a Cadillac—and let it be known that he himself had gone around the White House at night turning off unnecessary lights. This was something new, and the *Wall Street Journal* purred with pleased editorials. Edwin Neilan, the most conservative Chamber of Commerce president in some years, volunteered after a talk with Johnson that he might even vote for him. "Not the least interesting aspect of President Johnson's job-cutting directive," observed the New York *Herald-Tribune*, "was the way he announced it. . . . He promised he would be a better economizer than his predecessor. . . . He can reasonably hope to pick up some support among voters for whom Mr. Kennedy's image was too 'liberal.' " [4]

Johnson succeeded Kennedy just when the crucial decisions were to be made on the fiscal 1965 budget, and while public attention was focused on the possibility that a tightfisted attitude might chop spending to the $100 billion level, Johnson privately decided after his first meeting with Budget Director Gordon, two days after the Kennedy assassination, on a much more dramatic goal: he would bring in a budget not only smaller than Kennedy's restrained plan for fiscal 1965, but actually reduced from Kennedy's last budget, for fiscal 1964. And this he did—announcing a budget calling for $97.9 billion in expenditures, down $500 million from the 1964 estimate.

Johnson thus ran more of a risk than Kennedy seemed willing to take that the Government's fiscal policies would be deflationary. He placed all of his reliance on the tax bill—

passage of which was now virtually assured—and at the same time, solidified his position with the business community, which hadn't enjoyed the spectacle of federal budget cutting since Eisenhower turned the trick in fiscal 1960. Yet labor couldn't be too offended, since there was, within the reduced budget, an additional $1.5 billion requested for welfare programs and a New Dealish "war on poverty."

The LBJ economizing campaign was a brilliant political *tour de force*. In a few, swift months in the White House, Johnson cut the ground out from under conservative Democrats who had threatened to desert the party for Barry Goldwater in 1964. Yet he was careful to touch base on all sides—when he met with or briefed business leaders, he met with labor and farm groups as well.

The main theme of Lyndon Johnson's Administration, nevertheless, was the main theme of the business world—economy in government—and the applause Johnson won from the business community was unstinting and complete. And the rapport between him and the big wheels of Wall Street, Pittsburgh and Detroit went deeper. For three years, most American businessmen had been skeptical of a strong-willed, young, intellectual, and adventuresome President Kennedy who might—and sometimes did—challenge their tested and comfortable system. Kennedy was a man of words and the spirit, out of place among boards of directors.

Lyndon Johnson, the way the businessman sees him, is a more "typical" American President, more mature, a wheeler and a dealer, a man of action, a man "you can do business with." He is, as James Reston has said, "a part of their world." His own ranching interests, his closeness to the petroleum industry, the extensive Johnson family broadcasting holdings, make him, in a real sense, a businessman himself. The average big businessman had a proper respect for Kennedy's wealth, but regarded him as a rich man's son who had no real understanding of the role of profit or other business problems. "But they feel that they can get along with Johnson," sighed one of the Kennedy staff men who stayed on at the White House, "and Lyndon feels that he understands their problems. It's a relationship that Jack Kennedy never could have achieved."

Johnson is not a latecomer to the philosophy of fiscal integrity. Before the 1960 Democratic convention, he said in an interview with me that he was a strong believer in "fiscal stability." Except in time of emergency, he argued, "the Government ought to be run a good deal like you run your own business or your personal finances. . . . We should take in as much as we spend." [5] To visitors in his first few weeks in the White House, Mr. Johnson said that "the country wants some evidence of fiscal soundness—it needs some evidence of fiscal prudence." The new President was aware that for all the effort Mr. Kennedy had made, the business world simply hadn't trusted him, and he was determined that things would be different in his Administration. When the Business Council came to the White House just twelve days after Mr. Kennedy's assassination, Johnson pointedly told the group: "Gentlemen, I say banish your fear and shed your doubts and renew your hopes. We have much work to do together." Johnson took the time to be photographed individually with the 89 businessmen attending the session, and prints were promptly dispatched to each with an LBJ autograph. (There was never a memento like this from JFK.) And when Johnson invited the Business Council to dinner for a preview of the State of the Union Message, the members left starry-eyed. Exulted one as he left the State Dining Room: "It's the first time in our [31-year] history that we've been invited to dine in the White House—it didn't even happen under Ike!"

There were other evidences for the business world of a new era of good feeling. For example, Johnson's first major appointment was the designation of his Texas friend, Thomas C. Mann, to take command of all U. S.-Latin American policy posts. Mann is a career diplomat warmly regarded by conservatives, and a devotee of the private investment route to Latin American growth and progress. Under Kennedy, Mann had been yanked out of his State Department post, and demoted to an ambassadorship in Mexico.[6] Businessmen also were in tune with Johnson's concentration on domestic rather than international matters. Inherently isolationist and suspicious of new ventures abroad, many leaders of the American business community had the vague feeling that Kennedy was preoccupied with world affairs and esoteric matters like international liquidity, when he could have been paying more attention to things at home. And they liked the official "guidance" from the LBJ ranch at Christmas time, 1963, that Johnson firmly believed fiscal prudence "is no longer a rich man's issue" and that "the massive federal budget burden is staggering traditional liberalism in the United States." [7]

Although Johnson outdid Kennedy on the expenditure control front by many turns of the screw, some of his economies had their roots in Budget Bureau and Defense Department management techniques begun earlier. Even the Johnsonian "dollar's worth for a dollar spent" had a familiar ring. On August 13, 1962, in a speech to the nation when he rejected the proposed "quickie" tax cut, Kennedy had said: "I want to make it clear that we are not talking about Federal spending getting out of control. On the contrary, we are attempting to provide a dollar of service for the dollars we spend. . . ." [8] In August, 1963, Kennedy had demanded of Budget Director Gordon an explanation of the rise in federal payrolls. He had issued instructions that there be no net addition to federal employment in fiscal 1965. But it was President Johnson who made that order a reality. And as the American people rallied behind him, proud of the smooth transition in a time of terrible crisis and grief, only a bold few pointed out that the emphasis on reduced spending—as distinguished from the elimination of waste —could put a crimp in the health of the economy.

The story of the budget for fiscal 1965 goes back to the summer of 1963, when liberals in the Kennedy Administration and their allies in the labor movement lost a fight to set the expenditure figure at $105 billion. That was a mere hope—a bargaining total; the liberals hoped for a budget of around $103 billion, which would give the economy about as big a push as it had gotten in earlier Kennedy years. But President Kennedy, fighting for the tax bill, wouldn't go this high. At the time of Kennedy's assassination, the Budget Bureau "guideline" was $101.5 billion—and the President had not yet gotten down to the tough job of reviewing the final figures. (On the Wednesday before Kennedy died, Kermit Gordon made a date to see him on the following Wednesday—the day before Thanksgiving—for the beginning of the final budget-cutting sessions, to be continued at Hyannisport after Thanksgiving.)

The year before, Mr. Kennedy had whacked about $2 billion

off the fiscal 1964 budget in the final go-around, pushing the expenditure total well under the $100 billion mark. It is a reasonable assumption, Budget Bureau men who worked under Kennedy agree, that the late President would have done a similar job, chopping the 1965 budget figure to about $100 billion, or perhaps a shade under, gambling on the tax cut to stir the economy to new heights.

President Johnson came along and did everything that Kennedy would have done—and more. His additional savings may spell trouble for the economy. A growing nation can not afford pinchpenny budgets any more than it can afford to waste money on obsolete military installations. There is a difference between economizing that eliminates waste, and budget slashing that is offered as a tribute to the anti-intellectual bloc of Southern Democrats and hidebound Republicans. As Harvey Siegel wrote in an excellent piece in the Washington *Post*:

> [Mr. Johnson] is assuming a great and unnecessary risk. . . . Those who would make a hostage of the tax bill in the Senate are not likely to be deterred by the conservative appeal of a tight budget. . . . The case against a tight budget on economic grounds is far stronger. . . . The safest course for President Johnson to follow would be to budget Federal expenditures in the $103 to $104 billion range. At that level, the budget would exert a positive force for expansion until such time as the impacts of tax reduction are diffused throughout the economy.[9]

John F. Kennedy, with an ever-present sense of history, took special pains with a foreword he wrote for the 1962 volume of the *Presidential Papers*. In it, he observed that certain goals "still elude us and therefore will demand even more thoughtful and urgent attention in the years to come." Besides peace and civil rights, the President included among these objectives full employment and "accelerated economic growth."

President Kennedy was emotionally committed to a high growth rate goal—it was one of the centerpieces of the 1960 campaign. But sticking to a high target proved to be impossible for Kennedy, and may be for President Johnson as well. For no matter how you slice it, a consistently high growth rate trend implies a commitment to larger Federal spending, and faced with this as a reality, President Kennedy relinquished his eagerness to grapple with the problem.

Despite the advance of nearly $100 billion in gross national product in the Kennedy years (to which the President pointed with great pride in his final speeches in New York, Florida, and Texas in November, 1963) the proper statistical measure shows that the recent U. S. long-term annual growth rate, including the Kennedy years, was only 3.3 percent. This is a creditable showing compared to the 2.9 percent rate achieved since the turn of the century. But it wasn't enough—unemployment and poverty are still with us—and it doesn't compare well with the 3.8 percent growth rate in the first post World War II decade.

Just how difficult it is to rack up even small increments in growth was explored in a study by economist Edward F. Denison in 1962.[10] Denison's main conclusion—and Kennedy was impressed with his argument—was that it would take a massive effort during the period 1960-1980 to improve the U. S. growth rate by even a fraction above 3.3 percent. For example, Denison said, to boost the average rate from 3.3 to 3.4 percent would require one of the following: a doubling of the rate of immigration; an addition of one hour to the workweek; a halving of the time lost to sickness or accidents; or adding 18 months' education for all those in school between 1960 and 1980.

If Denison is right, it puts the growth problem in perspective; there is no easy-turning spigot to reach for. But a monumental effort would produce extraordinary dividends, too. Denison's calculations show that even a one-tenth of a point increase in the growth rate from 3.3 to 3.4 percent would add $20 billion to the GNP by 1980. Eventually, President Johnson or one of his successors will have to decide whether the effort should be made to lift our sights. Eventually, I am certain that some courageous leader will galvanize the country into action, for real expansion will not only help us meet the economic challenge in world affairs posed by our friends and enemies alike, but will raise our standard of living, for poor and well-to-do alike.

No other nation can match the long-time growth record of this country going back 120 years. The Joint Economic Committee under the direction of economists Otto Eckstein and James W. Knowles estimated that from 1839 to 1879, the U. S. growth rate averaged 4.3 percent; from 1879 to 1919, 3.7 percent; and from 1919 to 1959, 3.0 percent.[11] But the pace in the post-World War II era slowed down. Kennedy was making a political mark—but was accurate nonetheless—when during the campaign in 1960 he observed that the growth rate under Eisenhower from 1953 to 1958 had slumped to 2.1 percent, compared to a resounding 4.6 percent average in the Truman years of 1947 to 1952.

The Rockefeller Brothers report in 1957 suggested a 5 percent national target—a high level, but one that caught the public's imagination. Men as far apart in their thinking as Richard M. Nixon and Leon Keyserling think such a goal acceptable. And the authoritative Joint Committee report suggested that with "no change in our economic way of life," the nation could grow at a 4.5 percent rate.[12] For much of 1962, President Kennedy was entranced with the fact that growth rates of 5, 6, 7 percent, and better, were common in Western Europe, and he instructed Heller's council of economic advisers to study Europe's experience, including planning activities. Some explanations for the fast pace in Europe were obvious: postwar reconstruction, much of it financed by Uncle Sam, provided Western Europe with a quick conversion to modern plants, and with them, increases in productivity. Moreover, Europe could—and did—borrow from American technology. The Common Market was an underlay, feeding the whole process.

But there were other reasons, the most important being an acceptance of long-range planning, and open resort to deficit spending. Heller wrote President Kennedy in a private analysis: "The biggest single difference between Europe on the one hand and North America on the other is probably that they had pretty continuous full employment during the 1950's while we were having three recessions. They say—and they're right—that high levels of demand, and the confident expectation of continued prosperity help to generate the optimism, the risk-taking, and the investment that produce rapid growth." In France, this national determination to set high levels of demand was underwritten by "le Plan," a total effort to boost output, sector by sector, with the full cooperation and participation of business, labor, and the academic community.

President Kennedy was also struck by the fact that rapid economic growth in Europe was not accompanied by a runaway inflation, even though the labor force was so fully occupied that the jobless rates were minuscule. Under constant pressure to cut spending, it was natural for the President to marvel at the European accomplishments. Kennedy knew, of course, that Western European planning techniques would not be easily transferable to this country; "planning" still shocks people here. But there were other difficulties; for example, part of the success of "le Plan" in France is the ability to control capital investment, at least one-third of which is funneled through nationalized industries.

Moreover, there is a cartel tradition in many European countries which encourages businessmen to make their industrial plans in concert. The French deliberately limit the uncertainties of the market place by their elaborate blueprinting of the economy. A French businessman who knows America says with a smile: "Here, we say that in America, 'le Plan' would put the planners in jail for 94 years."

But Kennedy tried to direct attention to the confidence the Europeans had in the vitality of their system—and their determination to make their economies stronger. And to a President troubled by frictions with the business community, there was a fascination with the relationships of European businessmen to their governments. "French businessmen," former Council member James L. Tobin reported to Kennedy, "do not regard government as their natural enemy."

The studies of Western Europe's success encouraged Kennedy to move to a planned deficit in fiscal 1963. But the key lesson that Kennedy's advisers felt could be drawn from European experimentation is that one element in getting to and maintaining high growth rates is the very existence of a national determination to do so. Jean Monnet, that great patriot of the Western world, told me during an interview in 1962 in Paris that any country, including the United States, could modify "le Plan" to its own use. "The secret, if there is any," Monnet said, "is very simple. Everyone here has knowledge of the total needs of the economy, not just his own sector. 'Le Plan' doesn't impose anything on anybody, but it gets all sectors of the economy to participate in a collective action."

But it takes more than wishful thinking. Knowles insists: "Our economic growth is within our own control. If the Government pursues growth-facilitating policies, the economy will expand near the upper limit of the range [3.5 to 4.6 percent]. If, on the other hand, the Government, as a matter of policy, sacrifices economic growth to the pursuit of other objectives, our economy will perform sluggishly, will add less to our capacity. . . ."

Early in the Kennedy Administration, Heller initiated one experiment in trying to raise the sights on growth—and promptly got his head battered by the Business Council. This occurred in the fall of 1961, when Heller presented a report called "Full Employment Perspective, 1963" to a group of the Business Council economists, only to get it brushed off as a useless, theoretical exercise.

Carefully labeled "tentative," the Heller blueprint for a fully employed economy in 1963 showed that GNP could hit $620 billion ($35 billion more than was the actual result) and profits could rise an astonishing $16.5 billion from the then prevailing rate of $45.5 billion. The figures themselves were not particularly startling; the new idea in the "Perspective" was Heller's suggestion that various key industries supply "detailed estimates that will put flesh on the bones of the skeleton." Given the over-all numbers, Heller felt that industry could then estimate what would be required, in terms of tons of steel, volume of business loans, amount of consumer credit, and other components, to meet the goals. "This will help us spot the bottlenecks to full employment," Heller said. He argued that a fairly full picture could be developed by a systematic survey of the individual needs of companies based on the Government's "Perspective" supplemented by data supplied by labor, farm groups, and university economists.

But this very tentative step—more of an informational approach than a full-blown plan—was shouted down by the business world and quietly laid to rest. The Business Council economists labeled it "numbers talk," and the business leaders themselves expressed the fear that once they participated in setting targets, the next step might be government controls to insure their achievement. The thought that the business community could play a significant role, along with labor, farm, and other experts, in actually determining the economic future of the country didn't appeal to these giants of industry. It was too great a risk with Kennedy in the White House. But perhaps President

Johnson can cash in on his newly won status with business to revive the notion.

Just a few days before the Tampa speech, Mr. Kennedy flew to New York to tell the AFL-CIO convention that "this group more than any knows how much we still have to do." Labor was indeed impatient with Kennedy's pursuit of business approval, and wished it could get him to mount a frontal attack on the unemployment problem.

Kennedy's dilemma, and it was evident from the omissions in his speech to the AFL-CIO, was that a major attack on unemployment or an effort to accelerate economic growth would interfere with the posture of "fiscal integrity" that he found necessary to display as the exhorbitant price of the tax cut. The audience at the Americana Hotel didn't know it, but to the dismay of his own labor advisers, Kennedy took out of his speech at the final drafting a section which restated a willingness to spend money for broad social welfare objectives. This single paragraph was all that remained:

> But tax cuts are not enough. More jobs are not enough. Higher earnings and greater growth and record prosperity are not enough—unless that prosperity is used to sustain and support a better society. We can take real pride in a $600 billion economy and 70 million jobs only when they are underwriting to the fullest extent the measures we need to improve our schools, rebuild our cities, counsel our youth, assure our health and care for our aged and infirm.

The sentiment was genuine, but President Kennedy's labor and liberal friends searched for a specific timetable. It wasn't there, because Mr. Kennedy apparently felt that he wouldn't even get the business support for a tax cut if he pushed too hard on the welfare front. Kennedy's worries were well based. "Business attitudes toward the New Frontier have frequently been suspicious and hostile," Tobin observes. "Evidently many businessmen believe that the frontier where the Kennedy Administration wishes to advance is the frontier between government and business. . . . These fears are misplaced. The frontier between government and business in the United States is in reality static and quiet—very possibly as inactive as at any time in the twentieth century. The defense outcries from the business side of the frontier seem to me an obsolete ideological reflex, to which businessmen became conditioned in the days of the New Deal and the Fair Deal.

"This time-honored reaction to a Democratic Administration is, I think, not only misdirected; worse, it is diverting the business community from the many real problems along the active frontiers of the seventh decade of this century." [14]

The 1962 steel episode was, to be sure, a departure from peaceful relationships. Kennedy's crackdown on Roger Blough shook the business world—but he moved decisively, and almost immediately, to show that it was the grand exception, not the guiding principle, of his Administration. Blough himself later acknowledged that "it seems fairly clear that efforts are being made to create an atmosphere which is good." [15] Not only did the Administration produce tax and depreciation incentives for all business, but in 1963 it allowed the steel industry to raise prices on about 70 to 80 percent of its products with no objection. The first wave of steel price advances was a "selective" increase in April, 1963. Mr. Kennedy gathered his advisers for a round of secret meetings; but this time, he was annoyed, rather than angry. It was quickly decided that little could or should be done to head off the round of price increases, so long as the price boost could be labeled "selective" and not "across the board." (President Kennedy did remark privately on the fact that the first increase—by Wheeling Steel—came on the anniversary of the big fight the year before, and he didn't believe it was a coincidence.) In the fall of 1963, the industry, newly deft, raised prices again—and the Administration, having made the basic decision in the spring against renewing its battle with the industry, found there was little it could do about the new round.

For all of the bravado displayed in the steel crisis of 1962, the Kennedy Administration became jittery. When it established antitrust policy, the Justice Department moved supercautiously —although strict enforcement of the antitrust laws ought never to be related to an examination of pro-business or anti-business attitudes. Antitrust enforcement is, rather, a duty of the Government which *protects* the business community. Yet, over the years, businessmen have evidenced an obsessive preoccupation with federal antitrust policy, regardless of the party in power.

They have a distaste for the man charged with enforcing the antitrust laws (whether or not his name is Robert Kennedy) akin to a stereotyped hostility to the tax collector. Business's fear of antitrust action is deeply rooted in a conviction that a vigorous policy is an intrusion into the freedom of private enterprise to make its own decisions on what constitutes unfair competition, monopoly, or price fixing.

The late Mark W. Cresap of Westinghouse had the courage to say that in the electrical cases, "the government agencies . . . were carrying out . . . the responsibilities assigned to them by law. And I do not believe that careful and responsible enforcement of the antitrust laws should subject the Government to attack from business."

Cresap added that, in his belief, the overwhelming majority of American people, including businessmen, support the antitrust tradition as one of the powerful weapons to control monopolies and promote competition; which is another way of saying that if the phrase "free enterprise" is to be something more than a hollow-sounding fiction, it must go hand in hand with a strong antitrust posture. It would be sad if the American people were led by a shortsighted element of the business community to believe anything else.

Business leaders regularly insist that the antitrust laws must be "fair, not punitive." The exact meaning of this isn't clear. But it suggests that antitrust officials would be "fair" if they turned the other cheek to business excesses. It is hardly a secret that many business leaders openly detest such ardent guardians of the antitrust laws as Representative Emanuel Celler of New York, and the much-maligned late Senator from Tennessee, Estes Kefauver. In the jargon—and conviction—of the business world, these are mere headline hunters. Both men, being politicians, were not indifferent to publicity, but the persistent efforts of Celler and Kefauver, over the years, have helped strengthen the framework of the antitrust laws, which are in the best interests of the American people, and indeed in the best interests of American business. Corporation executives who railed at Kefauver's "fishing expeditions" would have little to worry about had the Senator not been dangling his line in well-stocked waters.

The Kennedy Administration's antitrust program was no

more stringent that Eisenhower's. Robert A. Bicks, Assistant
Attorney General in charge of the antitrust division under
Eisenhower, was actually a "tougher" trust buster than his suc-
cessor in the Kennedy Administration, former Judge Lee
Loevinger. Except for a somewhat stronger posture on bank
mergers, the Loevinger operation (now in the hands of William
H. Orrick, Jr.) was inhibited by the charge that the Kennedy
Administration was "anti-business." Loevinger freely admitted
that the antitrust division was sticking to tested, orthodox ap-
proaches.

Professor Walter Adams of Michigan State University, testifying before a subcommittee chaired by Senator William Proxmire, Wisconsin Democrat, quoted this Loevinger assessment,
and suggested that it fairly characterized the mood of the antitrust division. "It is not going to rock the boat," said Adams.
He noted that the Federal Trade Commission was also timid.
One of the FTC commissioners, Philip Elman, was quoted as
saying that there was in effect at the FTC "a kind of Gresham's
law, where the trivial and inconsequential cases leave little
room for and tend to drive out the substantial and the significant." [16]

In the spring of 1964, there was a flurry of antitrust activity,
starting with the carbon steel indictment (see Chapter VI). That
was followed by an anitrust suit to bar acquisition by the giant
Humble Oil and Refining Co. of the Tidewater Oil Co.'s western operations, promptly called off when Humble knuckled
under to the Justice Department demand. An additional series
of cases suggested that the Johnson Administration, for all of
its sweet-talking to business around the White House dinner
table, might give the trustbusters somewhat freer rein. This will
not be proved out, of course, until Johnson wins an election of
his own, and designates his own Justice Department aides.

There were other and cumulated evidences that the intention
of the Kennedy Administration was to get along with business.
Over the strong objections of Senator Kefauver and other
liberals, Mr. Kennedy entrusted communications satellites to
private enterprise—an extraordinary transfer to private hands
of infinite wealth and power that might have been, properly, a
public trust. Kefauver fought valiantly against the Kennedy
Administration's proposal, which he labeled "the most gigantic

giveaway" in the history of this country. The bill, he said, "would turn over to a governmentally created private monopoly the benefits of hundreds of millions of dollars of taxpayers' money which have been invested in the development of space and satellite communications technology." [17]

But Mr. Kennedy in the summer of 1962—still looking for a kind word from business—was not about to embark on a fight to make the satellite corporation a public entity. The President insisted that the statute protected the public interest and that "no single company or group will have the power to dominate the corporation." [18] This was an insufficient rebuttal of the Kefauver challenge, but it was renewed evidence that the Kennedy Administration was not trying to affect the basic division of economic power between government and the private sector. There was no disposition at all on Kennedy's part to disturb the allocation of functions—although Senator Goldwater in his unexcelled devotion to nineteenth-century dogma would remand the TVA to private enterprise. The single area in which Kennedy proposed new responsibilities for government was the extension of the Social Security system to provide medical care for the aged.

On the whole, any reasonable businessman in 1963 should have been content, and labor and liberals impatient, with the economic scorecard. Unemployment was at the 5.5 percent mark, but business was buoyant, profits at an all-time peak, productivity was soaring—and so was the stock market. Some few Business Council members confided to me in October, 1963, that Kennedy was "improving" in his relationships with business. They were pleased by a promise he had made to the CED in May, 1963, that the Federal Government would not undertake new electric power projects unless there was a compelling reason to do so. Kennedy said that the "burden of proof" is on the Government to demonstrate that public rather than private financing should be used for specific projects. Business approved that kind of talk—but it wanted more of it.

Why did John Kennedy fail in his attempt to woo the business community? It is probably true that Kennedy didn't understand the average businessman too well. He believed that there were many who were crass and greedy. He did admire some—

like Tom Watson, Jr., of IBM, in whom he found a concern for the country that goes beyond his own business. To the businessman, Kennedy was a bit aloof, a man of the softer world of society, not of the rough-and-tumble world of production, prices, dollars and profits. He was a man more comfortable with artists and intellectuals than with salesmen—businessmen knew it and so did he. And out of his Irish Catholic heritage, he found a close bond with the leading labor bosses, a fact which didn't escape attention in the executive suites. It took a Lyndon Johnson to have the Business Council in to dinner for the first time at the White House—preceded by cocktails in the second-floor living quarters.

Astute politician that he is, Johnson took the Kennedy program and imprinted his own image on it. First, he used the budget as a vehicle to hammer away at the economy theme. But having established himself in the public mind as a prudent man, he moved quickly to show that he was a humanitarian, too, by charting a "war against poverty." The fact, of course, is that the groundwork had been laid by Kennedy: just three days before his death, Kennedy—who had been impressed by Michael Harrington's *The Other America*—told Heller to rough out the lines of a program.

One of Johnson's very first decisions was to seize on the antipoverty theme as a cornerstone of his Administration; it was the counterbalance, in effect, to the economy drive. Who could be against a man who was steadfast against waste—but who would commit monies for the nation's poor?

Johnson could quite honestly claim the antipoverty program as his own. Kennedy had taken no actual moves to formulate the attack—and there were no provisions for it in the budget. Thus, a simple "no" would have ended the idea. But fighting poverty had a great appeal to Johnson. He has a real feeling and a warmth for people, and an attack on poverty was completely in character with his own humble beginnings. "Johnson had a 'gut' reaction to the whole idea," said one of Kennedy's aides.

LBJ was lucky, to be sure, to find the antipoverty idea ready and waiting to be exploited. He was also fortunate to move into the White House while the economy was riding the crest of a prosperous business cycle, and soon fell into the habit of announcing a raft of bullish economic barometers at the beginning of each press conference.

Business was prospering under Johnson, and he was making obvious political capital out of that happy situation. But business had also prospered under Kennedy—a fact that many tycoons found hard to concede. Kennedy came into office when the dollar was in trouble, and he shored it up, dumping some of his pet campaign promises in order to protect the balance of payments. Why, then, business mistrust? One cannot ignore the wounds of the battle over steel. But there is something more. A persistent critic of business, the *New Republic's* columnist who signs himself "T.R.B.," says that "most businessmen are plain dumb." [19] One doesn't have to agree with T.R.B. to observe that most businessmen, clearly, were so overwhelmed by their own built-in prejudices that they failed to acknowledge or perceive how closely in tune the Kennedy Administration was with business objectives. "The prevailing attitude toward the good times of Autumn, 1963, is apathy, toward Kennedy, distrust," wrote *Business Week* magazine. "Businessmen don't wax rhapsodic over the gains of the Kennedy years, and any gain they give the Administration is given grudgingly." [20] The *Wall Street Journal* complained, in commenting on Kennedy's Tampa appeal to businessmen, that "business remains tied up in the tangle of Federal regulations. . . . Only in one specific area—transportation—has it proposed significant de-regulation, which is very much to its credit." [21]

Against such a standard, Mr. Kennedy could never have achieved rapport with business unless he abdicated all responsibility and deregulated everything. He once made an observation along those lines, when a questioner at a conference of editors asked how his support of the free market system "jibes" with farm price supports. Mr. Kennedy answered:

> We have been attempting in this Congress, with some success, but no total success, to provide that those who receive the supports will not plant an unlimited amount.
> . . . But I think that those members of the business community who feel that the solution is a total withdrawal of the Government's support program, I don't think we are going to see that in the very near future, and, Number 2, I am not sure

that it would serve our long-range interests. But there are, of course, limitations.

The transportation industry is regulated. There are, of course, limitations on the free market. But basically, this is a free market economy, and the fact of the matter is that it is the freest market economy of any industrialized society in the world today, and I think we can take some satisfaction in that. It is the freest in the world.[22]

This emphasis on the "free market economy" was the essence of Mr. Kennedy's philosophy. It formed the basis for the decision on communications satellites, and Mr. Kennedy bragged about it in Tampa. It led the Administration not only into its role as creator of new tax incentives for business, but into protectionist support of the textile industry which wanted discriminatory quotas against Japanese goods. It proved the framework for the Clay Committee report, which influenced Congress to deny foreign aid funds to state-owned enterprises such as the Bokaro steel mill in India, with the result that the Indian Government in 1964 reluctantly turned to the Soviets to build Bokaro. Thus a parochial insistence on exporting our own kind of capitalism helped, merely, to entrench the Communist influence in India. Such a total emphasis on the "free market economy" concept also laid the basis for Dillon to castigate broadened spending in the public sector at home as just another name for "bigger central Government." [23]

Mr. Kennedy, in a word, was a true but not blind defender of the free enterprise system, one of the best friends that the business community ever had in the White House. There are some few, reflective businessmen who agree that this is so. Yet most would deny it. If T.R.B. is wrong, and businessmen are not stupid, then most must have paid excessive attention to the Kennedy rhetoric about the unfinished business of the nation. Kennedy did put forward a wonderful range of goals for education, conservation, health, employment, and care for the aged, stated with vigor and perception. He saw the need for a vast step-up in growth—but he reached only cautiously to achieve it. He knew better than many of his critics of the need for an enormously enlarged manpower training program and sympathized with the structuralist argument on unemployment more than did Walter Heller—but he hesitated to ask for the necessary monies. He would have loved to see a wide reform made in the budget document, and privately urged his friends to publicize the need to change the accounting system so it would show the true nature of federal investments. But he feared the repercussions of making such a move himself. What the business community failed to realize was that John F. Kennedy in action was a most temperate man, striving to win to himself the conservative elements in his own party and in the community. His friend and biographer, James MacGregor Burns, wrote just after his death in Dallas: ". . . There were really four Kennedys—the rhetorical radical of the stirring campaign promises and New Frontier idealism; the policy liberal who showered specific proposals on Congress; the fiscal moderate who sought to balance the budget even while stepping up spending; and the institutional conservative who opposed major changes in the executive or legislative branches of Government." [24]

Yet, John Fitzgerald Kennedy accomplished a great deal—and as he told the AFL-CIO, there was a long way to go. Given a chance, he might have led the nation to greater achievements. In his final days, he had seen the sickening barriers of racial prejudices lowered, if not removed. And the upswing from the last Eisenhower recession had erased the squeeze on profits, even if unemployment was still a pressing problem. He had made a start, too, on cleaning up stock market excesses, even though reform legislation which had speeded through the Senate on its own momentum, needed a push in the House.

In the tragic and painful hours following Kennedy's assassination, Arthur Schlesinger, Jr., Walter Heller and other of the President's friends and aides insisted that the second term would have been different. Even the Kennedy pledge for spending restraint, they feel, would have been washed away in the wake of a new mandate from the people. This, one will never know, although I do not believe that Congress would have been much different in makeup and disposition, whatever the measure of popular support President Kennedy would have received, had he lived.

But a lesson is here for the Johnson Administration: there is never time to wait. The next year, the next term may never come. If, as President Johnson tells the country, he supports the Kennedy goals, the time to move is now. If the war against poverty is to be more than an election-year battle cry, it will have to be expanded enormously—to clean out the slums, beef up federal education programs, clean up the narcotics rackets, and (courageously) foster a meaningful birth control program. A President Johnson moving in this direction will find that the liberal groups in the nation, denied a full measure of influence by the efforts Kennedy made to sway the business community, will respond to his call for positive action. President Kennedy took one of the boldest steps of his all too-brief Presidency when, at the start of 1963, he budgeted a deficit in order to stimulate a lagging economy. He refused, then, to pay tribute to the conventional wisdom of business, which would have been to cut spending in a fruitless chase for a balanced budget.

Such a budget would have been a fiction, and Mr. Kennedy wasn't tempted. The complicated problems of today's America, as Kennedy came increasingly to believe, necessitate more attention to a balanced economy, and less to a balanced budget. In his Tampa speech, President Kennedy tried to demonstrate to businessmen that there was much more to the Federal budget than one simple figure showing a net surplus or deficit. Since ways must be found to increase public spending for public needs, is it too much to hope that President Johnson will give real attention to revising the form and structure of the National Budget? He could make a place for himself in the history books by appointing a blue-ribbon Presidential Commission to Study the Revision of the Federal Budget. Many of the myths that Mr. Kennedy sought unsuccessfully to dispel derive from the American fixation on the traditional, or "administrative" budget which can overstate the real amount of Federal spending by ignoring enormous assets in people and things. As President Kennedy learned from his studies of Western Europe, no modern government there—indeed, no modern American corporation—keeps its books the way the Federal Government of the United States does. If they did, most of them would be "in the red" most of the time.

So many of our troubles—so many of the painful overtures to the ultraconservatives in Congress and in the business community—are occasioned by this simple truth about the budget that some change is overdue. President Kennedy expressed a great interest in published discussions of this problem; it was one of the reasons behind his great interest in European economic growth. What better monument to John F. Kennedy could there be than a study which might help, one day, to eradicate some of the economic myths with which he tried to cope? It should be done soon. As Mr. Kennedy said when he concluded his speech to the AFL-CIO in New York, just seven days before he died:

> We ask your help, not next year, but now.
> Marshal Lyautey, the great French marshal, went out to his gardener and asked him to plant a tree. The gardener said, "Why plant it? It won't flower for 100 years."
> "In that case," the Marshal said, "plant it this afternoon."
> That is what we have to do.

Notes

Chapter I

1. Macmillan, 1962.
2. R.I.A. poll of 1,400 businessmen, published in the July-Sept. 1963 issue of the *General Electric Quarterly*.
3. *U. S. News,* interview, Jan. 28, 1963.
4. Interview with David Broder, Washington *Evening Star,* Oct. 7, 1963.
5. *The Economics of the Political Parties,* Macmillan, 1962.
6. CBS telecast with Howard K. Smith, June 15, 1961.
7. This comment was made to me during an interview for the *Newsweek* story on Washington columnists, Dec. 18, 1961. It did not appear in the article. Lippmann himself, writing in the January 21, 1963 issue of *Newsweek,* said: "During his first two years . . . the President did not think he could convince Congress or a majority of the people that economic growth can be promoted deliberately. He knew he would be charged with quackery, with attempting sleight of hand, and his Administration would be impugned as unsound and rather disreputable. In fact, though the economists have been preponderantly on the side of the Administration, General Eisenhower and the mass of the people have been against it." Lippmann apparently meant here that Kennedy didn't feel he would have popular backing for an expansionist economic policy.
8. "Rights of Man," Democratic Platform, published at Los Angeles, July 13, 1960.
9. *Challenge,* N.Y.U., Jan., 1961.
10. Response to Scripps-Howard Newspapers question, as reproduced in Washington *Daily News,* Sept. 26, 1960.
11. April 24, 1958, address to the American Newspaper Publishers Association.
12. Response to Scripps-Howard Newspapers question, as reproduced in Washington *Daily News,* Oct. 1, 1960.

Chapter II

1. *Report of Council of Economic Advisers,* 1963, discussion of fiscal policy and Appendix.
2. *Ibid.,* p. 29.
3. *Hearings,* Joint Economic Committee, 1961, Appendix, pp. 703-711.

4. Ibid.
5. Paul A. Samuelson, "Economic Policy for 1962," *Review of Economics and Statistics*, Vol. 44, Feb. 1962.
6. Wilfred Lewis, Jr., *Federal Fiscal Policy in the Postwar Recessions*, Brookings.
7. Testimony of Walter Heller, James L. Tobin, Kermit Gordon, members of the Council of Economic Advisers before the Joint Economic Committee, *Hearings*, 1961, pp. 309-392.
8. *Ibid.*, p. 360.
9. *American Scholar*, Autumn 1961 Issue, p. 536.
10. Aug. 22, 1963.
11. Lewis, *Federal Fiscal Policy in the Postwar Recessions*, Brookings.
12. A portion of this quote was used in my article in *Harpers*, July, 1962, titled: "Washington's Unseen Powerhouse: David Bell and his Budgeteers."

Chapter III

1. 1963 Report, Council of Economic Advisers, p. 29.
2. Labor News Conference, Mutual Broadcasting System, Jan. 21, 1962.
3. SEC-Commerce Department Surveys of Business Intentions for Expenditures on Plant and Equipment, 1963; also see Corporate Profits Table, 1964 Economic Indicators.
4. Treasury Department Press Release, TP-18, Sept. 1, 1963.
5. Address before Empire State Chamber of Commerce, IRS Commissioner Mortimer Caplin, May 1, 1962.
6. Tax Message, April 20, 1961.
7. Speech, May, 1962.
8. Letter to Wilbur D. Mills, March 22, 1962.
9. Release, Bureau of Internal Revenue (now IRS) S-2979, Feb. 26, 1952.
10. IRS Study, April, 1961, Report to Congress by the Secretary of the Treasury.
11. *New York Times Magazine*, March 20, 1960, "There's No Business Like Lunch Business," and many similar articles in other periodicals.
12. *Wolfe vs. U.S.*, 58-2 USTC #9934, 261 F. 2d 158 (CA-6) cited by Caplin in December, 1961, Speech to University of Chicago Tax Conference.
13. IRS Press Briefing, March 29, 1963; also see Release IR-628, Aug. 27, 1963.
14. Caplin Article: "Legitimate Business Expenses are Deductible," *American Road Builder*, Aug., 1963.
15. Press Conference, March 29, 1963.

Chapter IV

1. This article won the Sigma Delta Chi award for Magazine Reporting in 1960.
2. Indianapolis, Ind., *News*, Sept. 21, 1960, column headed "Happy Talk."
3. See story by Bernard D. Nossiter, Washington *Post*, Feb. 15, 1961.
4. Luther Hodges, *The Business Conscience*, Prentice-Hall, 1963. Secretary Hodges' book is worth reading for a firsthand account of how his old friends in the textile business tricked him out of a price increase when he was an OPA executive, then confronted him years later with the observation: "We certainly bilked old Luther out of more than a million dollars that day. . . ."

5. Hodges' testimony before Senator Paul Douglas' subcommittee studying depressed areas legislation, Feb., 1961.
6. Transcript of Hodges' press conference, April 4, 1961, p. 24.
7. Charles Bartlett, article in the Washington *Evening Star*, July 9, 1961.
8. These are pretty substantial "small" businessmen. None of them runs a corner grocery. But their operations *are* smaller than General Motors, the Ford Motor Co., and the Standard Oil Co. of New Jersey, to run down a few of the more typical names on the BAC roster.
9. *The New York Times*, July 11, 1961.
10. Bartlett article, July 9, 1961.
11. Informal remarks by McGeorge Bundy, Sept. 21, 1961, as released by the White House press office.
12. F. R. Kappel, Address before Commonwealth Club, San Francisco, Dec. 1, 1961.
13. Hobart Rowen, "Keys to the Economy—Steel and Blough," *Newsweek*, Jan. 22, 1962, p. 71.
14. *Ibid.*, p. 70.

Chapter V

1. Interview with Anthony Lewis, *New York Times*, June, 1961.
2. Interview, *U. S. News and World Report*, April 24, 1961.
3. Feb. 12, 1961, p. C-3.
4. *The New York Times*, Feb. 28, 1961.
5. *Fortune Magazine*, April, 1962, p. 132; and May, 1962, p. 161.
6. Speech before the Harvard Business School Club at George Washington University, Washington, D. C., Nov. 1, 1961.
7. Theodore L. Thau, "The Business Ethics Advisory Council," The Annals of the American Academy of Political and Social Science, Sept., 1962.
8. Professor Arthur S. Miller, page ix, Foreword to Annals, Sept., 1962.

Chapter VI

1. See *Newsweek* cover story, "Blough vs. Kennedy: The Price Wasn't Right," issue of April 23, 1962.
2. Hobart Rowen, "Keys to the Economy—Steel and Blough," *Newsweek*, Jan. 22, 1962, p. 71.
3. As one of many examples, see speech to the Industrial Union Department, AFL-CIO, Washington, D. C., Nov. 17, 1961.
4. Telegram, released Feb. 6, 1962, to steel unions and to McDonald, from Secretary Goldberg "speaking on behalf of the President."
5. Economic Report of the President, Jan. 20, 1962, p. 17.
6. Hobart Rowen, "Arthur Goldberg and the Labor Unions," *The Reporter*, April 20, 1962.
7. There have been many accounts of the dramatic 72-hour period that began with the steel price increase. This chapter relies largely on my own day-by-day reporting of the events for *Newsweek*, much of which appeared in the

April 23 cover story cited above. Another extensive report by a group of reporters appeared in *The New York Times,* April 23, 1962.

8. "United States versus United States Steel," *The Economist,* April 21, 1962, p. 223.

9. Interview, *U. S. News and World Report,* Jan. 28, 1963, p. 57.

10. From Council "White Paper," quoted by Roy Hoopes, "The Steel Crisis," John Day, 1963.

11. Interview in Japan with Rafael Steinberg, *Newsweek,* April 23, 1962, p. 19.

12. Associated Press account, as published in the Washington *Post* and other newspapers, April 13, 1962.

13. Russell Baker article, p. 1., *New York Times,* April 20, 1962.

14. Washington *Post,* April 20, 1962.

15. Transcript of Blough press conference, April 12, 1963, as duplicated and released by U. S. Steel, p. 16.

16. Interview with Hobart Rowen, *Newsweek,* May 14, 1962.

17. Transcript of interview with the President by William H. Lawrence, George Herman, and Sander Vanocur, at the White House, Dec. 16, 1962.

18. *Look* Magazine article by Roger Blough, Jan. 29, 1963.

19. *The Kiplinger Washington Letter,* April 14, 1962.

20. Editorial, *Wall Street Journal,* April 19, 1962.

Chapter VII

1. Columnist Peter Edson once suggested that the total output of the two organizations about equals the White House's. See the Washington *Daily News,* April 27, 1962, p. 23.

2. Tally provided me by Mr. Earl Steele of the U. S. Chamber. On one of the two occasions Eisenhower missed, he sent Nixon. On the other, he sent a letter of greeting—as Kennedy did in 1961.

3. See an excellent column by Marquis Childs, Washington *Post,* May 2, 1962: ". . . The President should probably be rated a conservative in his outlook. On taxes, the budget, fiscal responsibility and the problem of the gold outflow his stand surely falls in the conservative category. The course of the economy in the next 12 or 18 months will prove him right or wrong."

4. *The New York Times,* May 1, 1962.

5. Sterling F. Green, Associated Press story in the Washington *Post,* July 14, 1962.

6. *Newsweek,* May 14, 1962, p. 78.

7. See Richard Strout, *Christian Science Monitor,* May 1, 1962.

8. Interview with Hobart Rowen, *Newsweek,* May 14, 1962.

9. For example, see comments by noted labor relations expert George W. Taylor, proceedings of the White House Conference on National Economic Issues, final session, May 22, 1962. Taylor's point of view was that the averages of the guidelines were relatively unimportant in themselves. They were significant only as the end product of some wages rising more, some rising less. Labor Secretary Goldberg, in the opening session of that conference, observed: "I am not suggesting, nor has the Council of Economic Advisers suggested, that their principles or guidelines are an inflexible formula to be applied

mechanically to every collective bargaining situation. . . . The principles
. . . are intended as reminders of the economic realities. . . . The important
thing . . . is that total bargaining come out right in the end, or as near right
as it can."

10. Economic Report, 1962, p. 189.

11. Text, as actually delivered, released by the White House, May 8, 1962.

12. "The Stock Market Under Stress," the N. Y. Stock Exchange, March, 1963,
p. 3.

13. "Free and Responsible Collective Bargaining and Industrial Peace," a report
to the President from the Labor-Management Advisory Committee, May 1,
1962, pp. 7 and 8.

14. Transcript, White House Conference on National Economic Issues, morning
session, May 21, 1962, p. 1.

15. Transcript, afternoon session, May 21, 1962, p. 61.

Chapter VIII

1. For this and subsequent references to the statistics of the three-day break I
have relied on "The Stock Market Under Stress," a research report published
by the New York Stock Exchange in May, 1963; and on Chapter XIII of the
Special Study of the Securities Markets, "The Market Break of May 1962,"
released by the SEC's study group in July, 1963.

2. *Business Week* story, Aug. 25, 1962, as cited by the SEC study group.

3. SEC report on the composition of savings, March, 1963.

4. In a conversation with Sidney Weinberg, just before the May 28 break, he
gloomily predicted: "I don't like to say it, but we could have a panic."
Weinberg complained that Kennedy had surrounded himself with "a bunch of
professors with a lot of theories, who don't have much business experience."
As a result, Kennedy had been persuaded to overload Congress with "too
much welfare state legislation."

5. Without using Gudeman's name, I quoted these remarks in a Newsweek
story written for the June 11, 1962, issue, attributing them only to a high
government official. Since Gudeman has left the Government, I feel free to
make the direct quotation.

6. "The Stock Market Under Stress," p. 3.

7. *Ibid.*, p. 10.

8. White House Conference on National Economic Issues, May 21, 1962.

9. Remarks by the President at the Yale University commencement exercises,
June 11, 1962.

10. *Newsweek*, June 25, 1962, p. 18.

11. *Ibid.*, p. 19.

12. Chapter XIII, Special Study, p. 1.

13. Murray Rossant, in *The New York Times,* Sept. 16, 1963.

14. *Newsweek*, May 14, 1962, p. 75.

15. Chapter XIII, Special Study, p. 2.

16. Dillon speech to New York Financial Writers Association, June 4, 1962. This
was a remarkably blunt address, which helped to reinforce the Wall Street

view that Dillon had abandoned all ties with the conservative community.
17. 1963 Economic Report, p. 15.
18. "The Stock Market Under Stress," p. 5.
19. Chapter XIII, Special Study, Section E: Summary, conclusions, and recommendations.
20. See discussion by Sylvia Porter, column in Washington *Evening Star*, July 21, 1963.
21. Speech to the Association of the Bar of the City of New York, "Current Problems in the Securities Field," May 20, 1963.
22. The Re & Re case and the American Stock Exchange: see SEC proceedings against Re & Re, May 12, 1960; hearings, January 23, 1961; staff brief, April 27, 1961; argument before Commission and expulsion order, May 4, 1961; announcement of study of American Stock Exchange, May 15, 1961; study group report, Jan. 6, 1962; and summary by Commission, Sept. 21, 1962. Also, *Newsweek*, issues of May 15, May 29, June 5, July 10, July 24, 1961; Jan. 15 and 22, 1962; *The New York Times*, Sept. 11, 1963; and special study group report, 1963.
23. Public Affairs Press, Washington, D. C., 1962.
24. Hearings, Subcommittee on Securities, Senate Banking and Currency Committee, on S. 1462, June 18-21, and 24-25, 1963.
25. Wharton Report, transmitted by the SEC to Congress, Aug. 29, 1962.
26. Associated Press Report, Washington *Post*, Sept. 26, 1963.
27. Interview with Hobart Rowen, *Newsweek*, Aug. 19, 1963, p. 65.

Chapter IX

1. Seymour Harris, article in the *New Republic*, Oct. 30, 1961.
2. For a thorough exposition of Heller's economic philosophy just prior to his appointment, see his address June 6, 1960, to the 87th Annual Forum of the National Conference on Social Welfare, Atlantic City, N. J.: "An Economic Prognosis for the Sixties." Also, an address on Nov. 1, 1960, to the Pennsylvania Citizens Association in Harrisburg, published by the PCA as Vol. IV of PCA Reports, Dec. 6, 1960.
3. Krock column, "Kennedy Fiscal Policy," *New York Times*, Jan. 7, 1961.
4. Hobart Rowen, "Kennedy's Economists," *Harper's*, Sept., 1961.
5. Transcript, afternoon session, White House Conference on National Economic Issues, May 21, 1962.
6. Interview with Lewis. Also see *Newsweek*, June 3, 1963.
7. Ackley speech, "The Economic Policies of the Kennedy Administration," Midwest Economics Association, St. Louis, April 26, 1963.
8. Tobin told me this story, and I used it in the *Harper's* article cited above; it has been widely quoted since.
9. *Hearings*, Joint Economic Committee, August, 1962.
10. Presidential Press Conference, June 28, p. 478, Vol. 1, *Public Papers of the Presidents*, John F. Kennedy, 1961.
11. Paul Samuelson, speech to American Bankers Association, Washington, D. C., Feb. 25, 1963.

12. Report of the Commission on Money and Credit, Prentice-Hall, 1961.
13. *Hearings* on the Economic Report, Joint Economic Committee, Jan., 1963, p. 45.
14. Separate views of Republicans, Report of the House Ways and Means Committee on H. R. 8383, p. c9, Sept. 13, 1963.
15. Originally, the White House understood that Keyserling had said that his "cook knew more economics than Walter Heller." But even the correct version didn't help to better the cool relationships between Keyserling and Heller.
16. See the President's speech to the Economic Club of New York, Dec. 14, 1962; also his remarks to the Advertising Council in Washington, March 13, 1963; and the Budget Message of the President for fiscal 1964.
17. *Public Papers,* p. 398.
18. Text of Kennedy letter to Senator Clark, dated August 7, 1961, concerning the Clark Bill, S. 986.
19. Press Conference, Aug. 30, 1961, *Public Papers,* p. 575.
20. Hobart Rowen, "Kennedy's Economists," *Harper's,* Sept., 1961.
21. Kennedy Address, July 25, 1961, "Report to the American People on the Berlin Crisis." The $3.2 billion increment to military spending programs was settled on by the President as a "low-key" response to the Berlin crisis. Alternate programs considered at the time ranged from $2 billion up to $15 billion, and if anything much larger than the $3.2 billion had been chosen, it's probable that there *would* have been a tax increase proposed also. The desirability of avoiding a tax increase, as the President finally saw the issue, thus may have played a role in the "low-key" response to Mr. Khrushchev.
22. Both the Hansen and Samuelson observations are from "Economic Policy for 1962: A Symposium," *Review of Economic Statistics,* Vol. 44, Feb., 1962.
23. Kennedy statement to Cabinet officers and agency heads, *Public Papers,* p. 681. Also, see Hobart Rowen, "David Bell and his Budgeteers," *Harper's,* July, 1962.
24. First National City Bank letter, Dec., 1961, p. 138.
25. Editorial, *Wall Street Journal,* "Admirable Aims, Misbegotten Methods," Jan. 22, 1962.
26. Walter Lippmann, "Philosophy of the Budget," Washington *Post,* Jan. 21, 1962.
27. Dillon speech to New York Financial Writers Association, June 4, 1962.
28. See transcript, briefing on 1963 Budget by Dillon and Bell, Jan. 17, 1962, pp. 35-36 of dittoed copy.
29. See article "The Kennedy Republicans," *Newsweek,* Jan. 29, 1962.
30. *Newsweek,* Jan. 28, 1957. For a study in depth of the ramifications and impact of Humphrey's outburst, see Richard Neustadt's valuable book, *Presidential Power,* John Wiley & Sons Inc., 1960.

Chapter X

1. *The Economist,* March 31, 1963.
2. Washington *Post* and *New York Times,* Jan. 23, 1962.

3. Private interview with me at the AFL-CIO executive council meeting, Bal Harbour, Fla., Feb., 1963.

4. See *Newsweek* cover story, March 6, 1961; also my story, "Arthur Goldberg and the Labor Unions," *The Reporter*, April 20, 1962.

5. See Goldberg speeches to the Industrial Union Department, AFL-CIO, Washington, Nov. 17, 1961; to the AFL-CIO convention, Miami Beach, Fla., Dec. 5, 1961; to the Chicago Medical School Annual Dinner, Chicago, Ill., Dec. 5, 1961; his testimony before the Joint Committee on the Economic Report, Jan. 31, 1962; and a speech before the Executives Club, Chicago, Feb. 23, 1962. For Wirtz' views, see his speech when still Undersecretary before the American Management Association Personnel Conference, Chicago, Feb. 14, 1962, and the Beloit, Wis., commencement address, June 3, 1962; and as Secretary, before the Economic Club of Detroit, May 27, 1963.

6. Executives Club Speech, *op. cit.*

7. Morning session, May 22, 1962, transcript, p. 8.

8. Economic Report, Jan., 1962, pp. 185-190. The section on guidelines was largely drafted by Council Member Kermit Gordon, now Director of the Bureau of the Budget.

9. Seminar, Business Research Advisory Council, Washington, D. C., May 22, 1963. Lewis, a professor at Indiana University, replaced Gordon.

10. See Frank C. Porter's excellent analysis of the third-man role in collective bargaining, Washington *Post*, Jan. 13, 1963.

11. Column: "Compulsory Arbitration," as it appeared in the New York *Herald Tribune*, Aug. 20, 1963. Lippmann in other and earlier writings has been less averse to compulsory arbitration than most other critics, observers, or politicians.

12. "The Strike and Discontent," *Monthly Labor Review*, June, 1963, pp. 645-651.

13. Press Conference, executive council meeting, AFL-CIO, Bal Harbour, Fla., Feb., 1963.

14. Speech to National Press Club, Sept. 25, 1962.

15. Figures supplied by research staff, United Steelworkers of America; analysis my own. April 1962 ingot tonnage, 9,235,881; production workers employed, 453, 277. April 1963 ingot tonnage, 10, 695, 362; production workers employed, 423,439. I do not yield to the temptation to work out the arithmetical increase in productivity, since productivity should be measured over a longer span. But the figures are clearly illustrative of a dramatic trend.

16. Editorial, "The Vanishing 40-hour Week," *Steel Labor*, August, 1963.

17. Private Interview. See Note 3.

18. Sept. 25, 1962.

19. See my article on Van Arsdale, syndicated by North American Newspaper Alliance, *Chicago's American* and other papers, Jan. 30, 1962.

20. "The Benefits and Problems Incident to Automation and other Technological Advances," a report by the committee to the President, Jan. 11, 1962.

21. Press conference at AFL-CIO Executive Council Meeting, Feb., 1963. Despite many confused stories at the time, notably one in the Baltimore *Sun*, which was enjoying an even wider general readership than usual because of the New York newspaper strike, Wirtz did not advocate a 35-hour week in his remarks on or off the record.

22. Tom Wicker, *The New York Times*, Sept. 29, 1963.
23. Testimony by Ewan Clague, Commissioner of Labor Statistics, before House Education and Labor Subcommittee, June 10, 1963.
24. "Old Before Its Time: Collective Bargaining at 28," Center for Study of Democratic Institutions, Santa Barbara, Calif., June 17, 1963. Jacobs is director of the Center's study of the trade-union movement.
25. "Decline of the Labor Movement," Solomon Barkin, Nov., 1961.
26. Kenneth Fiester, AFL-CIO public relations staff, in an article called "Where 'Powerful' Labor Stands Today," *The American Scholar*, Fall Issue, 1961.
27. Unless otherwise noted, this and other quotations from George Meany are from a personal interview in May, 1963.
28. Speech to University of California symposium on collective bargaining, Fairmont Hotel, San Francisco, May 28, 1963.
29. *Monthly Labor Review*, Dept. of Labor, June, 1963, p. 616.

Chapter XI

1. See the President's special message to the Congress, February 2, 1961, esp. pp. 43 and 44, *Public Papers of the President*, 1961.
2. *Economic Report of the President*, Jan., 1962, p. 86.
3. Article, Washington *Post*, Sept. 1, 1963.
4. One of the best introductions to the operations of the FRB is the Board's own handbook, "The Federal Reserve System—Purposes and Functions," published in 1954. See also Robinson, Morton, and Calderwood, *An Introduction to Economic Reasoning*, the Brookings Institution, 1956, Chap. 7.
5. Wirtz speech to National Press Club, Sept. 25, 1962.
6. See Hobart Rowen and Clem Morgello, "Tighter Money: The Backstage Drama," *Newsweek*, April 23, 1956; and "The Federal Reserve and the Political Gantlet: 1956," mimeograph, by the Federal Reserve System, 1956.
7. James Tobin, *Challenge* magazine, Feb., 1961.
8. Asher Achinstein, "Federal Reserve Policy and Economic Stability, 1951-1957," Senate Banking and Currency Committee report, Oct. 10, 1958.
9. See Burns' speech at the University of Chicago, inserted in the *Congressional Record* by Rep. Tom Curtis of Missouri, April 27, 1961, p. A 2885-7.
10. This and other Martin quotations not attributed to a specific source are from interviews with me.
11. Transcript, panel discussion before 19th Annual Advertising Council Conference, Washington, D. C., March 13, 1963.
12. President's press conference, Feb. 1, 1961, *Presidential Papers*, 1961, p. 36.
13. Lewis speech, White House Conference on National Economic Issues, May 21, 1962.
14. Clayton Gehman, *Measuring and Analyzing Economic Growth*, Federal Reserve Bulletin, Aug., 1963.
15. George W. Mitchell, address at Carroll College, Waukesha, Wis., Dec. 11, 1962.
16. Transcript, panel discussion before 19th Annual Advertising Council Conference, Washington, D. C., March 13, 1963.
17. *Hearings*, House Banking and Currency Committee, July 22, 1963.

18. Excerpt from President Johnson's prepared text, as released by the White House Press office.

Chapter XII

1. For example, see Heller statement August 8, 1962, before the Joint Economic Committee: ". . . The basic case for easing the net tax drain on the economy, as well as the broad principles which should guide tax reduction, are reasonably clear in the light of our unsatisfactory economic experience of the past five years." As we have seen, Kennedy turned down this argument when made for a quickie tax cut, but accepted it as the basic rationale for his 1963 tax program.
2. See text as actually delivered, including questions read by Charles G. Mortimer and Murray Shields, with answers by President Kennedy.
3. Separate views of the Republican minority, House Ways and Means Committee Report on H. R. 8363 offer a good review of the theory that tax cuts should be accompanied by expenditure reductions. Also, see the National City Bank Letter for June, 1963, *Tax Reduction vs. Expenditure Increase.*
4. *Forbes Magazine,* Jan., 1963.
5. Official transcript, press seminar with Walter W. Heller on the issuance of the Economic Report for 1963.
6. Transcript, panel discussion before the 19th Annual Advertising Council Conference, Washington, D. C., March 13, 1963.
7. Heller's basic justification of the Administration's tax cut proposal—repeated in scores of speeches in 1963—is contained in Chapter Three of the 1963 Economic Report, titled "Fiscal Policy in Perspective," and in the Council of Economic Advisers' January 28, 1963, testimony before the Joint Economic Committee.
8. Tax message of the President, January 1963.
9. *The Reporter,* June 6, 1963.
10. *Ibid.*
11. P. 11, Budget Message of the President, the Budget of the United States Government for fiscal 1964, Jan. 17, 1963.
12. See excerpts from President Kennedy's remarks, as published in *The New York Times,* Feb. 26, 1963, p. 4.
13. For example, see *New York Times* story by Eileen Shanahan, Aug. 13, 1963.
14. "The Tax Bill—The Need for Reform," a speech by Senator Paul Douglas released by his office Nov. 1, 1963.
15. Hobart Rowen, "Let's Spend More," *The New Republic,* May 25, 1963.
16. In his Oct. 28, 1963, testimony before the Senate Subcommittee on Labor and Public Welfare, Heller said that calculations "which purport to show" a rising cost in adding jobs to the economy are "misleading." Yet Heller's own data showed such a rising cost—less, by his analysis, than Goldfinger's, but still a rise. When I first called attention in *The New Republic* article cited above to the "cost" of stimulating employment, I received a message from President Kennedy, who had read and enjoyed the article. He was sympathetic with the main point of the article, even though it was critical of those who placed

sole reliance on the tax cut. On Sept. 12, 1963, when Prof. Seymour Harris wrote the President calling attention to "the need of knowing more about the job equivalent of government spending programs," Kennedy asked Budget Director Gordon to analyze such data. In conversation with friends, President Kennedy constantly stressed the tremendous difficulty of expanding job opportunities, despite the steady gains in gross national product. It was a problem that perplexed him, and he referred to it constantly in the weeks immediately prior to his death.

Chapter XIII

1. Unless otherwise noted, quotes in this chapter attributed to Secretary Wirtz are from a series of interviews and talks with him during 1962 and 1963.
2. Washingon *Post*, Sept. 29, 1963.
3. See, especially, testimony by Prof. Charles C. Killingsworth, Michigan State University, before Senate Subcommittee on Employment and Manpower, Sept. 20, 1963; testimony by Seymour L. Wolfbein, Director of Department of Labor Office of Manpower, Automation and Training, before Senate Small Business Committee, June 20, 1963; and transcript of Wirtz press conference, Oct. 10, 1963.
4. *Commentary*, July, 1962.
5. Oct. 3, 1963, before Senate Labor Subcommittee on Employment and Manpower.
6. Fiscal and Monetary Policy conference sponsored by the Labor-Management committee, Nov. 14, 1962, printed proceedings, p. 29.
7. *Ibid.*, p. 20.
8. Transcripts of President Johnson's address, Dec. 4, 1963.
9. Address by President Kennedy, Sept. 1963, Statler-Hilton Hotel, Washington, D. C.
10. Gordon's report, transmitted to Kennedy in September, 1962, made detailed suggestions for improvements in collection and presentation of the monthly labor force data. But it showed conclusively that unemployment was as high in this country as the figures suggested, and much higher than in other industrial countries of the world.
11. *The Economist*, Aug. 31, 1963.
12. White House Conference on National Economic Issues, May 22, 1962, transcript, p. 22.
13. Testimony before the Senate Subcommittee on Employment and Manpower, Sept. 26, 1963.
14. Testimony before Senate Subcommittee on Employment and Manpower, Oct. 28, 1963.
15. Seymour L. Wolfbein testimony before the Senate Select Committee on Small Business, June 20, 1963.
16. A compilation by the Department of Labor shows the decline of jobs in various key industries from recent peak levels to 1962:

Industry	Peak	*1962*
Steel	726,100 (1953)	597,500
Railroads	1,557,000 (1947)	801,400
Aircraft	895,800 (1957)	707,300
Textiles	1,332,000 (1948)	880,600
Telephone	768,200 (1957)	689,500
Mining	994,000 (1948)	647,000
General Bldg.		
Construction	1,074,600 (1956)	831,000
Auto	917,300 (1953)	723,500

17. See Economic Reports for 1961, 1962, and 1963; also Proceedings of the Fiscal and Monetary Conference, Nov. 14 and 15, 1962.
18. Manpower Report of the President, March, 1963.
19. Special Labor Force Report No. 38, "Work Experience of the Population in 1962," Samuel Saben, reprint No. 2429 from the *Monthly Labor Review,* January, 1964.
20. See a comprehensive article, "The Erosion of Jobs and Skills," the AFL-CIO *American Federationist,* October, 1963.
21. See Wolfbein testimony, Sept. 26, 1963, cited above.
22. Remarks of the President before the United Steel Workers Union, District 36-G, Tampa, Fla., Nov. 18, 1963.

Chapter XIV

1. Remarks of President Kennedy before the Florida Chamber of Commerce at Tampa, the Fort Homer Hesterly Armory, Nov. 18, 1963.
2. *Atlantic Monthly,* April, 1962.
3. Dec. 4, 1963.
4. Editorial, "Mr. Johnson as Economizer," Dec. 27, 1963.
5. Hobart Rowen, "Talking Business With the Candidates," *Newsweek,* April 25, 1960.
6. For a detailed account, see James A. Wechsler, "Wrong Man?" New York *Post,* Dec. 26, 1963.
7. See accounts in daily newspapers Jan. 2 and 3, 1964; for example, story by Garnett D. Horner, Washington *Star,* Jan. 2, 1964.
8. *Public Papers of the President,* John F. Kennedy, 1962, p. 615.
9. Washington *Post,* Jan. 6, 1964.
10. "The Sources of Economic Growth in the United States and the Alternatives Before Us," published by the Committee for Economic Development, Dec., 1962.
11. "Employment, Growth, and Price Levels," by the staff of the Joint Economic Committee, Dec. 24, 1959. It is interesting to observe that this monumental study was the "bible" on economic topics for Kennedy's speech writers during the 1960 campaign.
12. *Ibid.,* p. 101. See also "The Potential Economic Growth in the United States," by James W. Knowles, Joint Committee Study Paper No. 20, Jan. 30, 1960.
13. Hobart Rowen, "The European Economy—How It Goes—and Grows," *News-*

week, June 25, 1962. See also "French and Other National Economic Plans for Growth," European Committee for Economic and Social Progress, June, 1963 (obtainable from the Committee for Economic Development, New York).

14. Address, economic outlook conference, University of Michigan, Nov. 15, 1962.
15. Interview, Washington *Star,* Oct. 27, 1963.
16. Hearings, Joint Economic Committee, Aug. 1962.
17. Senate speech on Satellite Communications Bill, H. R. 11040, Aug. 9, 1962.
18. President Kennedy's remarks upon signing H. R. 11040, Aug. 31, 1962.
19. *The New Republic,* Nov. 31, 1963, just after Kennedy's death.
20. *Business Week,* Nov. 16, 1963.
21. Nov. 19, 1963.
22. Transcript, as published in the Washington *Post,* Sept. 27, 1962.
23. Testimony before the Senate Finance Committee, Oct. 15, 1963.
24. *New York Times Magazine,* Dec. 1, 1963.

Index

Achinstein, Asher, 218, 219
Ackley, Gardner, 43, 158, 160, 212
Adams, Phelps, 97
Adams, Sherman, 84
Adams, Walter, 290
Advertising Council, 224, 237
Adzhubei, Alexei, 161
AFL-CIO, 36, 75, 76, 85, 92, 113, 117, 126, 184, 186, 190, 194, 197, 200, 201, 202, 204, 205, 228, 234, 251, 256, 261-62, 287, 295, 297
Aircraft industry, 118, 120
Aluminum industry, 196
American Bankers Association, 242, 244
American Broadcasting Company, 109
American Medical Association, 121
American Motors Corporation, 203
American Scholar, 42
Americans for Democratic Action, 35, 163
American Stock Exchange, 144
"America's Most Powerful Club," 62-63
Anderson, Robert B., 41, 209, 211
Antitrust cases, 80-84, 85, 96, 106, 288-90
Armco Steel Corporation, 101, 104, 105, 106
Associated Business Publications Conference (1960), 29
Associated Press, 103, 145
Automation, 116, 194, 195, 196, 198, 200, 206, 207, 251, 255, 257-58, 263, 264-66, 269
Automobile industry, 195

Balance of payments, *see* Payments-balance problem
Bal Harbour, Florida, 92
Ball, George, 103, 123, 180

Bank for International Settlements, 179, 229
Barkin, Solomon, 200
Bartlett, Charles, 67, 105
Bator, Francis M., 276
Bay of Pigs disaster, 170
Beckley, West Virginia, 267
Beirne, Joseph A., 190-91, 194
Bell, Daniel, 206, 207
Bell, David E., 37, 44, 66, 159, 172, 173, 176, 208, 214
Berlin crisis, 24, 70, 72, 90, 171, 219
Bethlehem Steel Company, 101, 103, 104, 105, 106
Bicks, Robert A., 81, 290
"Big Four" meetings, 208, 210
Big Steel crisis, 89-112; *see also* Steel industry
Bills-only policy, 159
Birth control program, 296
Black Monday's stock market crash, 112, 130-35, 143, 174
Block, Joseph L., 101, 102, 103, 104, 125, 138
Block, Joseph W., 194
Block, Leigh B., 102
Block, P. D., 102
Blough, Roger Miles, 16, 61, 64, 65-66, 68, 69, 70, 71, 73, 77, 79, 87, 89-90, 92, 93, 94-100, 102, 103, 105-07, 108, 109, 110, 114-15, 116, 118, 120, 122-23, 124, 139, 158, 288
Bokaro steel mill, India, 294
"Breakfast Group," 166
Britain, 45
Brookings Institution, 44, 159, 180
Brotherhood of Sleeping Car Porters, 262
Buckmaster, Lawrence C., 60

Budget, federal, problems and policies, 23-24, 33, 40, 43-44, 70, 73, 167-68, 172, 173-74, 219, 220, 235, 242-43, 273, 277, 278, 281-82, 292, 296
Budget Bureau, 172, 251, 281
Budget in Brief, 278
Bundy, McGeorge, 73, 74-75, 135, 166
Burns, Arthur F., 23, 211, 215, 218
Burns, James McGregor, 19, 295
Business Advisory Council, 28, 37, 61-79, 82, 99-100, 113, 122, 124, 127, 280, 284, 286
Business Committee for Tax Reduction, 243, 260, 271, 273
Business Conscience (Hodges), 87
Business Council, 69, 70, 72, 73, 76-77, 82, 87-88, 107, 112
Business ethics, 80-88
Business Ethics Advisory Council, 84, 85-87
Business Week magazine, 237, 247, 293
Byrd, Harry, 15, 50, 51, 55, 156

Cabinet appointments, 19-21
"Call to Action" (1962), 87
Caplin, Mortimer M., 50, 51, 56, 57, 58, 59, 60
Capp, Al, 207
Carlyle Hotel, New York City, 105, 106
Cary, William L., 143, 146
Celler, Emanuel, 85, 289
Census Bureau, 268
Center for the Study of Democratic Institutions, 184
Central Intelligence Agency, 21
Challenge, 159
Chamberlain, Neville, 17
Chamber of Commerce, U. S., 72, 112, 113-17, 118, 121, 127, 234, 261
Champion Spark Plug Company, 48
Chicago Association of Commerce and Industry, 60
Chicago & Illinois Restaurant Association, 60
Chrysler Corporation, 84, 85
Clague, Ewan, 263
Clark, Joseph, 23, 170, 172
Clay, Lucius, 62 n.
Clay Committee report, 294
Clifford, Clark, 105
Cloister, Sea Island, Georgia, 65
Code of ethics for business, 85-88
Cohan, George M., 56

"Cohan rule," 56
Cohen, Manuel F., 144
Cohen, Milton H., 134, 138, 143, 144, 149
Cohen study group report, *see* SEC Study Group report
Cold war problems, 24
Collective bargaining, 91, 92-93, 94, 124-25, 186, 188-89, 190, 192, 194, 199, 200, 202-04, 205-06, 207
Colorado Fuel and Iron Corporation, 101, 104-05
Commerce Department, U. S., 61, 63, 66, 68, 69, 70, 74, 272
Commission on Money and Credit, 163
Committee for Economic Development, 127, 234
Common Market, 284
Communication satellites, 290-91, 294
Communication Workers of America, 190
Compulsory arbitration, 183, 192-93
Conference on Economic Progress, 35
Conway, Jack, 205-06
Cooper, R. Conrad, 93, 94, 160
Cordiner, Ralph J., 63, 64, 73, 82-83, 122
Cormier, Frank, 145
Corporate tax reduction, 47, 240
Council of Economic Advisers, 21, 22, 25, 35, 43, 46, 71, 72, 120, 140, 153-82, 189, 191, 211, 249, 250, 255, 259, 272
Country club dues deduction, 59
Cox, Archibald, 50
"Credit card" economy, 19
Cresap, Mark W., Jr., 83, 289

Daane, Dewey, 217, 218
Daniel, James, 261
Davidson, Roy, 193
Dean, Arthur H., 73
Debt management, 214
Decision Making in the White House (Sorensen), 161
Decker, William C., 87
Defense Department, U. S. (Pentagon, the), 104, 108, 281
Defense spending, 44, 70, 170
Deflation, 226
Del Monte Lodge, Pebble Beach, Calif., 65
Democratic National Committee, 21
Democratic Party, 29, 36, 184, 238

Denison, Edward F., 283
Depreciation allowance, 47-48, 49, 77, 123
Depressed areas, 267
Depressed Areas bill, 39
Depression, 132, 177, 235
Dillon, Douglas, 19-21, 34, 38, 41, 42, 50, 53, 59, 67, 72, 76, 77, 79, 106, 134, 140, 141, 153-54, 158, 160, 161, 166, 167, 168, 171, 172, 173, 174-78, 179, 180, 208, 209, 211, 214, 220, 224, 225, 230, 232, 234, 236, 237, 240, 241, 242, 243, 244, 246, 277
Discount rate, 225-26, 227-28
Discrimination, *see* Racial discrimination
Donahue, Alphonsus J., 68
Douglas, Paul, 47, 51, 161, 176, 213, 215, 216, 220, 247
Dow-Jones industrial index, 130, 131, 132
Dulles, Allen, 21
Dungan, Ralph, 71, 73, 103
Dunlap, John B., 56
Dunlop, John T., 189, 263

"Easy money" policy, 213, 214, 215
Eccles, Marriner, 215, 224
Eckstein, Otto, 160-61, 283
Economic expansion programs, 19, 22-33, 41, 45, 114, 161, 173, 282-86
Economic "gap," theory of, 40-41
Economic Report (1962), 93, 120, 189, 190; (1963), 140, 162; (1964), 217, 249, 264
Economics of the Political Parties (Harris), 17
Education program, 72, 272
Eisenhower Administration, 19, 20, 23, 24, 25, 27, 43, 62 n., 90, 113, 131, 172, 173, 187, 209, 210, 211, 216, 218, 234, 242, 251-52, 277, 290
Elman, Philip, 291
Employment, full, 75, 183, 198, 205-06, 244, 259, 272
Employment Act (1946), 42, 44, 153
Employment Service, U. S., 39
Ethical problems of businessmen, 86-87
Ethics, business, 80-88
Expense account deductions, 55-58, 59-60
Exports, 45, 70

Featherbedding, 116, 195, 214
Federal Aid for Dependent Children Act, 39
Federal Bureau of Investigation, 103, 108
Federal debt, *see* National debt
Federal Housing Administration, 39
Federal Reserve Act, 26
Federal Reserve Bank and System, 25-26, 29, 30, 33, 39, 159, 178, 179, 208, 209-30
Federal Reserve Bulletin, 222
Federal Trade Commission, 291
Federationist, 204
Feldman, Myer, 71, 166
Financial Writers Association, 140
"Flash prices," 130
Florida Chamber of Commerce, 274-75
Folsom, Marion B., 124, 127
Forbes, Malcolm S., 235
Forbes Magazine, 235
Ford, Henry, 195
Ford, Henry, II, 71, 83, 124-25, 243
Foreign-aid program, 16, 45, 294
Foreign income regulations, 55
Fortune Magazine, 83
Foster, William C., 123
Fowler, Henry H. (Joe), 73, 76, 77, 102, 103, 123, 214, 242, 243, 246
France, 79, 285
Freeman, Orville, 39, 106, 155
Free market economy, 294
"Full Employment Perspective, 1963," 286
Funston, Keith, 123, 144

Gagarin, Yuri, 170
Galbraith, John Kenneth, 20, 22, 27, 135, 155, 160, 161, 208, 210
Ganey, J. Cullen, 80, 82, 84
Gehman, Clayton, 222
General Electric Company, 48, 63, 81, 82-83
General Motors Corporation, 48, 61, 142
Germany, 79; *see also* Berlin crisis
Gift deductions, 59
Gilpatric, Roswell, 73, 76
Goldberg, Arthur, 37, 38, 39, 49, 61, 85, 90-91, 92, 94, 95, 98, 101, 102, 103, 105-06, 118, 125, 158, 161, 169, 171, 172, 183, 185, 190, 197, 205
Goldfine, Benjamin, 84
Goldfinger, Nat, 251

Goldwater, Barry, 22, 160, 163, 165, 279, 291
Gordon, Aaron, 261
Gordon, Kermit, 36, 95, 155, 159, 160, 166, 168, 242, 278, 281
Government, role of, 17, 27-28; size and shape of, 135-36, 275-76
Government-spending program, 18, 26-29, 40, 43, 135, 171, 176, 177, 241-42, 260, 272, 275, 276, 277, 281
Great Stock Market Crash of 1929, 131, 143
Greenberg, Leon, 263, 264, 270
Griffiths, Martha W., 163-64, 165
Gross National Product (GNP), 40, 46, 79, 140, 141, 168, 191, 231, 250, 251, 256, 260, 275, 283, 286
Gudeman, Edward C., 65, 69, 72, 76, 102, 103, 133
"Guideposts for Noninflationary Wage and Price Behavior," 189-90

Hall, Joseph P., 62-63
Halleck, Charles, 40
Hamilton, Fowler, 76
Hand, Learned, 56
Hansen, Alvin, 172, 176
Harper's Magazine, 62, 63
Harriman, Averell, 128
Harrington, Michael, 292
Harris, Louis, 245
Harris, Seymour E., 17, 20, 42, 128, 154, 155, 217-18
Harrison, Gilbert, 161
Hatcher, Andrew, 95
Hauge, Gabriel, 117, 119, 121, 122
Heller, Walter W., 19, 21, 22, 23, 34, 36, 37-38, 39, 40, 41, 42, 43, 47, 51, 71, 76, 77-78, 79, 91, 95, 99, 103, 106, 108, 119, 121, 123, 127, 135, 140, 141, 153-82, 190, 208, 209, 210, 211, 214, 217, 219, 220, 221, 226, 228, 232, 233, 234-35, 236, 237, 238, 245, 248, 249, 255-56, 257, 258, 264, 276, 286, 292, 294, 295
Highway program, 39
Hill, Herbert, 262
Hodges, Luther Hartwell, 36 n., 39, 49, 61, 63-66, 67, 68, 69-70, 72, 76, 77, 80, 81, 83, 84-87, 88, 102, 111, 274-75
Hoffa, James R., 183
Homestead, Hot Springs, Virginia, 65, 67, 68, 74, 76, 77, 107, 112, 122, 177

House Banking and Currency Committee, 228
House Interstate and Foreign Commerce Subcommittee, 144
House Judiciary Committee, 85
House Ways and Means Committee, 51, 53, 54, 165, 175, 179, 225, 240, 245-46, 248
Howard, Alvin, 68
Human Relations Committee (steel industry), 202-03
Humble Oil & Refining Company, 290
Humphrey, George M., 62 n., 67, 177, 210, 211, 215, 277
Humphrey, Hubert, 157, 216

"Incredible Electrical Conspiracy, The," 83
India, 294
Indianapolis (Ind.) *News,* 63
"Industrial statesmanship," 92
Inflation, 32, 42, 70, 75, 77, 109, 120-21, 139, 155, 183, 219, 221, 230, 284
Inland Steel Company, 101-02, 103, 105, 106
Interest rates, 26, 33, 42, 211, 223
Internal Revenue Service, U. S., 55, 58, 59, 60, 62
International Business Machines Corporation, 139, 207
International Monetary Fund, 24, 179, 180, 235
Investment Company Institute, 149
Investment tax credit, 34-35, 46-50, 60, 72, 128, 274

Jacobs, Paul, 200, 202
Jacobsson, Per, 24, 99, 139, 235
Job retraining program, 170, 185, 222, 268
John Kennedy—A Political Profile (Burns), 19
Johnson, Lyndon Baines, Anderson a friend and adviser of, 41; anti-poverty campaign, 248-49; appointments, 280; automation commission requested by, 207; business acceptance of, 18-19, 277-80; Business Council and, 77, 87; dealings with business and labor, 116; Economic Report (1964), 191; economy campaign, 278-79, 281; Federal Reserve Board and, 217, 218, 230; fiscal policy, 279-80,

281-82; full employment and, 200; Heller and, 166-67; inheritor of the Kennedy program, 295-96; member of the "Breakfast Group," 166; railroad strike threat and, 183, 193-94; tax reduction act signed by, 246; unemployment and, 271-73; war against poverty program, 292-93, 296

Joint Economic Committee, 36, 40, 160, 163, 174, 178, 196-97, 221, 224, 248, 283

Jones and Laughlin Steel Company, 101

Justice Department, U. S., 68, 81, 82, 104, 288, 290

Juvenile delinquency, 268

Kaiser, Edgar, 103, 104
Kaiser Steel Corporation, 101, 102, 103, 104, 105, 203, 206
Kappel, Frederick R., 77, 78, 87
Kaysen, Carl, 180
Kefauver, Estes, 106, 289, 290-91
Kennedy, John Fitzgerald, accomplishments, 274, 294-95, 296-97; appointments, 19-22, 158; assassination, 274, 295; balance of payments problem, 16, 17, 31-33; Blough and, 89-90, 94-95, 98, 9-100, 105, 107; budget policy, 23-24, 33; Business Advisory Council and, 63, 65, 67, 69, 70-74, 76, 77-79, 87-88; business ethics and, 84, 87-88; business hostility to, 15-18, 113-20, 123-29, 132-34, 274-75, 291-92, 293-94; Council of Economic Advisers and, 153-82; Dillon and, 174-76, 209; economic growth and, 282-87, 294-95; Economic Issues Conference address, 125-26; Economic Message to Congress (1962) 93, (1963) 259; economic programs, 19, 22-33, 41, 45; Federal Reserve Board and, 208-30; Florida Chamber of Commerce address, 274-76, 294, 296; "free market economy," 294; Heller and, 157-60, 162, 163-64, 166, 167-69, 171, 172-73, 179, 181-82; Inaugural Address, 50, 89; investment tax credit policy, 46-50; labor movement and, 183-207; Martin and, 208-12, 214, 217-20, 223, 226, 227, 229-30; New York Economic Club address, 232, 235, 237, 241, 244; rapprochement, 113-29; "State of the Union" message (1961), 38; steel industry crisis and, 89-112; stock market collapse and, 132-50; tax message of 1961, 50, 52, 53; Tax Reduction Act (1964) and, 231-52; tax reform program, 47, 50-60; UAW Convention address, 121-22; unemployment and, 254-60, 271-73; U. S. Chamber of Commerce address, 113-16, 118; Yale University address, 135-38, 275

Kennedy, Robert, 18, 71, 81, 83, 95, 98, 103, 104, 105, 289
"Kennedy market," 133, 135
Kerr, Clark, 203-04, 205
Kerr, Robert S., 51
Keyserling, Leon H., 20, 22, 127, 165-66, 176, 244, 284
Khrushchev, Nikita, 73, 162, 171
Kingson, Justin, 68
Kiplinger Letter, 110
Klein, Herb, 29
Knowles, James W., 283, 285-86
Korean War, 266, 276
Krock, Arthur, 155-56

Labor Department, U. S., 120, 154, 188, 204, 257, 268, 269, 270
Labor leaders, 16, 17, 24, 43, 73, 75, 85, 92, 115-16, 120, 121, 183, 184-85, 186, 189, 190-91, 193, 194, 196-98, 199, 200-01, 204-06, 262
Labor-Management Advisory Committee, 43, 101, 124, 185, 186, 198
Labor movement, 183-207
Labor Statistics Bureau, 199, 260, 263
Laos crisis, 70, 170
Lawrence, David, 156, 178
Lawrence, John, 103
Lawrence, William H., 109
Lewis, John P., 158, 191-92, 221-22, 256-57
Lewis, Wilfred, 40, 43
Lincoln, Evelyn, 94, 95
Linder, Lee, 103
Lippmann, Walter, 23-24, 174, 192
Living standards, 183, 204
Livingston, Joseph A., 104
Lobbies, 54, 113
Lodge, Henry Cabot, 20
Loevinger, Lee, 81, 290
Loftus, Joseph A., 75
London *Economist,* 98, 184, 261
"Long Range Sharing Plan," 203, 206

Look magazine, 168
Lovett, Robert A., 108
Lukens Steel Company, 104
Luna, Charles, 193

Mack, Peter F., Jr., 144
Macmillan, Harold, 45
Magill, Roswell, 67
Mann, Thomas C., 280
Manning, Robert, 166
Martin, Edmund F., 103
Martin, William McChesney, 21, 25, 26, 33, 38, 39, 134, 137, 155, 158, 162, 171, 172, 178, 179, 208, 209-30, 254
Maudling, Reginald, 180, 181
McClellan, John J., 187
McCollum, Leonard F., 65
McCone, John, 21
McCormick, Edward T., 145
McDonald, David J., 75, 91, 92, 93, 98, 196
McLouth Steel Company, 101
McNamara, Robert S., 22, 39, 103, 104, 176
Meany, George, 16, 92, 101, 184-85, 186, 195, 197, 198, 203, 204-05, 217, 277
Medical care for the aged, 291
Meet the Press (TV show), 156, 164, 237
Michigan University survey center, 142-43
Mills, Wilbur D., 50, 53, 54, 55, 160, 233-34, 242, 245
Missile industry, 120, 187
Missile Sites Labor Commission, 187
Mitchell, George W., 140, 210, 217, 223
Mitchell, James P., 90
Monetary and fiscal policy, 33, 38-39, 40, 43, 136, 153, 172-73, 208-30, 241, 252, 278-80
Monetary devaluation, 235
Monnet, Jean, 285
Monopoly power, 124-25
Monthly Labor Review, 194
Moon-shot effort, 169, 170
Moor, Roy, 250
Morris, Edwin, 86
Morse, Wayne, 202
Morton, Thruston, 176
Mutual funds industry, 138, 142, 147-49
Myrdal, Gunnar, 271

Narcotics rackets, 296
National Association for the Advancement of Colored People, 262, 263
National Association of Manufacturers, 72, 117, 118
National Cash Register Company, 139
National debt, 25, 156, 275, 276
National Industrial Conference Board, 74
National Mediation Board, 202
National Planning Association, 234
National Press Club, 49, 61, 197
National Restaurant Association, 59-60
National White House Conference on Economic Issues, 125-27
Natural resources development, 31
Neilan, Edwin, 278
Newberg, Mr., 85
New Frontier, 50, 51, 61, 63, 79, 88, 95, 178, 181, 276
New Republic, 161, 293
Newsweek, 23, 64, 67, 96 n., 108, 149
New York Economic Club, 232, 235, 241
New York *Herald Tribune*, 111, 278
New York Stock Exchange, 111, 112, 123, 130-32, 133-34, 138, 144, 145-46, 147, 148
New York Times, The, 67, 75, 96 n.
New York University, 159
Nixon, Richard M., 16, 17, 20, 28-29, 90, 218, 284

O'Brien, Lawrence, 160, 166
O'Donnell, Kenny, 94, 95
Oil lobby, 15
Okun, Arthur, 160
"Operation Nudge," 38-39, 212, 221
Organization for Economic Cooperation and Development (OECD), 36, 169, 235
Orrick, William H., Jr., 290
Other America, The (Harrington), 292
Ottenberg, Miriam, 82
"Over the counter" securities, 146

Pacific Maritime Association, 206
"Paris Club," 180
Parks, James L., Jr., 103-04
Patman, Wright, 213, 216, 217
Paxton, Robert, 82
Payments-balance problem, 16, 17, 31-33, 41, 42, 44, 46, 75, 91, 114, 127,

160, 166, 180-81, 183, 209, 225, 227, 228, 229, 230

Pechman, Joseph A., 159, 239, 240, 243

Pecora, Judge, 133

Pentagon, the, *see* Defense Department

Percy, Charles H., 76-77

Petersen, Howard, 123

Philadelphia electrical cases, 80-84, 85, 289

"Plan, le," 285

Plant modernization programs, 33, 34-35, 46-48

Plumley, H. Ladd, 117, 118

Polaroid Company, 140

Poverty abolishment program, 18, 292-93, 296

Presidential Papers, 282

Price-fixing cases, 80-84, 85, 111, 289

Price stability and policy, 16, 30, 33, 70, 75, 77, 79, 91-93, 94-96, 97, 98-99, 109, 111, 114, 115, 116, 117, 119, 120-21, 191, 230, 259

Profit margins, 79

"Progress Sharing Plan," 203

Proxmire, William, 220, 290

Public interest, 186, 187-88, 291

Public works program, 169-70

Racketeering, 116

Racial discrimination, 81, 183, 257, 261-63, 295

Rail Labor Crisis of 1964, 18, 183, 193-4

Railroad Brotherhoods, 207

Railway Labor Act, 183

Randolph, Philip, 262-63

Raskin, A. H., 203

Reader's Digest, 261

Re & Re case, 144-45

Recessions, 25, 26, 32, 34, 36, 41-42, 44, 132, 141, 176, 179, 191, 231, 235, 244-45, 295

Republican National Committee, 176

Republican Steel Company, 101

Research Institute of America, 17, 18

Reston, James, 279

Reuss, Henry, 23, 39, 217, 220

Reuther, Walter, 43, 120, 121, 185, 196, 200, 201, 203, 204

Revenue Act (1962), 55, 56-60; (1964), 47, 231-52

Ribicoff, Abraham, 171

"Right Remedy But Late and Little," 238

"Rights of Man" declaration, 24

Robertson, J. L., 218, 223, 226-27, 228

Rockefeller Brothers' report (1957), 29, 284

Roosa, Robert V., 21-22, 72, 179, 180, 208, 214, 215, 230

Roosevelt, Franklin D., 28, 41, 128

Roosevelt, Theodore, 28

Roosevelt Revolution, 128

Ruder, William C., 69, 84

Rusk, Dean, 22, 61, 166

Ruttenberg, Stanley H., 47-48, 76, 217

Salant, Walter S., 180

Salinger, Pierre, 166

Samuelson, Paul A., 20, 22, 23, 34, 36, 37, 40, 155, 157, 158, 160, 162, 163, 166, 171, 172, 197, 213, 254-55

San Francisco State College, 43

Saul, Ralph S., 149

Saunders, Stuart T., 243

Savings deposits, rise in, 139

Schlesinger, Arthur, Jr., 20, 22, 135, 163, 252, 295

Securities and Exchange Act, 145

Securities and Exchange Commission, 124, 143, 144, 145, 146, 147, 148, 149, 150; Division of Plans and Programs, 149; Division of Trading and Exchanges, 149; Study Group report, 133, 134, 138, 142, 143, 145-50

Seligman, Ben B., 256

Senate Finance Committee, 51, 55

Senate Labor Committee, 256

Shriver, Sargent, 248

Siegel, Harvey, 282

Smith, Alfred E., 60

Smith, George Albert, 86

Smith, John F., Jr., 102

Snyder, John, 257

Socialism, 18

Social Security program, 39, 185, 291

Social Security taxes, 236

Social welfare programs, 26-28, 39, 287

Société d'Economie Politique, 238

Solow, Robert, 160

Sorensen, Ted, 38, 43, 95, 113, 135, 158, 159-60, 161, 166, 172

Soviet Union, 161, 170

Speyer, Howard B., 48

Sproul, Allan, 215
Stam, Colin, 51
Steel industry, 15, 16, 62, 70-71, 89-112, 115, 195-96, 202-03, 288
Steel strike of 1959, 90, 91
Stevens, Robert T., 62 n., 71
Stock market, 122, 123, 128, 130-50, 220; break of 1962, 169
"Stock Market Under Stress, The," 133
Strikes in basic industries, 90, 91, 192, 194, 204
Supreme Court, U. S., 185, 217
Surrey, Stanley, 35, 50-52
Sweden, 192
"Symmetrical" approach, the, 91, 92

T. R. B. (*New Republic* editorial writer), 293, 294
Taft-Hartley law, 116, 124, 188
Tax bill (1963-64), 157, 225
Tax "drag" theory, 232
Tax revision program, 33, 34, 40, 47, 50-60, 72, 160-61, 163-65, 167-68, 171, 174-75, 184, 217, 224, 230, 231-52
Taylor, George, 118
Technological changes, 188-89, 206-07, 254, 263, 265-66; *see also* Automation
Television industry, 84-85
Tennessee Valley Authority, 291
Textile industry, 49, 294
Textile Workers Union, 200
Thirty-five-hour work week, 196-200, 256
Thomas, Woodlief, 210
Tidewater Oil Company, 290
"Tight money" policy, 25, 155, 213, 217, 219, 229, 230
Tobin, James L., 25, 39, 43, 75, 76, 155, 159, 160, 209, 215, 216-17, 219, 285, 287
Trade Expansion Act, 233, 274
Travel deductions, 59
Travell, Dr. Janet, 208
Treasury Department, U. S., 46, 48, 55, 77, 128, 157, 177, 180, 213, 214, 224, 228, 239, 244, 247
Trefethen, Gene, 102
Trippe, Juan T., 71
Truman, Harry S., 165
Tyson, Robert, 105

U. S. News and World Report, 156, 178

Unemployment compensation, 185
Unemployment problem, 25, 30, 36-37, 47, 71, 94, 140, 141, 170-71, 191, 196, 207, 221, 222, 228, 231, 250-51, 253-73, 276, 295
Union membership, 201-02
Union officials, *see* Labor leaders
Union shop contracts, 118-19
United Automobile Workers of America, 120, 121-22, 191
United Press International, 164
United States Steel Corporation, 64, 89, 93, 94, 96, 97, 103, 104, 105, 106, 142
United Steel Workers of America, 91, 92, 98, 112
University Club, New York City, 69
Urban Affairs Conference (1960), 26

Van Arsdale, Harry, Jr., 197-98, 199
Veterans Administration, 39
Vietnam crisis, 70

Wage stability and policy, 30, 33, 73, 75, 76, 77, 78, 91, 93, 97, 114, 116, 117, 119, 120-21, 127, 186, 230
Wagner, Richard, 72, 113, 115, 117, 124
Wallich, Henry C., 42
Wall Street Journal, 48, 103, 111, 173, 178, 278, 293
Wall Street's Shady Side (Cormier), 145
War Production Board Steel Division, 101
Warren, Dean, 50
Washington *Evening Star*, 82
Washington *Post*, 164, 245, 282
Washington World, 117
Watson, Thomas J., Jr., 69, 71, 108, 126, 207, 292
Weinberg, Sidney J., 62 n., 65, 66-67, 74, 79, 108, 112
Westinghouse Electric Company, 81, 83
Wharton School of Finance, 148
Wheeling Steel Company, 101, 288
Whiskeytown, California, 199
White House Conference on Monetary Policy, 222
White House Conference on National Economic Issues, 107, 158
"White Paper," 106
Williams, G. Mennen ("Soapy"), 22
Wilmington *Evening Journal*, 104

Wilson, Charles E., 61, 62 n.
Wilson, Woodrow, 28
Wirtz, W. Willard, 47, 73, 76, 154, 185, 188, 195, 197, 198, 199, 202, 207, 214, 217, 221, 251, 253, 254, 258-59
Withholding tax on dividends and interest, 53-55, 60, 128

Wolfbein, Seymour L., 264-65
Women's National Democratic Club, 252
Worthington, Leslie B., 106

Yale University, 135
Youngstown Steel Company, 101